THE
FRANC
FOOTB
LEAGUE

CW00621845

1995
OFFICIAL
FANTASY
FOOTBALL
JOURNAL
AND
COMPUTER
GUIDE

DICK GIEBEL

THE
FRANCHISE
FOOTBALL
LEAGUE

1995
OFFICIAL
FANTASY
FOOTBALL
JOURNAL
AND
COMPUTER
GUIDE

DICK GIEBEL

A Fantasy Sports Properties Trade Paperback

A FANTASY SPORTS PROPERTIES PAPERBACK

Published by:
Fantasy Sports Properties, Inc.
PO Box 2698
Reston, VA 22091

If you purchased this book without a cover, you should be aware that this book is stolen property. It was reported as "unsold and destroyed" to the publisher, and neither the author nor the publisher has received any payment for this "stripped book."

Copyright ©1995 Fantasy Sports Properties, Inc.

All rights reserved. No part of this publication may be reproduced or transmitted in any form or by any means, electronic or mechanical, including photocopying, recording, or by any information and retrieval system (except excerpts which may be used for reviews) without the express written consent of the publisher, except where permitted by law.

FSPI, FBL, Franchise Baseball League, FFL, Franchise Football League, FBBL, Franchise Basketball League, Fantasy Basketball, FHL, Franchise Hockey League, and Fantasy Hockey are all registered trademarks of Fantasy Sports Properties, Inc.

Ultimate Football is a registered trademark of MicroProse Software

PRODIGY is a registered trademark of The Prodigy Services Company

CompuServe is a registered trademark of CompuServe, Inc, an H & R Block company

Microsoft and The Microsoft Network are registered trademarks of Microsoft Corporation

The FFL software and trademark are registered in the U.S. Patent and Trademark Office Patent No. 4,918,603 Registration No. 1,687,798

The FBL, FHL, and FBBL software and trademark are registered in the U.S. Patent and Trademark Office. Patent No. 4,918,603 Additional Patents Pending.

ISBN 0-9636895-4-1

Printed in the United States of America by Peake Printing, Washington, DC

Cover Design by Chris Larivey

June 1995   10 9 8 7 6 5 4 3 2 1

*This Journal is dedicated
with love and respect to
my three children,
Matt, Tim and Caitlin*

★☆★☆ACKNOWLEDGMENTS★☆★☆

You can round up the usual gang of suspects at the FSPI World Headquarters, for making this year, as every year, a winner for fantasy football fans everywhere. Kudos go out to Chris (Data) Yager, Mike (Dry Cleaners Rule) Hughes, and David (Preggo) Dewenter for all the hard work they've put into the 1995 FFL program. The new program continues to astound, and will confirm FSPI's status at the top of the fantasy football mountain. Dave Dewenter gets an extra-special thanks for the many hats he wears at FSPI. Thanks go out to Bill (Mr. Roster Almanac) Kelly, for his invaluable editing and other technical assistance. Your knowledge of the league and its players is almost as extensive as mine, and we couldn't have made this without you! Thanks go out to the rest of the FFL technical gang, for helping support a great product and a great company! My thanks go out to Kathy (Taxidermy) Rowland, for the many arduous hours she spent working on the 1995 FFL software manual. Thanks to my editor, Dave (Stevie Ray) Warner, for putting up with impossible deadlines, a hard-to-reach author, and all my "Giebelisms." (The editor would like to thank his family and friends for their unflagging support of the countless hours and deadlines associated with the FFL. (Hi Chris & Cortney!)) And of course, what can I say in thanks to Pat (Huggies Rule) Hughes and Cheryl (PMA Rules) Hughes, for their eight years of hard work and support of this *Journal*, and fantasy football fans worldwide. My eternal thanks go out to media consultant extraordinaire Michael Goodman, and my publishing guru Marty McGrath. A special thank you goes out to Sarah Vogel, for her critical technical assistance during the writing of this book. Larry Michael, Dave Douglas, Larry Weisman and John Weiss all took time out of their busy schedules to write the Team-by-Team reviews for this *Journal*, and my thanks go out to them as well.

★☆★☆CONTENTS★☆★☆

49ers ★ Seattle Seahawks ★ St. Louis Rams ★ Tampa Bay Buccaneers ★ Washington Redskins

★5★
Quarterbacks   140
Quarterback Review ★ Quarterback Ratings

★6★
Running Backs   160
Running Back Review ★ Running Back Ratings

★7★
Wide Receivers   177
Wide Receiver Review ★ Wide Receiver Ratings

★8★
Tight Ends   192
Tight End Review ★ Tight End Ratings

★☆★☆FOREWORD★☆★☆

This was the year fantasy football was to come out of the closet --and hit the big time!

In November of last year, I received the phone call I've been waiting for ever since 1987 when I conceived of the idea of how to market and promote fantasy football both to mainstream America and to the big leagues themselves. This call came from the National Football League! They said they were *finally* interested in pursuing ideas related to capturing the growing popularity of our game. They even hooked me up with one of their major television network partners. I thought this was all too good to be true, as I had almost been there before.

Even though we first received our licenses from both the NFL Players' Association (now NFL Players, Inc.) and NFL Properties (the licensing arm of the NFL) way back in 1988, we've never been able to break into the league's hierarchy, despite many tries. It was NFL Properties that directed Miller Brewing Company to us in 1989, where we ran Miller Franchise Football for three years in sports bars and taverns across the country. The promotion was one of Miller's most successful ever during its first year, thanks largely to John Madden, who was used in the beer distributor video sell-in.

In 1991, Larry King introduced us to the top brass at the NFL as he thought our proposed educational tie-ins were "terrific". In 1993, Al Michaels teamed up with Topps trading card company to promote Topps FantaSports. Al said, "it's the hottest thing in football today," and that "this has got to be the bigget news in pro football today!"

Well, here it is the start of the 1995 season, and still no league acknowledgment of the game. Even though we've heard that the NFL's legal beagles have said our game is OK, they're still playing it safe.

The time has come for me to ask for your help. I would like to hear about your league and how much it builds spirit and camaraderie among your league members. Tell me how you find it educational, or how it may instigate friendly competition and communication among family members or schoolmates.

Please write and tell us about your league, so that we can finally show the top brass and NFL big wigs to finally know the truths about fantasy football. Then, expect to see us on national TV in 1996!

Incidentally, FSPI has gone even further "online" this year, by allowing users to download our stat files through PRODIGY, CompuServe, The Microsoft Network, and the Internet. By the beginning of the football season, FSPI will have a World Wide Web site up and running, giving users around the world access to fantasy football information, product demos, etc.

We at FSPI feel that this year will be the biggest and best ever, and again we encourage to to share your league's history and stories with us. As always, I wish you, your league, and your franchise as much success as I had with mine last year!

Patrick J. Hughes
President
Fantasy Sports Properties
PO Box 2698
Reston, VA 22091

P.S. FSPI would like to extend our thanks to everyone that helped make the 1995 FFL program a success, especially those who helped us Beta test the program.

ABBREVIATIONS

QB - Quarterback
RB - Running Back
HB - Halfback
FB - Fullback
WR - Wide Receiver
TE - Tight End
PR - Pass Receiver
K - Kicker
P - Punter
S - Safety
C - Center
FS - Free Safety
SS - Strong Safety
DB - Defensive Back
CB - Cornerback
LB - Linebacker
OLB - Outside Linebacker
MLB - Middle Linebacker
ILB - Inside Linebacker

FG - Field Goal
PAT - Point After Touchdown
Yds - Yards
DT - Defensive Team
TD - Touchdown
Pts - Points
AVG - Average
REC - Receptions
NFL - National Football League
FFL - Franchise Football League

AZ - Arizona Cardinals
ATL - Atlanta Falcons
BUF - Buffalo Bills
CAR - Carolina Panthers
CHI - Chicago Bears
CIN - Cincinnati Bengals
CLE - Cleveland Browns
DAL - Dallas Cowboys
DEN - Denver Broncos
DET - Detroit Lions
GB - Green Bay Packers
HOU - Houston Oilers
IND - Indianapolis Colts
JAX - Jacksonville Jaguars
KC - Kansas City Chiefs
RAI - Los Angeles Raiders
MIA - Miami Dolphins
MIN - Minnesota Vikings
NE - New England Patriots
NO - New Orleans Saints
NYG - New York Giants
NYJ - New York Jets
PHI - Philadelphia Eagles
PIT - Pittsburgh Steelers
SD - San Diego Chargers
SF - San Francisco 49ers
SEA - Seattle Seahawks
STL - St. Louis Rams
TB - Tampa Bay Buccaneers
WAS - Washington Redskins
NFC - National Football Conference
AFC - American Football Conference

Introduction

There might be some of you out there who are reading this type of book for the very first time. Perhaps you've heard John Madden or Chris Berman mention fantasy football on TV. Maybe you've heard about it from some family or friends who participate in fantasy football. Or perhaps you are one of literally millions of fantasy football players ("franchise owners") who know how much fun and how addictive fantasy football can be. (Heck...maybe you just happened to see the snazzy cover and pick it up in a local bookstore...) However you got here, I say a hearty "Welcome!"

Every year, we expand our fantasy football coverage to keep up with all the real-life action happening in the NFL, and this year is certainly no different. This is the seventh year for this *Journal*, and in my humble opinion it keeps getting better each year. In addition to giving you the full complement of 1994 NFL statistics, 1995 NFL player projections and the full NFL schedule, we have now expanded our free agent section to cover the whole league--all thirty franchises are analyzed for how they fared in the million-dollar roulette wheel of free agency. Plus, other features such as the head coaches section, the Team-by-Team reviews, and more have been "tweaked" to respond to the way leagues all across America play, while giving you the information you need to know to have the upper hand in your fantasy league.

Each NFL season we hear stories of how our *Journal* helps commissioners administrate their league rules, or how the famous "Dick's Picks" section has helped a franchise take home the coveted annual league trophy. But if you are just starting out and just putting a league together, don't be intimidated by terms or concepts you may not yet understand: another goal of this book is to hold your hand and take you step by step through the sometimes-tricky process of setting up and running a league. This *Journal* has both the advanced information that the die-hard league commissioner needs, and the introductory information that can get even the most basic league up and running.

We encourage those of you just starting a fantasy league to read the information found in the first two chapters on how to start and run a league. If you are an experienced Commissioner and a die-hard information seeker, then your fun begins in Chapter Three, where we cover free agency and the draft. The information in Chapters Four through Eleven will give both novice and fantasy pro alike complex in-depth analysis of each NFL team, and each player position that leagues normally draft. In Chapter 13, we give you the complete computer guide for our 1995 FFL software. The 1995 software has a host of new features designed to truly make it every Comissioner's dream.

So, my friend, whether you are a seasoned pro or just a rookie, sit back and enjoy what we believe to be the most current, accurate and informative fantasy football Journal published today!

★1★

What is Franchise Football League?

WHAT IS FRANCHISE FOOTBALL?

Franchise Football is a game that allows you the opportunity to be the owner, general manager and head coach of your own NFL team. Now, you can't tell me that you wouldn't want to replace a Jerry Jones in Dallas, or an Eddie DeBartolo in San Francisco!

Of course, looking back at last year's Super Bowl winning 49ers, George Seifert sure looked like *he* was playing fantasy football. Any fantasy coach would give his left arm to have Steve Young, Jerry Rice, Brent Jones, Ricky Watters, Deion Sanders, William Floyd, Doug Brien...that's practically an All-Star Team right there!

Well, for ordinary folks like you and me (who just weren't *fortunate* enough to be called on to replace Bill Walsh in San Francisco) it doesn't have to be "just a fantasy." Now it can be fantasy football...the FFL way! You draft players, build your own team, and compete against other teams in your FFL league.

Imagine the feeling of matching your wits against your buddies, co-workers or family. Will your draft strategy work? Who will be the emerging scorers for 1995? Which quarterback will lead the league? Will it be Marino, Elway or Young? Will Emmitt Smith continue to prove he is the best running back in the NFL, or will Detroit finally get a clue and use Barry Sanders while they have him? Will Jerry Rice continue to be the best receiver in football, or will he be challenged by Andre Rison, Michael Irvin or Anthony Miller? Which rookies will jump into the limelight? What about Ki-Jana and Rashaan? Who will be a bust? Hmmm, all of these questions must be faced, and decisions will have to be made as you take charge and draft a fantasy team.

Hey, no one said these decisions would be easy...but these kinds of decisions are fun. So why delay starting a league and miss the fun? The choice is yours, and the choice is simple: either spend another season frustrated as you watch some inept play calling, or call your own shots and see how you rate as an FFL team owner. Fantasy Football makes you put up or shut up! The FFL--you will never watch football quite the same way again. Enjoy!

THIS BOOK WAS ON SALE IN OCTOBER, AND I MISSED THE OPENING KICKOFF--CAN I STILL PLAY?

Part of the intrigue of drafting an FFL team is the great unknown. Drafting a fantasy team several days before the NFL season kicks off is exciting because there are still many decisions to be made by NFL coaches--decisions such as starting players or who will be cut, traded, or placed on injured reserve.

So obviously, the FFL suggests forming a league prior to the start of the NFL season. However, if by chance you have just now discovered the Franchise Football League program and fantasy football, by all means, join in! It's simple to just hold your draft and play an abbreviated schedule. On the plus side, you and your cronies will know firsthand who's starting full-time, who's hot and who's not. Also, you will know who's injured. So, starting late shouldn't stop you. So play!

SO WHO DIED AND MADE ME AN EXPERT?

Well, now you have the opportunity to become something of an expert through Franchise Football's fantasy football program. This is my sixth book on fantasy football, an endeavor which is akin to projecting the upcoming year's stock market. In other words, I attempt my very best at predicting just who will be top scorers and potentially explosive picks.

What I do is not rocket science, but my recommendations are well thought-out and researched. Sometimes I'm on and sometimes I'm not, but that's what makes this game so enjoyable. Also, it gives *you, the reader* some responsibility. Shucks, I'm a realist: besides this book, you probably have purchased several other football magazines or books--therefore, this book should serve as an aid to you in making your selections. I'm trying to make *you* the expert.

I've been playing fantasy football for 13 years, and I have *never* walked out of a draft with every player that I wanted. In my dozen or so fantasy league years I have begrudgingly developed the realization that my league-mates are every bit as astute as I am (although only *I* got the book contract).

Playing in my league are men and women whom I have learned to appreciate and with whom I have developed great friendships. It's funny, but the league that I play in now has expanded to over 40 people, residing all over the country. We only really see each other two to three times a year--but what a party it is. (I know I'm kissing up here, but I may need to work some trades in '95.)

I know that this scene is replayed all over the country with FFL and fantasy leagues that have sprouted up over the last several years. I've been on countless call-in radio talk shows and have responded to many folks from many walks of life who have written me on PRODIGY, and the one constant is that you folks are not only knowledgeable about the world of sports, but a blast to talk and correspond with.

Also, it's quite evident just how popular fantasy football has become. Leagues are now part of the office, job site, universities and high schools, and are shared among families and friends.

I still remember the early days of playing fantasy football: only a few people understood the concept, and even fewer actually played. I still recall quizzical looks from those who were not playing and couldn't understand my enthusiasm over drafting players from NFL teams and cheering their every score.

I can remember sitting in the stands of RFK Stadium rooting for the Redskins against Dallas when I absentmindedly let out a roar as Tony Dorsett (who happened to be one of my FFL running backs) broke off a long run for a touchdown. I suddenly knew exactly how Miami kicker Garo Ypremian must have felt in the 1971 Super Bowl when he vainly attempted a pass (which looked more like a two-handed set shot), and the errant flub was picked off by Washington's Mike Bass for a touchdown. At that moment, the ex-soccer player looked mighty foolish.

Cheering for a Dallas TD in Washington in the late '70's was not an intelligent move--in fact, it was moronic. I quickly escaped the section of stunned and irritated patrons by urgently yelling "Look, a fumble!" as I did a 360 and dove for the nearest exit. It was at that moment that I realized that I would never be watching NFL football quite the same...*ever again.*

STATS, DON'T FAIL ME NOW!

You've heard the saying "stats don't lie?" In fantasy football, they can be very misleading. How so? Well, it's all about *context.*

As an example, in 1995, the Dolphins lost both Keith Byars and Terry Kirby to injuries, so Bernie Parmalee and Irving Spikes got to see some major playing time, and turned more than a few heads. But now, the Dolphins have all four guys back, so to draft Parmalee and Spikes and think they're gonna get the same or better usage they did last year means you're not seeing the whole picture. Stats are just part of the story. Certainly, Spikes and Parmalee are studs, and they will contribute, but you have to consider the context in which they performed well.

As another example, the way your league handles scoring has to decide who it is you draft. In my league, TDs are king and yardage means *nada*. Which means that in my league, a Barry Sanders is less valuable than a Marshall Faulk or Emmitt Smith (because Sanders gets lots of yardage but doesn't end up in the endzone as much as the other two). So you always have to consider your league, and how it scores its points. Don't have a league, or considering new rules changes? Let's take a look at the FFL way of doing things, and see why the FFL is considered by many to be the leader of this phenomena called fantasy football.

★2★

Starting a Franchise Football League

Occasionally, someone will ask me why one needs the FFL, the FFL software---or even my *FFL Journal*. Normally, upon regaining my composure after throttling such a nudnik, I explain it this way:

Thumbing through the sports pages today is like reading the obituaries. Players are dropping off teams and signing with others on what seems like a daily basis. Tracking all of these player moves is more difficult than keeping up with the latest Congressional scandal.

So, if even keeping up with the rosters appears complicated, wouldn't it be way too much hassle to form an FFL league and play fantasy football?

WHO'S ZOOMING WHO?

Look, don't get zoomed by all of this--simply play fantasy football the FFL way. If you've never been part of a league, don't fret--starting one is a breeze.

First of all, keep it simple and begin with people you know--family, friends and co-workers. One key suggestion for beginners: don't be overly ambitious and attempt to organize a 20-team league. Think simple; or, better yet, simply think! For the novice, large leagues are difficult to maintain successfully. My suggestion would be to stick with 8 to 10 teams at the start and, if successful, entertain expansion in the following year or two. It's best to select franchise owners who are likable, and, at the same time, fit the mold of fun-loving football fans interested in competing in a fantasy league for the entire season. This last point is important, because it only takes a couple of idiotic mental-midgets who lose interest during the season to bring down the entire league.

SETTING UP YOUR FANTASY LEAGUE

1. League Organization

Organize 4 to 16 "teams" to form your own league. A team can consist of one person or multiple partners, but a tip to the wise: try to keep your league down to 8 to 10 teams. Holding down the number of teams eliminates a watering down of your draft. Although you can start an FFL league with as few as four teams, the down side of a small league is that all the teams will be loaded with superstars, the scoring is higher, and there's less challenge and competition among team owners. The FFL software allows you to set up leagues of up to 30 franchises, but we tend to recommend to keep it to about 10 - 16, in order to not dilute the talent pool too much.

2. Select a Commissioner

Don't minimize the importance of a good commissioner. This is a time-consuming job consisting of keeping records, tracking weekly lineups and trades, and solving a whole lot of problems. The commissioner doesn't have to be a wizard or a know-it-all of fantasy football, just someone who can be firm in the handling of questionable scoring decisions, yet remain open-minded when dealing with franchise owners' concerns. Two big tips: it's best that the commissioner have the use of a computer; and choose a commissioner carefully--an order-taking wimp won't stand up and be accountable for important league decisions; on the other hand, a hard-headed bully will ruin your league.

3. Draft Day

Your commissioner sets up the league's fantasy draft. Tip: give plenty of notice but schedule your draft just prior to the NFL season opener. I realize many of you draft in late July or early August, but the problem I have with drafting this early is that many teams haven't made their cuts, players will get injured, and starters haven't been listed. Drafting later (just before Game 1) is a better move. The commissioner has the responsibility of running the draft on draft night. This is a time of celebration and exuberance--have fun and enjoy the draft!

4. Franchise Representation

By giving plenty of notice for the fantasy draft you will ensure that every franchise is represented. A missing franchise puts a damper on the draft, and having another franchise draft for the phantom team is both a drag and an inconvenience. It is difficult enough keeping track of who's drafting whom and deciding just what your own next move will be; adding the responsibility of drafting for another team is a complete bummer! Therefore, make it clear that all franchises are to be represented.

5. Draft Sequence

As a rule of thumb, an existing league generally will operate the draft just like the NFL--based on the final standings from the previous season. The last-place team receives the first pick, next-to-last gets the second pick, etc. Obviously, this sequence will give last season's champ the final pick in round one and the first pick in round two.

Example Sequence for 10 Teams

Round One	Round Two
Team #10 - 1st pick	Team # 1 - 1st pick
Team # 9 - 2nd pick	Team # 2 - 2nd pick
Team # 8 - 3rd pick	Team # 3 - 3rd pick
Team # 7 - 4th pick	Team # 4 - 4th pick
Team # 6 - 5th pick	Team # 5 - 5th pick
Team # 5 - 6th pick	Team # 6 - 6th pick
Team # 4 - 7th pick	Team # 7 - 7th pick
Team # 3 - 8th pick	Team # 8 - 8th pick
Team # 2 - 9th pick	Team # 9 - 9th pick
Team # 1 -10th pick	Team #10- 10th pick

Round three would lead off with Team #10 picking first--order reverses every round. If you are organizing a new league, just pick numbers from a hat--and sequence the draft.

    # 1 - # 10 (first round)
    # 10- # 1 (second round)
    # 1 - # 10 (third round)
    # 10- # 1 (fourth round)

Remember to reverse the order every round. The FFL software now lets you modify the draft order each round, or to change the draft order once and for all. For more information, see Chapter 13.

HOW TO RUN A SMOOTH DRAFT

1. Set The Draft Date

Just before the start of the NFL regular season, the league commissioner sets a date for the FFL fantasy draft. The commissioner must be prepared to list the players chosen round-by-round. An easel and a marker will help the commissioner or an assistant to record each round and will allow league members to review their choices.

2. Don't Let The Draft Drag

To move the draft along, set up a time limit per selection. (for example, many leagues suggest one minute between picks.) If you don't set a time limit initially, your draft will drag and tempers will flare. Trust me, without a time limit per selection, your draft will become a nightmare. Have fun, but move the selection process along to ensure a successful draft.

3. Suggested Number of Players to Draft

4 Quarterbacks   (QB)   2 Kickers (K)
6 Running Backs (RB)   2 Defensive/SpecialTeams (DT/ST)
6 Wide Receivers(WR)
2 Tight Ends   (TE)

These are the numbers of players the FFL suggests to draft per team. This is not a hard-and-fast-rule, but with these amounts you will have enough players at each position to cover situations such as the always-wonderful bye week, or injuries, etc. Many existing leagues change these numbers slightly, so use them as general guidelines. Clearly, if you have more than 15 teams in your league, you may only draft one defensive team.

Supplemental Draft

Do you remember just how smart you felt immediately after the draft? Now, several weeks later, you begin to notice your team fraying around the edges? Do you know what you need to give yourself a fixer-upper? My friend, you need a quick trip to the Supplemental Draft.

Many leagues hold Supplemental Drafts to fix "mistakes" (or, shall I say, those humongous "reaches" that you hung your hopes on). Not only will the Supplemental Draft correct Draft Night flaws, but it also is helpful in cases where your key players are injured, or worse, benched. I recommend that you hold the Supplemental Draft after Weeks 5 or 6, in order to supplement rosters with NFL players not chosen at the outset. I also recommend that you set a draft limit of six players to be selected for each team.

One other reason to hold the Supplemental Draft is that it is a great opportunity to get the whole gang back together. This is also a good chance to make trades, or just to trade barbs and banter!

Weekly Starting Lineups

Each franchise must submit a nine-player starting lineup (eight players and one defensive/special team) to the commissioner prior to the kickoff of the first game of the NFL/FFL week. If no starting lineup is submitted, the commissioner will assume that the team has no lineup changes. The FFL recommends the following starting lineup requirement:

1 Quarterback   (QB)
2 Running Backs (RB)
3 Wide Receivers (WR)
1 Tight End   (TE)
1 Kicker   (K)
1 Defensive/Special Team (DT/ST)

Some leagues will set Thursday evening as the time to call in their weekly lineups. Most commissioners, however, will give franchises until game time on Sunday to call in lineups. The commissioner should *never* accept any lineup change after games are in progress on Sunday! A good suggestion is to get an answering machine so each franchise can record his or her lineup. Believe me, if the commissioner takes every call, he or she will never get off the phone. And for the other franchise owners calling in lineups, a constantly busy phone line is a real drag. Therefore, it is imperative that the commissioner use a tape recorder/voice mail. This is the quickest and the most reliable method; besides, recorded lineup messages eliminate any confusion or errors--after all, you've got it on tape!

Trades and Waivers

As with real NFL teams, franchise owners can trade or transfer one or more NFL players from one franchise to another. However, all trades must be approved by the commissioner, and in order to play a traded player on that weekend, trades must be finalized in time for the weekly lineup exchange. No trades are allowed during the final four weeks of the season. (This is recommended to prevent real loser franchises from "selling" their talent to winning teams or teams in contention for the league championship.)

A franchise owner may also waive a player on his/her current roster and add a non-roster player up to a maximum of eight times during the season.

FFL SCORING SYSTEM

FFL scoring is based on actual plays made by NFL players each week during the NFL season. This is real scoring--not Nintendo® or Sega®. Only players listed as *starters* for each franchise receive points for that franchise. Points are awarded for rushing TDs, receiving TDs, passing TDs, points-after-TDs (PAT), 2-point conversions, field goals, and any TDs scored by defensive/special teams players, including safeties.

Also, the FFL has added performance scoring for yardage, receptions, interceptions, etc. We suggest using this scoring system, or modifying it to suit your league's rules.

14

Official FFL Scoring System

Regular Scoring Plays

	0-9 yds. Points	10-39 yds. Points	40+ yds. Points
QB pass for TD	6	9	12
RB run for TD	6	9	12
WR/TE catch for TD	6	9	12
DT/ST* or LB, DB and DL return for TD	6	9	12

	1-39 yds. Points	40-49 yds. Points	50+ yds. Points
Field Goal	3	5	10

Two-Point Conversion

QB pass for conversion	2
RB run for conversion	2
WR/TE catch for conversion	2
QB run/catch for conversion	4
RB pass/catch for conversion	4
WR/TE run/pass for conversion	4
K pass/run/catch for conversion	4

Bonus Scoring Plays

	0-9 yds. Points	10-39 yds. Points	40+ yds. Points
QB run/catch for TD	12	18	24
RB pass/catch for TD	12	18	24
WR/TE pass/run for TD	12	18	24
K pass/run/catch for TD	12	18	24

Optional Performance Scoring

QB Pass Yds.	5 points beginning at 250 yds. 1 point for every 10 yds. thereafter
QB Rush/Rec Yds.	5 points beginning at 50 yds. 1 point for every 10 yds. thereafter
RB Rush Yds.	10 points beginning at 100 yds.1 point for every 10 yds. thereafter
RB Pass/Rec Yds.	5 points beginning at 50 yds. 1 point for every 10 yds. thereafter
WR/TE Pass/Rush Yds.	5 points beginning at 50 yds. 1 point for every 10 yds. thereafter
WR/TE Receiving Yds.	10 points beginning at 100 yds.1 point for every 10 yds. thereafter

Safety scored by DT/ST or DB, LB, DL = **4 pts**. INT thrown/Sack received by a QB = **-1 pt**.
Point After Touchdown (PAT) = **1 pt**.   Sack or INT made by DT/ST or DB, LB, DL = **1 pt**.

Key: QB (Quarterback), RB (Running Back), WR (Wide Receiver), TE (Tight End),
K (Kicker), DT/ST (Defensive Team and Special Team), LB (Linebacker), DB
(Defensive Back), DL (Defensive Lineman), TD (Touchdown).

* If your league uses the defensive/special teams unit method (in which franchise owners
pick an entire defensive and special teams unit rather than individual players), and any
player from that unit scores a TD, the points, as specified above, are awarded to that
franchise.

League Newsletters

Communication with league members is crucial, and the best means is through a weekly newsletter. You should keep league members up-to-date with weekly information on stats, scores and league standings. Generally, since the commissioner keeps track of the stats, he or she should also do the newsletter. Make sure you include the following:

* Weekly winner
* The past week's scoring results, team by team
* Year-to-date league standings
* Weekly head-to-head schedules
* Any league business (trades, roster changes, etc.)
* Any rules interpretations

The FFL software program now allows the Commissioner to incorporate a newsletter directly into the weekly reports. See Chapter 13 for more information.

TEAM vs. TEAM SETUP

While some leagues still prefer a system where there is one weekly winner based on the number of starting points for the franchise, many Franchise Football leagues now supplement their league with the team-vs.-team (or head-to-head) format in order to give more teams a chance to stay in contention and win. It also provides a playoff structure similar to the NFL's. For ease and convenience, the FFL has structured a 17-week schedule to be used by 8-, 10-, 12-, 14-, and 16-team leagues.

One bit of advice on setting up leagues--don't get overly ambitious and set up a 20-team league. Besides being overweening, a 20-team league completely dilutes your player pool.

★3★

The Draft

FREE AGENCY, or "THE DRAFT ACCORDING TO GIEBEL"

This is now a critical chapter when preparing for your draft. Free agents in the past were thought of as semi-decent players that were picked in the later rounds. Scratch that antiquated thought process, because the free agents of 1995 can make or break your franchise. In fact, I am now starting to think strategically that in order to win, free agency players are the key to pulverizing the status quo of my league. In 1995 only a dimwit would not be prepared and totally updated on all the bazillion free agent player moves. Drafting a Barry Foster because you think he is still wearing a Steeler uniform only shows little knowledge and an ill-prepared draft plan.

Even the tiniest free agent move should be put under a microscope and examined. For example, Dallas signed very few free agents, yet they inked David Lang (ex-Ram, ex-Falcon). Small move, but what does Dallas have up their sleeve? Lang is a reliable pass receiver out of the backfield, so does this mean more passing on second and third down? Does this mean less wear and tear on Emmitt? Or...is Lang just fodder to see how good rookie Sherman Williams is?

Miami already had a rocking offense with WRs Irving Fryar, O.J. McDuffie, RBs Keith Byars, Bernie Parmalee and Irving Spikes...and yet they added TE Eric Green, WRs Gary Clark and

17

Randal Hill. You think Dan Marino just might have an incredible season if he stays healthy. Who catches balls out of the backfield better than Byars and Terry Kirby? Can you imagine the game-faced Marino and Clark grousing and sniping at slacking teammates during crunch time? With Marino's darts, the gritty Gary Clark could end up huge in 1995 if he too stays healthy. The Raiders running backs recently have run the football as if they are clutching a water balloon and fear it breaking open and soaking them. Yet they signed RB Derrick Fenner in the off-season. Fenner is a potential knucklehead and could prove to be another stiff like Nick Bell. But I think that the Raiders may be the team for this lovable lunkhead. Fenner can play. Fenner can score. Fenner is a load. Now is the time in Fenner's career to prove his value. Next year at this time I may be writing about what a steal Derrick Fenner was in 1995; then again, I may be writing about the latest in a disappointing string of Raider losers: Nick Bell, Harvey Williams and Derrick Fenner.

My advice to you is to study the list of free agents and review my section on the team-by-team gains and losses. During exhibition season watch closely for Ricky Watters and see how he fits in with Randall Cunningham and the Eagles offense. How about the Jets' Ron Moore--is he the go-to guy over Johnny Johnson? Will ex-Falcon Erric Pegram split duty or backup hard running second year back Bam Morris? How will Terry Allen be used in Washington? Do your research, scouting and preparation and your draft will be smooth...show up with only last season's sports info and you will be a bucketheaded loser. Period.

POS	PLAYER	OLD TEAM	1995 TEAM
QB	Frank Reich	Buffalo	Carolina
	Dave Krieg	Detroit	Arizona
	Chris Chandler	St. Louis	Houston
QB	Bill Musgrave	San Francisco	Denver
	Bubby Brister	Philadelphia	NY Jets
	John Friesz	Washington	Seattle

POS	PLAYER	OLD TEAM	1995 TEAM
	Mark Rypien	Cleveland	St. Louis
	Wade Wilson	New Orleans	Atlanta
RB	Ricky Watters	San Francisco	Philadelphia
	Terry Allen	Minnesota	Washington
	Derrick Fenner	Cincinnati	Los Angeles
	Dave Meggett	NY Giants	New England
	Derrick Moore	Detroit	San Francisco
	Erric Pegram	Atlanta	Pittsburgh
	Herschel Walker	Philadelphia	NY Giants
	Kevin Turner	New England	Philadelphia
	Lorenzo White	Houston	Cleveland
	Marc Logan	San Francisco	Washington
	Dexter Carter	San Francisco	NY Jets
	Ricky Ervins	Washington	Free Agent
	James Joseph	Philadelphia	Cincinnati
	Cleveland Gary	Miami	St. Louis
	Darrell Thompson	Green Bay	Chicago
	Randy Baldwin	Cleveland	Carolina
WR	Andre Rison	Atlanta	Cleveland
	Alvin Harper	Dallas	Tampa Bay
	Willie Anderson	St. Louis	Indianapolis
	Haywood Jeffires	Houston	Free Agent
	Ernest Givins	Houston	Jacksonville
	Don Beebe	Buffalo	Carolina
	J.J. Birden	Kansas City	Atlanta
	Michael Timpson	New England	Chicago
	Randal Hill	Arizona	Miami
	Ed McCaffrey	San Francisco	Denver
	Alexander Wright	Los Angeles (RAI)	St. Louis
	Johnnie Barnes	San Diego	Pittsburgh
TE	Eric Green	Pittsburgh	Miami
	Pete Metzelaars	Buffalo	Carolina
	Kerry Cash	Indianapolis	Los Angeles
	Scott Galbreath	Dallas	Washington
K	John Kasay	Seattle	Carolina

POS	PLAYER	OLD TEAM	1995 TEAM
	Dean Biasucci	Indianapolis	Free Agent
	Mike Cofer	Free Agent	Indianapolis
DB	Eric Allen	Philadelphia	New Orleans
	James Washington	Dallas	Washington
	Stanley Richard	San Diego	Washington
	Marquez Pope	St. Louis	San Francisco
	Vinnie Clark	New Orleans	Jacksonville
	Shaun Gayle	Chicago	San Diego
	Todd Scott	Minnesota	NY Jets
	James Williams	Arizona	Carolina
	Patrick Hunter	Seattle	Arizona
	Eric Thomas	NY Jets	Denver
	Gary Jones	Pittsburgh	NY Jets
	Brett Maxie	Atlanta	Carolina
	Lionel Washington	LA Raiders	Denver
	Mickey Washington	Buffalo	Jacksonville
	Tim Hauck	Green Bay	Denver
	Charles Mincy	Kansas City	Minnesota
	Harlon Barnett	New England	Minnesota
LB	Bryce Paup	Green Bay	Buffalo
	Darion Conner	New Orleans	Carolina
	Lamar Lathon	Houston	Carolina
	Rod Stephens	Seattle	Washington
	Broderick Thomas	Detroit	Minnesota
	Kurt Gouveia	Washington	Philadelphia
	Carlos Jenkins	Minnesota	St. Louis
	Pat Swilling	NY Jets	LA Raiders
	Sam Mills	New Orleans	Carolina
	Marvcus Patton	Buffalo	Washington
	Rufus Porter	Seattle	New Orleans
	Bobby Abrams	Minnesota	New England
	Britt Hager	Philadelphia	Denver
	Frank Stams	Cleveland	Carolina
	Darrick Brownlow	Dallas	Washington
DL	Joel Smeenge	New Orleans	Jacksonville

POS	PLAYER	OLD TEAM	1995 TEAM
	Henry Thomas	Minnesota	Detroit
	Ray Agnew	New England	NY Giants
DL	Jeff Lageman	NY Jets	Jacksonville
	Mike Fox	NY Giants	Carolina
	Tim Goad	New England	Cleveland
	Kelvin Pritchett	Detroit	Jacksonville
	Gerald Williams	Pittsburgh	Carolina
	Erik Howard	NY Giants	NY Jets
	Robert Harris	Minnesota	New York
	Michael Dean Perry	Cleveland	Denver
	Ted Washington	Denver	Buffalo

TEAM BY TEAM FREE AGENT REVIEW

ARIZONA
Gains: WR Rob Moore, QB Dave Krieg, G Duval Love, CB Patrick Hunter
Top Draft: WR Frank Sanders
Losses: QB Steve Beuerlein, RB Ron Moore, WR Ricky Proehl, WR Randall Hill, WR Gary Clark, DE Keith McCants

ATLANTA
Gains: RB Eric Metcalf, LB Darrell Talley, WR J.J. Birden, WR/RS Nate Lewis, CB Terry Taylor, P Dan Stryzinski
Top Draft: DB Devon Bush
Losses: WR Andre Rison, RB Erric Pegram, WR Clarence Verdin, P Harold Alexander, OT Mike Kenn (retired), S Brett Maxie

BUFFALO
Gains: LB Bryce Paup, DE Jim Jeffcoat, NT Ted Washington
Top Draft: OL Rueben Brown

Losses: LB Darryl Talley, WE Don Beebe, TE Pete Metzelaars, QB Frank Reich, CB Mickey Washington, LB Marvcus Patton, DE Oliver Barnett

CAROLINA
Gains: RB Barry Foster, QB Frank Reich, RB/RS Randy Baldwin, WR Don Beebe, WR Dwight Stones, K John Kasay, TE Pete Metzelaars, P Tommy Barnhardt, LB Lamar Lathon, LB Darion Conner, LB Frank Stams, DB Bubba McDowell, DT Mike Fox, LB Sam Mills, DB James Williams, DB Brett Maxie, OT Rick Cunningham
Expansion Draft: WR Mark Carrier, QB Jack Trudeau, RB Derrick Lassic, DB Rod Smith, DB Tim McKyer, NT Greg Kragen, OT Harry Boatswain
Top Draft: QB Kerry Collins, DB Tyrone Poole, OT Blake Brockermeyer, DE Shawn King

CHICAGO
Gains: WR Michael Timpson, RB Darrell Thompson, RB Anthony Johnson, DB Marty Carter
Top Draft: RB Rashaan Salaam
Losses: WR/RS Nate Lewis, DE Trace Armstrong, DB Maurice Douglas, DB Shaun Gayle, P Chris Gardocki

CINCINNATI
Gains: RB Eric Bienemy, RB James Joseph, LB Andre Collins, DE Mike Flores
Top Draft: RB Ki-Jana Carter
Losses: RB Derrick Fenner, DB Louis Oliver

CLEVELAND
Gains: WR Andre Rison, RB Lorenzo White, NT Tim Goad

Top Draft: LB Craig Powell, QB Eric Zeier
Losses: QB Mark Rypien, WR Mark Carrier, DL Michael Dean Perry, LB Frank Stams, DL James Jones

DALLAS
Gains: QB Wade Wilson, RB David Lang, C Ray Donaldson
Top Draft: RB Sherwin Williams
Losses: WR Alvin Harper, QB Rodney Peete, RB Derrick Lassic, C Mark Stepnoski, DE Jim Jeffcoat, DB James Washington, DB Kenneth Gant, DE/LB Matt Vanderbeek, LB Darrick Brownlow

DENVER
Gains: WR Ed McCaffrey, QB Bill Musgrave, DT Michael Dean Perry, RB Aaron Craver, OL Mark Schlereth, OL Bill Shultz, DB Eric Thomas, DB Lionel Washington, DB Tim Hauck, LB Britt Hager
Top Draft: OL Jaime Brown
Losses: LB Mike Croel, NT Ted Washington, LB Richard Harvey, WR Cedric Tillman, OT Kirk Scrafford

DETROIT
Gains: DT Henry Thomas, OT Zefross Moss, QB Don Majkowski, P Mark Royals, P Harold Alexander, DB Corey Raymond
Top Draft: DL Luther Ellis
Losses: QB Dave Krieg, KR Mel Gray, RB Derrick Moore, LB Pat Swilling, TE/LB Ty Hallock, DE Kelvin Pritchett, LB Broderick Thomas, DE Marc Spindler, DB Harry Colon, OT Larry Tharpe, OL Shawn Bouwens

GREEN BAY
Gains: TE Keith Jackson, WR Mark Ingram
Top Draft: DB Craig Newsome

Losses: WR Sterling Sharpe (Injured/Waived), LB Bryce Paup, TE Ed West, RB Reggie Cobb, TE Reggie Johnson, DB Corey Harris, QB Mark Brunell, RB Darrell Thompson, DL Matt Brock, DE Don Davey, OL Joe Sims, DB Terrell Buckley

HOUSTON
Gains: QB Chris Chandler, KR Mel Gray, C Mark Stepnoski
Top Draft: QB Steve McNair
Losses: WR Haywood Jeffires, WR Ernest Givins, RB Lorenzo White, LB Lamar Lathon, DB Bubba McDowell, DT Tim Roberts, DB Bo Orlando, OL Bill Shultz, QB Cody Carlson

INDIANAPOLIS
Gains: QB Craig Erickson, WR Willie Anderson, TE Ed West, P Chris Gardocki
Top Draft: DT Ellis Johnson
Losses: TE Kerry Cash, QB Don Majkowski, OT Zefross Moss, OT Cecil Gray, P Rohn Stark

JACKSONVILLE
Gains: DE Jeff Lageman, DE Kelvin Pritchett, LB Joel Smeenge, DB Mickey Washington, QB Mark Brunell, DB Vinnie Clark, OL Dave Widell, OL Shawn Bouwens, TE/LB Ty Hallock, QB Andre Ware
Top Draft: OT Tony Boselli, RB James Stewart
Expansion Draft: QB Steve Beuerlein, TE Derek Brown, RB Reggie Cobb, WR Desmond Howard, WR Cedric Tillman, LB James Williams

KANSAS CITY
Gains: WR Victor Bailey, DB James Hasty, DB Ronnie Lott, DB Brian Washington
Top Draft: OT Trezelle Jenkins

Losses: QB Joe Montana (retired), WR J.J. Birden, DB Charles Mincy, NT Greg Kragen

LOS ANGELES
Gains: RB Derrick Fenner, TE Kerry Cash, LB Pat Swilling, OT Cecil Gray
Top Draft: RB Napoleon Kaufman
Losses: WR Alexander Wright, DB Lionel Washington DB Donald Frank, LB Winston Moss

MIAMI
Gains: TE Eric Green, WR Gary Clark, WR Randal Hill, QB Dan McGwire, DE Trace Armstrong, DB Louis Oliver, DB Terrell Buckley
Top Draft: OT Billy Milner, OL Andrew Greene
Losses: TE Keith Jackson, WR Mark Ingram, RB Aaron Craver, RB Cleveland Gary, C Jeff Dellenbach

MINNESOTA
Gains: LB Broderick Thomas, DB Charles Mincy, DB Harlon Barnett, DB Donald Frank, OT Rick Cunningham
Top Draft: DE Derrick Alexander, OT Korey Stringer
Losses: RB Terry Allen, NT Henry Thomas, DE Robert Harris, DB Todd Scott, LB Carlos Jenkins, DB Anthony Parker, DB Vencie Glenn

NEW ENGLAND
Gains: RB David Meggett, C Jeff Dellenbach, DE Tim Roberts
Top Draft: DB Ty Law, DB Jimmy Hitchcock
Losses: RB Kevin Turner, DB Rod Smith, NT Tim Goad, OL Eugene Chung, DB Harlon Barnett, DE Ray Agnew

NEW ORLEANS
Gains: DB Eric Allen, LB Rufus Porter, LB Richard Harvey
Top Draft: RB Ray Zellars, LB Mark Fields
Losses: QB Wade Wilson, LB Joel Smeenge, LB Darion Conner, LB Sam Mills. DB Vinnie Clark, DE Frank Warren (retired), LB James Williams, P Tommy Barnhardt

NEW YORK GIANTS
Gains: RB Herschel Walker, LB Mike Croel, DE Robert Harris, DT Ray Agnew, DB Maurice Douglas, DB Vencie Glenn
Top Draft: RB Tyrone Wheatley, OT Scott Gragg
Losses: RB David Meggett, TE Derek Brown, DT Mike Fox, NT Erik Howard, DB Corey Raymond

NEW YORK JETS
Gains: RB Ron Moore, RB Dexter Carter, QB Bubby Brister, DE Matt Brock, NT Erik Howard, DB Todd Scott
Top Draft: TE Kyle Brady, DE Hugh Douglas, OL Matt O'Dwyer
Losses: WR Rob Moore, QB Jack Trudeau, RB Anthony Johnson, DE Jeff Lageman, DB James Hasty, DB Gary Jones, DB Ronnie Lott, DB Brian Washington, DB Eric Thomas, OT Jeff Criswell, OL Dwayne White

PHILADELPHIA
Gains: RB Ricky Watters, RB Kevin Turner, QB Rodney Peete, TE Reggie Johnson, LB Kurt Gouveia, OL Raleigh McKenzie, OL Joe Sims, DT Rhett Hall, WR Kelvin Martin
Top Draft: DE Mike Mamula, DB Bobby Taylor, OT Barrett Brooks
Losses: RB Herschel Walker, QB Bubby Brister, DB Eric Allen, WR Victor Bailey, RB James Joseph, DE Mike Flores, LB Britt Hager, P Bryan Barker, DL William Perry (retired)

PITTSBURGH
Gains: RB Erric Pegram, OL Tom Newberry, P Rohn Stark
Top Draft: TE Mark Bruener, QB Kordel Stewart
Losses: RB Barry Foster, TE Eric Green, WR Dwight Stone, NT Gerald Williams, DB Gary Jones, DB Tim McKyer, OL Duval Love, P Mark Royals

ST. LOUIS
Gains: WR Alexander Wright, RB Cleveland Gary, DB Anthony Parker, LB Carlos Jenkins, DE Keith McCants, OL Dwayne White
Top Draft: DE Kevin Carter, OT Zack Wiegart
Losses: QB Chris Chandler, WR Willie Anderson, RB David Lang, DB Marquez Pope, OL Tom Newberry

SAN FRANCISCO
Gains: RB Derrick Moore, DB Marquez Pope, DB Clifford Hicks, DE Oliver Barnett, DE Shane Collins, OT Kirk Scrafford
Top Draft: WR J.J.Stokes
Losses: RB Ricky Watters, RB Dexter Carter, WR Ed McCaffrey, QB Bill Musgrave, OT Harry Boatswain, DT Rhett Hall

SEATTLE
Gains: WR Ricky Proehl, QB John Friesz, LB Winston Moss, DB Corey Harris, C Jim Sweeney
Top Draft: WR Joey Galloway, TE Christian Fauria
Losses: K John Kasay, QB Dan McGwire, WR Kelvin Martin, C Ray Donaldson, LB Rod Stephens, LB Rufus Porter, DB Patrick Hunter, DB Terry Taylor

TAMPA BAY

Gains: WR Alvin Harper, WR/RS Clarence Verdin, P Reggie Roby, DE Marc Spindler, DB Kenneth Gant
Top Draft: DT Warren Sapp, LB Derrick Brooks, DB Melvin Johnson
Losses: QB Craig Erickson, DB Marty Carter, P Dan Stryzinski

WASHINGTON

Gains: LB Rod Stephens, LB Marvcus Patton, DB James Washington, DB Stanley Richards, LB Darrick Brownlow, DE/LB Matt Vanderbeek, RB Terry Allen
Top Draft: WR Michael Westbrook, C Cory Raymer
Losses: WR Desmond Howard, QB John Friesz, LB Kurt Gouveia, LB Andre Collins, DE Shane Collins, OL Raleigh McKenzie, OL Mark Schlereth, P Reggie Roby

KEEP A CURIOUS EYE ON PLAYERS ON A TEAM WITH A NEW HEAD COACH

We all know that Dennis Erickson was a highly successful college coach at Miami, but what will he be like in the pros? The current Seahawks are not young college recruits, and for the first time he will not have the greatest talent in the country (as he did as Miami's coach). He does have a solid young QB in Rick Mirer, but will Erickson bomb out or run with the challenge?

Mike White takes over the Raiders. White is renowned as a quarterback coach, which could just be the ticket for Jeff Hostetler and his receiving corps of Tim Brown, Rocket Ismail and James (Grounded) Jett. But will White's players accept him over Art Shell? Can he pump up that dreadful running (on empty) backfield? So, my artful fellow drafters, take heed and give the new head coaches the once-over and try to surmise the direction that they will take (i.e. offensive or defensive).

PHILADELPHIA EAGLES

What can Ray Rhodes do to stem the bleeding from last season? First, he needs to sit Randall down and explain that if he doesn't get the job done within the offensive system that he will become an also-ran--another great athlete who never won the when the crunch time was prevailing. Rhodes has no choice but to make the streaky but primetime player Ricky Watters into a primary cog in the offense. Watters will be returning to his home state in Pennsylvania and I think he will live up to his superstar billing!

As for the defense (which was Rhodes' specialty), Ray has hired ex-Redskin defensive back coaching guru Emmitt Thomas. Therefore, it's a good guess that we will see plenty of "D" in Philly. But hold the phone, doesn't Rhodes have the much-maligned Randall Cunningham? (Psssst: don't you notice how Randall and much-maligned seem to go hand-in-hand lately?) Expect Rhodes to rejuvenate Randall and put more bite into the Eagles--remember that they were streaking last season until they fizzled at the end. I hope that Randall Cunningham will heed his advice and become the winner that he should be.

His free agent signings were sharp (LB Kurt Gouveia, QB Rodney Peete, OL Raleigh McKenzie) and drafting straight-shooting DE Mike Mamula was top notch. In my opinion Ray Rhodes will become a very successful head coach.

SEATTLE SEAHAWKS

In the past few years Dennis Erickson certainly has faced a media maelstrom over the situation at Miami with the Hurricanes and his DWI charge. Erickson's straight-as-an-arrow-image suffered a wee bit of tarnish and now he will be hounded if the Seahawks don't get out of the gate quickly. Erickson's philosophy tends to be OFFENSE...OFFENSE...OFFENSE, so expect him to cut loose from the Seahawks' past image of stationary football. Rick Mirer to Brian Blades, Ricky Proehl and Joey Galloway should wake up the normally staid "Zzzzz"-hawks!

You gotta like the fact that the 'Hawks drafted TE Chris Fauria with their number two pick--this guy has incredible hands and gives Rick Mirer an additional quality receiver. Now picture this...four quality receivers and a big, bruising running back with speed and goal line vision (Chris Warren). I am excited already at the prospect of an Erickson offense with a young, steady quarterback like Rick Mirer at the controls. With the emergence of superfly rookies (Galloway and Fauria), and the signing of always consistent yet constantly underrated Ricky Proehl, I expect Brian Blades to shine for the Seahawks and become their go-to guy. I have the utmost respect for Blades and feel that he is very similar to a Sterling Sharpe. Once Dennis Erickson can put the University of Miami and the DWI mess behind him, he will find peace and success at perhaps the only place that he can control his destiny--the ball field.

DENVER BRONCOS

Mike Shanahan suffered the embarrasment of bombing with the Raiders several years ago; in fact, he was practically run out of town. So he goes to San Francisco, and all he did there was prove his value by developing Steve Young and Company into a veritable juggernaut and, in case I didn't mention it, a world champion. Now everyone wants to clone Shanahan's offense. First, Shanahan will look to copy success with John Elway and his charges. He is bringing with him to the Broncos a possession receiver in Ed McCaffrey and backup QB Bill Musgrave, both of whom have intimate knowledge of his system. He'll obviously develop Glyn Milburn into more of a nimble runner/pass receiver (the Ricky Watters role) and maximize the tight end position (the Brent Jones role) with Shannon Sharpe. Although Denver does not have a Jerry Rice (does anyone?), Anthony Miller can play every play with intensity. He will be a top five NFL receiver. A healthy Mike Pritchard (if he returns) could really open up this offense. As far as the Broncos defense, I still don't see that changing...points will be scored on Denver again. As for Shanahan's chances this time? I think Mike Shanahan will be a winner the second time around!

HOUSTON OILERS

It was really tough watching a class act like Jack Pardee suffer the humiliation of losing his job during the 1994 season. Jeff Fisher took over in the interim and frankly fared no better than Pardee. Houston made the correct decision to give the former Chicago Bear and Buddy Ryan disciple the job for 1995. Fisher needs to rebuild (especially after losing Haywood Jeffires, Ernest Givins, Lorenzo White *and* Cody Carlson). Fisher can start with rookie QB Steve "Air" McNair--hey, why not? Let Air take the reigns and learn on the job--he'll be exciting! For now I expect to see Chris Chandler initially inheriting the QB job. He has proven to be a capable backup, but not a fulltime star.

One guy who needs a wakeup call is Gary Brown. Last year Gary Brown had a nauseating season (I am not being cruel, but if you drafted Brown last year, your stomach was churning, huh?). With Lorenzo White signing with Cleveland that leaves GB as the main RB in Houston. On a team with zero receivers...Jeff Fisher is going to have to put a lot of faith in Gary Brown. Therefore, expect Fisher to sooner or later bring in the exciting strong-armed, feets-a-moving, look-ma-no-hands-can-touch-me Steve "Air" McNair.

For all of you doubters that think Air can't cut it because he played for a small school: Whaddaya, nuts? This guy throws pigskin missiles; the only dying quails you'll see will be if a feathered flock get caught mid-air with a McNair air-strike. The only concern is exactly who McNair or any of the Oilers' armsmen will be throwing to. Unless Fisher can solve this problem, I expect his future to be shorter than his short sleeves. If he's not careful, he could end up being the water boy for Buddy's Boys real quick-like.

ST. LOUIS RAMS

Oh boy...this is going to take a while for me to get used to calling the Rams a St. Louis team and the Cardinals an Arizona team. I've been practicing calling the Raiders a Baltimore team, but that appears a no-no, as well as a no-go.

Back to the Rams, what will this move mean to them? How about shaking off some of that laidback LA attitude and perhaps developing an actual *winning* attitude?!? New head coach Rich Brooks has a heck of a college resume, but just exactly how will that relate to the pros? Relating or not, Brooks first needs to get Chris Miller off the carpet long enough to play more than half a season. Expect Brooks to re-establish the running game under the pile-moving strides of Jerome Bettis. Expect Brooks to miss NCAA Saturday afternoons by mid-season if Miller and Bettis don't stay off the Red Cross top ten List.

What I do like that Brooks did was sign some good defensive free agents: CB Anthony Parker, LB Carlos Jenkins, and DE Keith McCants. Add his number one draft pick DE Kevin Carter (fierce *and* mean) and the Rams look like a team with teeth.

The offense could click with speedster receiver Alexander Wright and the improving second-year player Isaac Bruce. But if Brooks is to move the yardsticks he needs a serious Jerome Bettis and TE Troy Drayton to pitch in and hustle. Brooks should have a easy time in St. Louis this season--but he better build a winner, because this town knows the difference between a contender (hail Jim Hart) and a slacker (anybody seen Bill Bidwell?)

NEW YORK JETS

Last season I thought that Rich Kotite got a raw deal with Philadelphia and their new owner (Jeffrey "Mr. I-Am-Hollywood-Look-At-Me" Lurie). Just when I was expecting to find Kotite working as a driving instructor at a local Philly high school, the Jets came a-calling like a jilted schoolboy looking for a prom date. Love struck and the rest is his-to-ry. Kotite will not be airing the ball out with Boomer Esiason, but he will be ramming the ball down the oppositions throat with a solid running game (Ron Moore and Johnny Johnson) and a double tight end extraordinaire (Johnny Mitchell and Kyle "# 1" Brady). By the way, the drafting of Brady at number one produced jeers from the Jet fans attending the draft.

Brady responded with verve, style and humor. (Watch out Jet fans: you just may fall in love with this super-talented, lovable lug).

But it should be noted by all that the Brady selection was Kotite's and that pick should show that Rich is in charge. Also NT Erik Howard and DB Todd Scott were solid free agent pick ups. Too bad Rich Kotite is playing in the AFC East, where Miami and New England are lethal and...oops...Indianapolis no longer wears the welcome mat on their backsides.

LOS ANGELES RAIDERS

I already mentioned that Mike White is a solid offensive mind and that he should ease Jeff Hostetler's mind with some improved offensive schemes. What he needs to do is load up on Derrick Fenner and see if he can get some yardage for the Raiders. If the Raiders have hopes of competing for the AFC crown, Hoss *cannot* be their leading rusher!

I like the drafting of Napoleon Kaufman and he should be a terrific player scooting out of the backfield. Memo to a MR. AL DAVIS: remember the success you had with those little scatbacks like Greg Bell? Visit the past (as it is, he dresses like he's stuck in 1978) and enjoy Kaufman! With this receiving corps and perhaps half of football's best returners, this will be an exciting and dangerous team downfield. Let's see...Tim Brown (very fast), Raghib Ismail (rocket-fast) and James Jett (ok...you quessed it...jet fast)? Add a tough scooter like Napoleon Kaufman and I am winging that ball everywhere.

Let Derrick Fenner bruise up the middle and toss a few short-yarders to the reliable TE Kerry Cash...heck, folks could confuse the Raiders for that other California team, the Niners. If I am Mike White, I open up the offense and roll into the playoffs. Only three teams stand in the Raiders' path: Miami, Cleveland and New England. Folks, don't look now but the AFC is closing that wide gap with the NFC!

★4★

Team-by-Team Reviews

DRAFTING HEAD COACHES

One fun part added to the *FFL Journal* last season was an idea presented by you, the reader. (See...I really do listen, gang!) People had written in to suggest including head coaches as part of their leagues. This little addition added even more fun and helped tweak the game. Obviously, you don't want to draft a head coach who appears headed for the gallows (this year, that would be Jacksonville's leader)--so even if this pick won't turn your season around, it could help out and allow you to squeak out a weekly victory in a close head-to-head game.

Now buck up here if you don't draft head coaches...because you should be aware of any player that you want to draft that could be on a real stink-a-roo of a team. For example last season the Houston Oilers fell completely apart. When a team begins to smell foul...the whole team eventually begins to perform like boneheads. In 1993 running back Gary Brown was a terrific pickup for many a proud franchise. In 1994 Mr. Brown looked sluggish...injury prone and, frankly, was a terrible pick (in many cases a first or early second round choice). So a tip here is to study the head coaches and regardless if you agree with my assessment, think about drafting players that will see action...can score...and can gobble yardage on a team that isn't losing 20-0 two minutes after the opening kickoff!

COACH	TEAM	PROJECTED '95 WINS	INSIDE SKINNY
George Seifert	SF	12	Gotta knock out the champ. Young to Rice still the best in NFL. J.J. Stokes will find success quickly. William Floyd is ready for a 1,200 yard, 14 TD season if he gets the ball. Watch for RB Derrick Moore...solid player and can score!
Don Shula	MIA	12	Don and Dan's Adventure-- Super Bowl; bound. Barring injuries...can't miss. Loaded up well with Eric Green, Gary Clark and Randal Hill. Shula's looking perhaps like a 12- 14 game winner.
Bill Belichick	CLE	12	Off-season aggressiveness with solid pickups (Andre Rison, Lorenzo White) should pay off. I am on the Vinny Bandwagon...he should have a awesome season...YO VINNY!
Barry Switzer	DAL	11	Troy, Emmitt and Michael still rule. Off season FA and NFL Draft produced very little. I think the C'Boys will be tighter in '95. Don't underestimate

COACH	TEAM	PROJECTED '95 WINS	INSIDE SKINNY
			Jerry and Barry...Kevin Williams will deliver results!
Bill Cowher	PIT	10	Surprised in '94 and should have grabbed the brass ring to the Super Bowl. Won't surprise in '95:Will O'Donnell be less erratic? Bam Morris is super but will he share with Erric Pegram?
Bill Parcell	NE	10	Quick-learning Pats still may be a season away. Drew Bledsoe is another Dan Marino. David Meggett was a gem of a FA. Watch rookie RB Curtis Martin, could surprise and start. Ben Coates is an All Pro, but I like Vincent Brisby BIG in '95!
Teddy Marchibroda	IND	9	Good move in acquiring Craig Erickson-- Marshall Faulk is a workhorse-Emmitt Smith clone. Nice job in picking up WR Willie Anderson and TE Ed West, to join with WRs Floyd Turner

COACH	TEAM	PROJECTED '95 WINS	INSIDE SKINNY
			and Sean Dawkins. Very improved team but needs kicker. Mike Cofer is a disaster waiting to happen.
Mike Holmgren	GB	9	Really going to miss Sterling Sharpe as he was the heart and soul to the offense--Brett Favre is key. Need a content Keith Jackson, renewed Mark Ingram and a big year from Edgar Bennett. I'd like to see RB LeShon Johnson finally.
Steve Shanahan	DEN	9	John Elway will benefit from his mentor Shanahan. Offense will explode with Shannon Sharpe, quick Glyn Milburn and Leonard Russell. Anthony Miller should be tighter with Elway in '95. Mike Pritchard is a big time player that hopefully will be back from an injured kidney.
June Jones	ATL	9	Loses Rison, but teamwork should improve. Jeff George has finally grown up to potential. I like

COACH	TEAM	PROJECTED '95 WINS	INSIDE SKINNY
			Terance Mathis and J.J. Birden with Jeff George. Plus Eric Metcalf will love George (and vice versa). Ironhead Heyward could be a big FFL player in the one back!
Ray Rhodes	PHI	9	Rhodes just may be the saving grace for Philly. A renewed Randall is also needed. Some question Ricky Watters as a major cog...Don't forget the guy is a primetime player and catches great and runs even better...He could strike it big with Philly.
Wayne Fontes	DET	9	Crucial time for Scott Mitchell to stand up and be counted. Johnnie Morton needs to help Herman Moore and Brett Perriman. I say this year let Barry Sanders...be BARRY!
Buddy Ryan	AZ	9	Dave Krieg will get Buddy 8-9 wins, but the eyes will be on Garrison Hearst. Defense will hold fort but Krieg is key. Rob Moore is phenomenal when he puts

COACH	TEAM	PROJECTED '95 WINS	INSIDE SKINNY
			forth effort. He'd better because Buddy's dog house is like Alcatraz.
Dave Wannstedt	CHI	9	Super job coaching in '94, but the Bears need Erik Kramer, not Steve Walsh to push playoffs. Gained good receiver in Michael Timpson to join Curtis Conway. If Rashaan Salaam shows up as a hard body then watch out for Bears!
Mike White	RAI	9	Hostetler and receivers (Tim Brown and Co.) will like Mike White. Nap Kaufman will excite and Derrick Fenner must be a factor. Hint: Someone introduce James Jett to offense...this guy is incredible!
Bobby Ross	SD	9	How did the Chargers do it in '94? Need a healthy Humphries. Offensive key is Natrone Means, without him this is a 5-11 team despite fine defense.
Dennis Erickson	SEA	8	Much improved offensively and will drive for more

COACH	TEAM	PROJECTED '95 WINS	INSIDE SKINNY
			scores in '95. Mirer will get chance to stretch his game with burner WR Joey Galloway, and solid Pro's Brian Blades and Ricky Proehl. Chris Warren is in the elite at RB.
Dan Reeves	NYG	8	Great running backs (Rodney Hampton, Herschel Walker and Tyrone Wheatley), but can Dave Brown lead? Will Thomas Lewis step up as a receiver? Good defensive FA pickups.
Dennis Green	MIN	8	Terry Allen leaves big shoes to fill--Good receivers (Carter & Reed) for Warren Moon. Lost some very solid defensive players. Will it be Amp Lee or Robert Smith running...or both?
Jim Mora	NO	8	No hocus-pocus here...if Jim Everett plays like he did in '94...Saints will contend. Mario Bates is a stud, while Ray Zellars could be a nice scorer as well. Michael Haynes

COACH	TEAM	PROJECTED '95 WINS	INSIDE SKINNY
			needs to be used more in '95.
Sam Wyche	TB	8	Sammy Wyche is in a now or never situation and really needs wins. Good cast, but is Dilfer ready? Receiving corps is one of NFL's best; Erricht Rhett is an exciting, solid RB.
Marv Levy	BUF	7	A whole lotta folks jumped ship and Jim Kelly sure was battered in '94. Defense will like Bryce Paup and Jim Jeffcoat...but where's the offense? Just Andre Reed and Thurman Thomas?
Norv Turner	WAS	7	Rebuilding effort underway. Defense looks solid but can Shuler become consistent and will RBs run? Rookie WR Michael Westbrook will become a bigtime player...another Michael Irvin? Can Henry Ellard play any better than his sensational '94 season? Is Reggie Brooks physically back?

COACH	TEAM	PROJECTED '95 WINS	INSIDE SKINNY
Rich Brooks	STL	7	This is a feelgood season for St. Louis. Need a healthy Chris Miller and an enthused Jerome Bettis. WR Alexander Wright has speed and could develop with Miller. Gained some terrific FA defensive gems. Troy Drayton and Bettis need to play with full-out potential.
Rich Kotite	NYJ	7	Cram the ball down the defenses throat with double TE's and RBs Ron Moore and Johnny Johnson. We may see Dexter Carter used much like David Meggett and Eric Metcalf.
Marty Schottenheimer	KC	7	Black arm band season with No Joe. Too many question marks on the Chiefs. Will it be Pro Bono? WR Victor Bailey was a bust in Philly and KC will miss J.J. Birden. WRs Willie Davis and Lake Dawson need to pick up pace.
David Shula	CIN	8	I really think the Bengals are becoming a really fun

COACH	TEAM	PROJECTED '95 WINS	INSIDE SKINNY
			and exciting team. Add Ki-Jana and Bengals roar. Jeff Blake was exciting in '94. Can he deliver again in '95? Exciting receivers in Pickens and Scott!
Jeff Fisher	HOU	3	Let's start all over in Houston. Air McNair should take over early and begin his field generalship. Houston looks no good for '95.
Dom Capers	CAR	2	Not a bad squad, but with any new franchise you are going to find a thin layer after the first line of talent. I like the lineup of Reich, Foster, Beebe, Carrier, Metzelaars and Kasay.
Tom Coughlin	JAX	0	In about three years we can really discuss this squad. Rookie RB James Stewart is fun, but the Jags are no Panthers!

PROGNOSTICATIONS
Or
"Just a Super Bowl Guess"

The one thing I enjoy about writing a book is that I get to make up reasons why I think so and so will win the Super Bowl! Yeah, as if I have some special power to predict the Super Bowl winner...uh-huh...okay, right. For the record over the past ten years I have been right three times. So I have a 30% shot at coming up with the best solution for the Super Bowl. The funny thing is that every season picking the Super Bowl pick looks easy. This season my mind hits and gets stuck on the Miami Dolphins and the San Francisco 49ers. The only other clubs that come close are the Cleveland Browns and the Dallas Cowboys. Frankly the rest of the group look like 9-and 8-game winners. This season we will really experience P-A-R-I-T-Y. After all the free-agency moves and the cutting and releasing of high-priced veterans--who knows who will do what?

Hey gang, the NFL is playing FANTASY FOOTBALL! Look around and tell me all this switching around doesn't remind you of your own sweet league. Franchises moving players like an FFL chess board on Draft Night. Free Agency is like a crazed auctioneer on a sugar high dealing players quicker than you can say "hey, whatever happened to...Buffalo's 1994 starters Don Beebe and Pete Metzelaars?" So before my editor Dave Warner slaps me silly and says "ahem...nice bit of sidetracking now will you finish your wandering, wondering thoughts on WHO will win the Super Bowl?"...back to reality...back to my deadline....here we go! The surprise teams for 1995 will be the also-rans of this decade: Tampa Bay, Indianapolis, and Cincinnati. In the past, these woeful squads (to steal a line from Bon Jovi)... "gave love..err football...a bad name" Combined wins would still keep them in the single digit win (can we say that) column. As for the Bengals they say a tiger never changes stripes...the players never changed uniforms because they were never dirty. The Colts seemed to be hexed by a spell ever since they moonlighted out of Baltimore in the Mayflower Van Lines trek to Indy. The Bucs were as stupid and lame as those insipid tangerine uniforms that send off gamma rays and bad vibes) in the sunlight...or an empty stadium. But take heed, gang, these teams are no longer slackers and inept unkempt pretenders. This season they will excite, score and especially win ...and probably play a round in the playoffs.

The real story is that the AFC has at least caught up with the NFC and may soon pass them up. After San Francisco and Dallas, the NFC contender list gets small. Green Bay, Philadelphia, Atlanta, Detroit, Tampa Bay and maybe Chicago will make runs. Questions abound in Arizona, New York, New Orleans, St. Louis and Minnesota. But look at the flashy Johnny-come-latelies in the AFC: Miami, Cleveland, Raiders, New England, San Diego, Indianapolis, Pittsburgh, Denver, Seattle, Cincinnati...etc. It's ironic that in the AFC, all of these franchises are on the move up while the three dominant AFC teams over the past 5 years (Buffalo, Kansas City and Houston) are disappearing. When I look at the Raiders, I see a team that could potentially explode if they can put together a consistent offensive game plan. If Derrick Fenner and Napoleon Kaufman can reawaken the dormant running game, we have a three-way AFC race to the end But in the end, the real winners will be from the AFC: Miami and Cleveland. In the NFC: San Francisco and Dallas. The Super Bowl will be San Francisco versus Miami. And the winner is: Miami Dolphins and one for the history books for Don Shula!

Most Fantasy Football publications generally give tunnel vision when it comes to discussing teams and players. Not us gang, as in this section I once again have the top notch insights of experts who cover the NFL. This section is designed to give you another set of eyes and viewpoints on teams and players. Because, my friends, in order for you to become the franchise winner of your league...you must be prepared and knowledgeable. I am once again honored to have Larry Michael (Mutual Radio), Larry Weisman (USA Today), and John Weiss and Dave Douglas (NFL Films) give their perspectives on the NFL Teams.

Larry Michael does a wonderful job with his play-by-play of NFL games for Mutual and I always enjoy the games when he hooks up with ex-Washington Redskin Doc Walker on radio casts. Listening to that duo is like sitting around the den with a couple of buddies and having a great time and a lot of laughs. If you haven't had the opportunity...check 'em out.

When I turn to the USA Sports page I always look for two writers: Larry Weisman and Rudy Martzke No one has a better grasp then Weisman when it comes to following the NFL beat and last year it was good to hear Larry being interviewed on several radio sports shows. Larry follows the NFL beat throughout the country and sees player and team developments and this knowledge has made him a very wise-man..or is that Weis-man?

As for Rudy, although I can't utilize his expertise (that he dishes out in his first rate TV Column), I certainly respect him for jumping the thin-skinned NFL and the TV networks for virtually ignoring the growing throngs of fantasy players who want shows and scores relating to the FFL. Pat Hughes and myself have been on many a radio show with Rudy and we always appreciate his candor concerning the NFL, network TV and the role fantasy football can play. I catch Rudy when I can, and sometimes his best can be heard on the incredibly funny Don & Mike National Radio Show (heard locally on WJFK in Washington, DC and on nearly 50 stations nationwide). Don & Mike is not a sports show, but they do converse quite a bit about sports and just everyday humor. Talent is something hard to hide and it is my hope that since WJFK radio in Washington is getting the Washington Redskins game action, I hope they utilize Don & Mike's vast entertaining abilities.

John Weiss and Dave Douglas (NFL Films), have been with the FFL Journal for several years. I have always appreciated their insight and their knowledge of the value of the FFL. In fact they were responsible for NFL Films first coverage of Fantasy Football. Of course, what else would you expect from NFL Films? After all, they have always had the best film footage of the NFL.

So without further ado, let's roll the videotape and get a team-by-team perspective of the 1995 NFL season!

★☆★☆ARIZONA CARDINALS★☆★☆

by Larry Weisman
Sports Columnist
USA TODAY

Buddy Ryan always acted as if offense meant nothing. Last year, he proved it.

The meddlesome Ryan defanged an offense that seemed on the verge of breaking through, changed quarterbacks the way other men change socks, and ruined the running game while he was at it.

Perhaps he'll let offensive coordinator Dave Atkins do what he was hired to do and stay with the defense, where he belongs.

QUARTERBACK

Ryan will put the ball in Dave Krieg's hands. The three-headed QB monster last year of Steve Beuerlein, Jay Schroeder, and Jim McMahon accounted for a pass rating of 64.1 and produced only 11 touchdown passes.

Krieg had a super year for Detroit once Scott Mitchell went down and has always been productive. He's also the NFL's all-time leading fumbler and we must wonder how many of those Ryan will tolerate before he goes to the hook.

When the hook is necessary, they do have Jay Schroeder, but he's just too inconsistent and injury-prone to be very effective.

Rookie Stoney Case is inexperienced at best, and Ryan better hope he doesn't need to see playing time early in the season, or Arizona is in deep, deep trouble.

RUNNING BACK

This is Garrison Hearst's biggest and best chance and the Cardinals are betting heavily he won't let it get away.

His off-season workouts were so good the Cardinals traded away Ronald Moore. Hearst's the guy and he'll do well with his breakaway speed and an upgraded offensive line. Look for some long, flashy touchdown runs.

Larry Centers is a do-it-all type who scored five rushing touchdowns and two receiving. He'll still be a receiving threat and a third-down back par excellence.

Chuck Levy didn't do much as a rookie, might figure more as a pass receiver.

WIDE RECEIVER

The Cardinals ditched Ricky Proehl and traded Randal Hill without much regard for what they would do next. They failed to sign Carl Pickens away from Cincinnati, then made their big move the day before the draft, picking up Rob Moore from the New York Jets in a trade.

Moore isn't a burner or a real home-run threat but he's steady and capable of making 80 catches and breaking 1,100. He could score as many as six touchdowns. He looks like the go-to guy.

Second-round draft pick Frank Sanders, a Moore-like receiver, is big and strong and able to make acrobatic catches in traffic. He's no burner but is the likely starter opposite Moore.

Anthony Edwards shows flashes and could be the third guy. The Cardinals will keep looking for depth. You should, too.

DEFENSE/SPECIAL TEAMS

The Ryan defense was toughest on the run. If the offense gets in gear, the defense will be truly dangerous. Ryan stresses turnovers and the Cardinals had 23 interceptions last year. Aeneas Williams is a terrific cornerback.

The Cardinals recorded 35 sacks, a number they can and will improve upon. Defensive tackle Eric Swann will be a force but Clyde Simmons needs to do more than get six sacks to justify his big contract.

The return game is nothing to get excited about. A play in the defense/special teams area is a bet that a Ryan defense will produce sacks, turnovers, and touchdowns. The Cardinals scored only one defensive touchdown.

KICKER

Greg Davis is fairly average. He made 20 of 26 FG tries. He would be a backup kicker in most fantasy leagues on the basis of limited range and lack of opportunities.

★☆★☆ATLANTA FALCONS★☆★☆

by Larry Michael
NFL Play-by Play Announcer
Mutual Radio Network

Another year, another attempt to build a contender. The Atlanta Falcons finished last season, their first under Head Coach June Jones, with a 7-9 record. In spite of the sub-.500 record and finishing out of playoff contention, there was a lot to be optimistic. The team ranked third in the entire NFL in first quarter points, quarterback Jeff George had a very strong year, and Craig "Ironhead" Heyward had more 1,100 yards from scrimmage. Failure to hold onto a lead late in a game, however, caused the Falcons to end up 7-9 instead of 12-4. The Falcons held a lead in the fourth quarter in 12 of the 16 games, and they only won 7 times!

QUARTERBACK

Finally last season, quarterback Jeff George showed why he's been highly touted since his high school days in Indianapolis. The enigmatic signal caller registered some tremendous numbers last year. He set both club records and career highs for yards passing and completions with his 322 completions and 3,374 yards! Overall in the NFL he ranked 7th in yards, touchdowns and completions. He was number ten scorer in the FFL last year with 216 points, firing 23 touchdown passes. With four of the tosses going for over 40 yards. Backing up George again this year will be Bobby Hebert, who threw for two touchdowns off the bench last year.

RUNNING BACK

Craig Heyward turned his career around last year. Probably the heaviest running back in the NFL, "Ironhead" entered his 7th NFL campaign with the label of underachiever taped on his helmet. The former #1 pick of the New Orleans Saints lost almost 40 pounds before 1994 training camp, and went on to career highs with 779 yards rushing, 1,114 total yards, and 8 TDs. His 4.3 average per carry tied him for 4th best in the NFL. He should go high in your FFL draft, but you better get a weight check before making the pick. The guess here is that "Ironhead" knows from last year's stats that weight makes a difference, and he should be ready to punish tacklers again this season. And how about this...for a change of pace this season, the electrifying Eric Metcalf will line up next to Heyward. There's more on Metcalf coming up.

WIDE RECEIVER

The aforementioned Eric Metcalf will see some time at wideout this season for Atlanta. The carpeted Georgia Dome should be ideal for the quick-cutting Metcalf. Last year he crossed the goal line seven times, including three times as a receiver. Jeff George's main beneficiaries last season were Terrance Mathis and Bert Emanuel. Mathis had a true Pro Bowl season with 111 catches and 11 touchdowns, with two of them over 40 yards. Second-round draft pick Bert Emanuel was a college quarterback, but in his rookie season last year he hauled in 46 receptions and four TDs. Even with the departure of Andre Rison, the addition of Metcalf makes the wide receiver corps of the Falcons as dangerous as any in the league.

DEFENSE/SPECIAL TEAMS

Eric Metcalf is one of the best return men in football. Once again, the indoor artificial surface in Atlanta should work to Metcalf's advantage. Defensively the Falcons need some help holding onto a lead, and in the draft they really looked to bolster their defense. First round pick Devin Bush of Florida State and third round pick Lorenzo Styles of Ohio State should lend a hand. Also former Buffalo Bills linebacker Darrell Talley should provide some leadership for what at times last year was a unit lacking confidence.

KICKER

Isn't Norm Johnson lucky? First in Seattle, now in Atlanta, the ideal kicking conditions of a domed stadium have been his to enjoy. And enjoy it he has, as Johnson has proven to be one of the league's most consistent kickers. Last season was another good one for Johnson, hitting on 21 of 25 field goals, 12-16 from 30 yards and out. In last year's FFL points, he was the 16th rated kicker. Take him as your kicker, and you probably won't regret it.

★☆★☆BUFFALO BILLS★☆★☆

by Larry Weisman
Sports Columnist
USA TODAY

It almost didn't seem like a Super Bowl without the Buffalo Bills.

Their remarkable four-year run of representing the AFC in the big game ended unceremoniously with a 7-9 record and a fourth place finish in the AFC East.

Jim Kelly underwent post-season knee surgery, though he should be ready for full duty during training camp. Defensive coordinator Walt Corey lost his job as the Bills' pass rush withered and the secondary sprung leaks. The offensive line no longer looks very dominant.

The road back to glory seems long indeed for the Bills but they still sport an explosive offense and some good players for fantasy play.

QUARTERBACK

Kelly, 34, takes a pretty good hammering every year. His ability to withstand much more on battered knees makes him a shaky choice, though he'll reward because the Bills like to throw. He threw for 3,114 yards and 22 touchdowns. More than ever, he needs protection.

Gone is capable backup Frank Reich, now the likely starter in Carolina. Rick Strom, who hasn't taken a snap since 1990 with Pittsburgh, is the No. 2 guy. No one knows what he might be able to do. No. 3 is Alex Van Pelt, who has been released by Pittsburgh and Kansas City.

The Bills picked Michigan's Todd Collins in the draft but coach Marv Levy steadfastly refuses to play rookies. The danger in drafting Kelly is the backup situation.

RUNNING BACK

Thurman Thomas will again be a good pick. He's a good receiver and the focus of the running game. He accounted for nine touchdowns, seven by rushing. Years of heavy duty have worn him down a bit and his rushing average dipped to 3.8 but he's the guy the Bills give the ball to. His 287 carries last season was his fewest in a year since 1990.

Carwell Gardner showed some flashes at fullback and looked great when the Bills played a two-back set. He scored four touchdowns as the short-yardage guy and should reprise that role.

Kenneth Davis has more outside speed than the slashing Thomas but never gets enough playing time to justify more than a backup role in fantasy leagues.

Journeyman rusher Bobby Humphrey was also signed in the spring, and could compete for a spot on the roster.

WIDE RECEIVER

The Bills need to replace reliable tight end Pete Metzelaars. Lonnie Johnson is not ready to be quite as dependable but the Bills do like to go to the tight end as their hot read. A.J. Ofodile sat out his rookie year with injuries.

Andre Reed had a terrific year, with 90 catches and eight touchdowns. He and Kelly have teamed for 58 touchdowns over the years, the fourth-best tandem in NFL history. He's still a good choice and he's in good shape despite the pounding of 10 NFL seasons.

Billy Brooks is mostly a possession receiver. The sleeper: Bucky Brooks. He had a great rookie training camp but coach Marv Levy doesn't like to play rookies. Brooks can run and gets good separation. He could slip in as the No. 3 receiver for the departed (and often injured) Don Beebe.

DEFENSE/SPECIAL TEAMS

Wade Phillips, the former Denver coach, takes over the defense and wants to put more life in the pass rush. Look for a 4-3 alignment. Bruce Smith dipped to 10 sacks in the face of double- and triple-team blocks but should be sprung more with free agents Jim Jeffcoat and Bryce Paup adding pressure.

The Bills need to replace Mickey Washington at left cornerback. They also need to make more than 16 interceptions, playing such pass-happy teams as New England and Miami twice. A bigger rush ought to open up the ball-hawking. Safety Henry Jones is a stud.

With linebackers Marvcus Patton and Darryl Talley lost as free agents, the Bills have to plug holes. Talley was the big play guy but the Bills scored only once on defense, a big drop from past performances.

The area of kickoff returns was a weak one. Bucky Brooks might get a look here. Jeff Burris did a good job handling punts as a rookie but the Bills did not score on returns.

KICKER

Steve Christie is one of the league's best. He made 16 consecutive FGs and 24 of 28. He's a clutch guy with excellent range and he can handle the tricky winds of Rich Stadium. He has made 72 of 90 FGs (80%) over the last three seasons. Grab him when you can.

★☆★☆CAROLINA PANTHERS★☆★☆

by Dick Giebel

Way back in 1976 when expansion teams Seattle and Tampa Bay entered the world of the NFL, there teams were stocked with castoffs and other teams' draft flops. These teams were jokes and real fodder for the other well-tooled NFL'ers. Nearly 20 years later, that is not the case, particularly when discussing the Carolina Panthers. Carolina trots out a very respectable offense--better offensive weapons, in fact, than several rebuilding teams like Washington and Houston. Offensively speaking, right now the Panthers are ahead of playoff contender Arizona Cardinals. Defensively they can crank out a linebacking corps that would rank fairly high: Lamar Lathon, Darion Conner, Sam Mills, and Frank Stams. Toss in All Pro bookend defensive ends Jeff Lageman and Kelvin Pritchett and the Panthers are solid. Don't be surprised to see this team not only jell early, but win several games.

QUARTERBACK

Frank Reich has always been a "What if?" quarterback. What if Reich actually had a starting QB spot at the start of the season? Well, we will soon find out, as Reich is The Dude in Carolina. The only weakness facing Reich will be the offensive line. The Panthers signed OT Derrick Graham and Harry Boatswain and in the draft literally stole the solid Blake Brockermeyer...but after those fellas, the line gets thin. Backing up Reich is the more experienced Jack Trudeau. Trudeau is a fine QB, but he is not durable and frankly could be hitting the brittle Chris Miller syndrome. Last (for now) in the QB parade is the guy Panthers GM Bill Polian is building around...rookie Kerry Collins. Nice job at

QB! The only reason that I am not predicting 7-8 wins is because this is an expansion team and injuries will deplete the quality players. It is hard to expect the second line Carolina players to be good enough as replacements.

RUNNING BACK

If Barry Foster (851 Yds/5 TDs) can come to Carolina with an "I-wanna-play" attitude, then the running game will be in good shape. Randy Baldwin has been a kick returner during his stint with the Browns, however maybe in Carolina he will get double duty-- check his stats during exhibition season. Derrick Lassic had to learn a thing or two backing up Emmitt Smith and he could develop into the role of receiving back out of the backfield. He could also see action like Ken Davis (BUF) does for the Bills. But for now, the key running back in Carolina is Barry Foster and this is the chance for the Panthers to control and win games with a 1,000 yard rusher.

WIDE RECEIVER

I like this veteran receiving corps: WRs Don Beebe (40 Rec/4 TDs), Mark Carrier (29 Rec/5TDs), Dwight Stone and TE Pete Metzelaars (49 Rec/5 TDs). This is a good crew and, like I stated earlier, they are a better receiving corps than a fair amount of NFL franchises today. My only question is will the offensive line be capable of holding the pass rush? As for speed, few receivers break out like speedy receiver duo of Beebe and Stone. As for quality hands guys...Carrier and Metzelaars are glue and both should have terrific seasons.

DEFENSE/SPECIAL TEAMS

Above I described several components of the Panthers defense that excites me: DE's Lageman and Pritchett, LBs Lathon, Conner, Mills and Stams. What I omitted was the other excellent players that will mesch into a solid group of defenders. In the NFL collegiate draft, they picked up the fabulously quick, solid defensive back Tyrone Poole and powerful DE Shawn King. These two will join NFL proven stalwarts DT Mike Fox, NT Gerald Williams, NT Greg Kragen and defensive backfield support from Bubba McDowell, Brett Maxie, James Williams, Rod Smith and Tim McKyer. If you look at that defense, it is as good if not better than many in the NFL.

Special teams will get a boost from the solid and succesful Randy Baldwin. Year in and year out Baldwin (26.9 return average on kickoffs) would always bring back a kickoff for a TD return at least once a season for Cleveland (last season he clipped off an 85-yd TD return). We may slso see the fleet-footed rookie Tyrone Pool become a returner during his initial campaign

KICKERS

I really like the moves they made by signing free agents John Kasay (K) and Tommy Barnhardt (P). Usually you would think that a kicker on an expansion team may be a poor pick in any fantasy league, but Kasay (20/24 FGs in '94) will get plenty of opportunities with this inspired offense. As for Barnhardt (43.6 Avg), he is a solid weapon and he can consistently pin the opposition deep in their territory.

★☆★☆CHICAGO BEARS★☆★☆

by Larry Michael
NFL Play-by Play Announcer
Mutual Radio Network

A masterful coaching job by Dave Wannstedt landed "'Da Bears" in the playoffs last year. This is not an FFL playoff team, however, as the 1994 Bears proved themselves to be one of the best teams in the NFL without a true "star" player. This could be the breakout year for them, though. Steve Walsh firmly established himself as the starter, while a lot is expected from Colorado Heisman Trophy winner Rashaan Salaam. The emotional Wannstedt could be on the verge of something big, having retooled Chicago in only a two year span. The NFL Central could again prove to be football's most evenly matched division, and if Salaam can even come close to matching his college numbers, the Bears will be in the hunt for the division crown.

QUARTERBACK

Last year's expected starter, Erik Kramer, was simply outplayed by Steve Walsh, who starts this season firmly entrenched in the starter's role. Walsh is steady but unspectacular, relying more on his intelligence and field vision than brute strength. Simply put, Walsh is a winner. For FFL purposes, however, Walsh is ranked 27th among quarterbacks, tossing only ten TD passes last season. Kramer returns as a solid number two man, and in fact could see starting action if Walsh falters. Kramer threw for eight TDs in 1994 before getting benched.

RUNNING BACK

Heisman Trophy winner Rashaan Salaam steps right into the starting lineup. Coach Dave Wannstedt has already said he expects the rookie from Colorado to carry a big part of the load. Wannstedt hopes running Salaam out of a pro set will benefit him more that the single-back sets that were used in Colorado. Talented Lewis Tillman is also in the backfield plans. Last season the undersized Tillman rushed for 7 TDs. Robert Green and Raymont Harris round out a backfield crew which has become deep and explosive with the addition of Rashaan Salaam.

WIDE RECEIVER

As good as the backfield looks this season for the Bears, the wide receiver crew is certainly in need of some help. 17 different players caught passes for the Bears last year, and none of them had more than four touchdowns. Chicago hopes free agent Michael Timpson of New England will become a major contributor. Last season Timpson caught just three TD passes from Drew Bledsoe. Anthony Morgan, Greg McMurtry, Chris Gedney and Keith Jennings will have a hard time making many FFL rosters this season.

DEFENSE/SPECIAL TEAMS

The Chicago defense will be young and mean with Alonzo Spellman and Chris Zorich anchoring a group of prototypical Bears. Last year's top draft pick John Thiery is expected to step up big this season as a defensive end Donnell Woolford anchors the secondary, while the kick return situation is a question mark right now.

KICKER

The Chicago kicker will again be Kevin Butler, one of the lasting links to the team's Super Bowl shuffle of 1986. The swirling winds of Soldier Field make it one of the toughest stadiums in the

NFL to kick a football. Somehow Butler continues to succeed, last year connecting on 21 field goals and 24 PATs, ranking him 14th in total points among FFL kickers.

★☆★☆CINCINNATI BENGALS★☆★☆

By Dave Douglas
NFL Films

1994 was a year of growing pains for David Shula's Bengals. Winners of only three games, they fought all season long not so much to win games but to find an identity. Defense, or more appropriately the lack of it, proved to be their most glaring weakness. Offensively, young quarterback Jeff Blake ignited a big play passing attack that made them exciting to watch and in This air game you'll find some terrific FFL performers. They will trail division rivals Pittsburgh and Cleveland early and often so they'll have to put it up, which could mean big points for you.

QUARTERBACK

The projected starter has to be Jeff Blake. Last season Blake took over and scrambled and fired away to breathe new life into a once dormant Bengal offense. He completed 156 of 306 for 2154 yards and 14 touchdowns and many of those scoring plays were the over 50 yard bonus variety. I don't believe there will be any letdown because he's an instinctive performer who loves to take risks and he has the targets to put up a 20 plus touchdown season. The Bengal ground game is so inconsistent that Blake will be the man and he'd be a great 3rd or 4th round pick. He took off on his own 37 times last year and rushed for a score so he's a definite threat in that regard.

David Klinger could win back his job in the preseason but it is unlikely. His 9 interceptions overshadowed his 6 touchdown passes and he seems to hold the ball too long in the pocket. Don Hollas is an undraftable reserve. BYU quarterback John Walsh slipped to the seventh round of this year's draft but he will be outstanding in the future. I thought he was one of the top three quarterbacks available.

RUNNING BACK

Ickey Woods where have you gone? Last year the backs were just plain icky. None rushed for 500 yards and none scored more than two touchdowns. Derrick Fenner is now a Raider. Steve Broussard (403 yds. and two TDs.) struggled so the Bengals added former Charger Eric Bieniemy through free agency. Both are better receivers than rushers so my rule is not to pick those kind of guys. You need carries and neither will tote the ball enough to hit the 100 yard Mark each week on a consistent basis. Harold Green (223 yds. and two TDs.) is a real enigma. I think he could be a 1000 yard rusher somewhere but for some reason he hasn't risen to the challenge in Cincinnati. James Joseph (203 yds. and three TDs.) was shipped in from Philly.

The story here is Penn State's Ki-Jana Carter, the first player chosen in the entire draft. I saw him play ten times the past season and he is nothing short of spectacular. He was the fastest player on the team and he is patient. He sets up blocks like a five-year pro. He could put up rookie numbers like Marshall Faulk did a year ago if the Bengal line can do anything for him. Pick him in the third round.

WIDE RECEIVER

Here is where you could hit the mother lode. They're loaded. Carl Pickens is a great one. He loves to go deep, he can sky, and Blake loves him. Pickens (71 catches -- 1127 yards -- 11 TDs.) Put up Rice, Sharpe and Rison numbers last season and he's just getting better. He's a sure second or third rounder. When he took one 70 yards last season did you have him? Darnay Scott was a rookie who played like a seasoned veteran. He caught 46 balls, averaged nearly 19 yards a catch and scored 5 times. He'd be a superb second receiver who'll catch 60 passes this season. Tight end Tony McGee (40 catches and one TD.) is a solid young blocker. Tim McGee (13 catches and one TD.) seems to be losing the battle to youth and will probably be relegated to the third receiver in the offense.

Blake will dial long distance with Pickens and Scott and if you have one of them you're in good shape. Fresno State's David Dunn was picked in the fifth round but he won't make an FFL roster.

DEFENSE/SPECIAL TEAMS

Last season the defense surrendered a whopping 406 points. One problem was the lack of pressure on quarterbacks as the Bengals managed only 31 sacks. Alfred "The Condor" Williams led them with nine and a half but then there was a severe drop-off. Top pick Dan "Big Daddy" Wilkinson started slow then came on a bit and finished with 5.5 sacks, but this season that number will approach 10. He had a year of seasoning and now he'll start to assert himself. Linebacker Steve Tovar is a true secret weapon who topped the team with 122 tackles and teammate James Francis could be a star with a little more support. In the secondary, the Bengals can lay you out but they lack the overall speed to really blanket receivers. Darryl Williams and Louis Oliver can hammer guys, but too often they're a step or two late getting there. Oliver's three picks led the team, and with the Bengals releasing Oliver in the offseason, improvement must be made in the takeaway area if the Bengals are to move up in the AFC Central.

Fleet Corey Sawyer handled the punt return duties and he's a true threat, returning one 82 yards for a score last season. Eric Ball was the kick returner, averaging an excellent 21.8 yards per try.

KICKER

Punter Lee Johnson is one the best and he boomed them, averaging 43.8 per boot last year. Kicker Doug Pelfrey has a huge leg. He nailed a pair from over 50 yards on his way to 108 points.

★☆★☆CLEVELAND BROWNS★☆★☆

By Dave Douglas
NFL Films

Last season, Bill Belichick's Cleveland Browns experienced a real franchise-turning season as they made the playoffs for the first time in five years. They won 11 games and nearly the division title. In the minds of many, they're an all-pro quarterback away from being a true Super Bowl contender. The defense is rock solid and always will be under defensive guru Belichick, and the running game is a counted on constant. If a big play passing game can develop, then the Browns could make a sustained run at the Steelers this season. When you think about it, aren't the Browns and Steelers almost a mirror image of each other?

QUARTERBACK

Last season, Vinnie Testaverde came of age behind an offensive line that allowed a league-low 14 sacks. He showed his leadership abilities and his escapability in his best season ever. The "Vin man" still tossed up 18 interceptions, but with the exception of the first Pittsburgh meeting, he played relatively error-free football...especially down the stretch. He passed for a respectable 2575 yards on 207 completions and found the endzone 16 times. He ran for two scores as well, which sort of qualifies him as an FFL bonus baby. Mark Rypien was the back up and completed only 59 passes and a mere 4 TD. passes. The Brownies made a bid for Phil Simms but it was only a half-hearted attempt. Perhaps a little lack of confidence in Vinnie? Gritty Georgia quarterback Eric Zeier was picked in the third round of the draft as the Brownies' passer of the future.

RUNNING BACK

The Browns' most explosive offensive weapon, Eric Metcalf, is off to Atlanta but he never really touched the ball enough to be a consistent FFL performer. Belichick likes pounders anyway and in Leroy Hoard, he has one of the best in the business.

Hoard is a complete back who rushed for 899 yards and caught passes out of the backfield for another 445. Five touchdowns rushing and four receiving...that's FFL balance.

Earnest Byner (219 yds.) is on a downslide and to make matters worse, Randy Baldwin was sent to the Carolina Panthers. Hoard is the pick among the backs easily. Tommy Vardell was sidelined by injury so check his status in the pre season.

WIDE RECEIVER

Former all-pro Falcon Andre Rison, hot temper and explosive personality aside, is a superb FFL receiver. He's a Brown now and he'll catch 80 balls and find the endzone at least a dozen times. He'll go in the first round in your FFL draft because he'll be out to reassert himself this year. If you can snatch him up, do it. Last season, rookie Derrick Alexander led the Browns in receiving with 48 catches and added a pair of touchdowns. With Rison doubled a lot, Alexander will improve on those numbers and thus is a solid second FFL receiver. Alexander averaged over 17 yards a catch so he's a homerun hitter for those bonus touchdowns. Brian Kinchen (24 catches, one TD.), Michael Jackson (21 catches for two TDs.) will play a supporting role but one of the two will be drafted depending on his pre-season performance. Speedsters Mike Miller (Notre Dame) and A.C. Tellison (Miami) were picked late in the draft.

DEFENSE/SPECIAL TEAMS

204 points allowed in 16 games...an NFL record. The defense held opponents to under 21 points in all but one game. Nine teams scored only a single touchdown against them. The secondary

allowed a league low 13 TD. Passes. The unit is very, very good...a mix of age and youth. They play hard for 60 minutes and nearly every year they seem to score a bunch of touchdowns off turnovers. Rob Burnett led the charge with 10 sacks while veteran linebacker Pepper Johnson was tops on the team with 203 tackles.

Eric Turner picked off a team high 9 passes and along with Antonio Langham made the Browns a tough club to throw against consistently. They are a tough unit that could emerge as one of the league's finest. One aspect that needs to be upgraded is sacks...only 38 last year. Michael Dean Perry is now a Bronco. Buckeye linebacker Craig Powell was Cleveland's first pick in the draft, a first rounder who can hit. With the losses of game-breaker Eric Metcalf (2 punt return TDs.) and Randy Baldwin (the AFC kickoff return leader), the Browns need to completely revamp their special team return tandem. Punter Tom Tupa averaged a solid 40.1 yards per boot and scored three times on two point conversions.

KICKER

Kicker Matt Stover quietly turned in an excellent season. Stover ran up 110 points and was 26 of 28. He only missed twice but he's rarely asked to make one from more than 50 yards. He's hit his last 20 in a row, a team record.

★☆★☆DALLAS COWBOYS★☆★☆

by Larry Weisman
Sports Columnist
USA TODAY

Two years ago the Dallas Cowboys seemed ready to establish themselves as the NFL's dynastic monarchs. They had the coach, they had the players, they had the cutting-edge management so critical in the new salary cap era.

Going into the NFC championship game against San Francisco last January, many still thought the Cowboys remained the NFL's team to beat. And the 49ers beat them.

Barry Switzer's second season won't be easy. The 49ers' loss exposed some flaws and another spate of free-agency defections puts a serious dent in an offensive line that is accustomed to dominating.

The corps of talent remains solid, the balance of the roster less so. Are the Cowboys now all hat and no cattle?

QUARTERBACK

It's hard not to like Troy Aikman. As a person, as a player, he is everything he should be. As a fantasy player, he is nothing to get excited about. Aikman threw only 13 touchdown passes last season and has lost preeminent deep threat Alvin Harper. His protection figures to be less solid than last year when he was sacked only 14 times.

The possible upside? If the Cowboys can't run with their old vicious effectiveness, Aikman must pass more. That's good for fantasy leagues, bad for the Cowboys.

RUNNING BACK

Just as the three key elements in real estate are "location, location, and location," Dallas' most important player is Emmitt Smith. You'd be crazy not to take him on the basis of past performance. Smith scored 21 rushing touchdowns and one more receiving and had more than 1,800 combined yards.

The danger signs are these: Smith suffered hamstring pulls in both legs last year. His rushing yards (1,484) dropped by two, but his carries increased by 83. His rushing average fell 1.3 yards to 4.0. Given that his blocking won't be as good, Smith doesn't figure to be quite as productive or durable. He has 1,630 career rushes in five seasons, and that's an awful lot of work.

Blair Thomas is clearly not the answer as the backup. Darryl Johnston doesn't get enough carries to make him a factor in fantasy leagues and his longest run last year was nine yards.

That means rookie Sherman Williams could play a key role. Of course, Smith almost never comes out of games and is a master of playing with pain.

WIDE RECEIVER

Alvin Harper tended to disappear at times but often hit home runs. He led Cowboys receivers with eight touchdowns but took his streaky talent to Tampa Bay. His absence only puts more pressure on Michael Irvin, who works well in traffic but is not the same sort of deep threat. Irvin remains an excellent choice because he'll catch 70-80 passes and will score at least six touchdowns.

The Cowboys will look to Kevin Williams to fill Harper's slot. He has good speed but is unpolished and sometimes undisciplined. Don't take him with a high choice.

Jay Novacek's production has dropped, especially around the end zone. He's no longer a premier tight end. The Cowboys don't have much depth here.

DEFENSE/SPECIAL TEAMS

The Cowboys got a reprieve when Charles Haley decided not to retire but their pass rush will be hurt without Jim Jeffcoat, gone as a free agent to Buffalo. Haley had 12 1/2 sacks and should hit double digits. The Cowboys re-signed Tony Tolbert for big dollars ($15 million for five years) but he'll have to pick up Jeffcoat's slack (and eight sacks). The Cowboys really need Shante Carver, last year's No. 1 pick, to emerge.

The Cowboys led the NFL in total defense and was third in points allowed (248). With the NFC East improving and their talent level barely holding steady, these numbers will slide. They put up 29 turnovers, a fair number, and scored off three.

Kevin Williams is fine return man, averaging 26.7 yards on kickoff returns. But Dallas' solid coverage teams lost a couple of key players in free agents Matt Vanderbeek and Darrick Brownlow, both to Washington.

KICKER

Chris Boniol's rookie year was a success. He hit on his first nine field goal tries and 22 of 29 for the season. His range remains a question. He made one FG from 45 yards but missed from 41, 43, 38, 43, 51. He had two blocked. What will he do under pressure?

★☆★☆DENVER BRONCOS★☆★☆

By John Weiss
NFL Films

So much for the Wade Phillips era in Denver. After two disappointing seasons as head coach, Phillips is out and Mike Shanahan is in, looking to revitalize a team that has become mired in mediocrity.

For Shanahan, this marks a third stint with the Broncos, having served as offensive coordinator on two previous occasions. Over the past three seasons, Shanahan has opened eyes around the NFL as offensive coordinator in San Francisco, and he became one of the league's hottest head coaching prospects when the unstoppable Niners' offense rolled to the Super Bowl XXIX title.

The good news for the Broncos is that in hiring Shanahan as head coach, they now have one of the NFL's brightest offensive minds guiding their team. The bad news is that Denver needs the most help on defense, which finished dead last in the NFL in 1994. So even if Shanahan works wonders with the offense, the Broncos won't improve much on their 7-9 record if they don't shore up football's most porous defense.

QUARTERBACK

John Elway was one of the hottest fantasy commodities going into last season, and though he had a Pro Bowl year, he didn't put up the huge numbers everyone expected. That shouldn't discourage you from making him one of your top picks in '95.

Being reunited with Shanahan, his former tutor, can only help Elway this season. And the fact that two of his star receivers now have a year in Denver under their belts should mean bigger numbers for Elway and the passing game.

71

Last season, despite missing two of the last three games with a knee injury, Elway completed 307-of-494 passes (62.1%) for 3,490 yards. But the stat that disappointed FFL fans was just 16 touchdown passes. If Elway can improve on that number, and he should, he'll once again be one of the top three or four quarterbacks fantasy owners look to in '95.

RUNNING BACK

The Broncos finished just 23rd in the league in rushing last season, and are still looking for a consistent feature back to carry the load.

Leonard Russell led the team in rushing with just 620 yards and a paltry 3.3-yard average before undergoing surgery to repair a ruptured disc in his neck. His one redeeming statistic was nine rushing touchdowns, fifth best in the AFC. If you want to gamble that Russell will be healthy and reach the endzone as often in '95, he's worth looking at as your second or third running back.

Rod Bernstine missed most of last season with a knee injury, and carried the ball just 17 times for 91 yards. He's been on injured reserve every year of his career, so he's a risk to look at for your fantasy backfield. Glyn Milburn made a big impact by catching 77 passes, the most among NFL running backs, and had three touchdown catches. But he doesn't get many carries and can't be counted on for any substantial yardage. The Broncos also signed former Dolphin Aaron Craver.

WIDE RECEIVER

This is where the Broncos are loaded with talent for your lineup. In 1994, his first season with the Broncos, Anthony Miller had a hard time fitting into the Denver system, and got off to a slow start. He picked it up at the end of the year to finish with 60 catches, 1,107 yards and five touchdowns. He should be more comfortable this season, and put up the kind of numbers that will make him one of the top point producers among fantasy receivers.

72

Equally as enticing is Shannon Sharpe. If you're looking to fill a tight end spot, there's not many out there better than Sharpe, who led the Broncos last season with 87 catches for 1,010 yards and four touchdowns.

Mike Pritchard's first season in Denver came to a painful end when he suffered a lacerated kidney, and he finished with just 19 catches for 271 yards and one touchdown. If Pritchard can play a full season, he gives Denver a third receiving threat capable of catching at least 70 passes for 1,000 yards. He'd make a great second receiver in your fantasy lineup. Derek Russell had 25 catches for 342 yards and a touchdown.

DEFENSE/SPECIAL TEAMS

As a unit, this defense doesn't have much to offer fantasy owners. The team registered just 23 sacks last season, and came up with only 12 interceptions, and 26 total takeaways.

Where do the Broncos begin trying to improve the NFL's 28th- ranked defense? Well, they started by plugging the middle of their line with two former Browns, Michael Dean Perry and James Jones. Perry had four sacks and Jones registered three last season. Other new additions include former Eagle linebacker Britt Hager and former raider cornerback Lionel Washington.

Among those returning, defensive end Simon Fletcher has become one of the league's most durable players, starting 124 consecutive games. But his seven sacks last season were his fewest since 1987. Shane Dronett was second on the team with six sacks.

Outside linebacker Elijah Alexander emerged last season to lead the team with 172 total tackles (105 solo). Safety Steve Atwater, the defense's lone Pro Bowler last season, was second with 125 tackles (72 solo). Cornerback Ray Crockett was one of the team's co-leaders with two interceptions.

On special teams, Glyn Milburn led the team in kick return yardage, but Butler By'not'e led in average with 22.7, fourth in the AFC. Milburn was the team's only punt returner with a 9.2 average, ranking sixth in the AFC.

KICKER

Jason Elam should certainly be one of the top five kickers on your fantasy draft list. He finished third in the NFL with 119 points last season, and his 30 field goals were also third best in the league. Overall, Elam hit on 30-of-37 field goals, including 1-of-3 from 50-plus yards.

With Denver's offense likely to put big points on the board again this season, Elam is a good bet to be one of the league's top scorers.

★☆★☆DETROIT LIONS★☆★☆

by Larry Michael
NFL Play-by Play Announcer
Mutual Radio Network

After a dismal performance in the first-round playoff game against Green Bay last season, the Detroit Lions must once again place themselves upon the giant shoulders of Barry Sanders and hope that he will lead them to the promised land. How can one man do so much? Overall, the Lions have not improved much during the offseason, so the heat is on Barry Sanders to have another tremendous year. The rest of the offense will be directed by quarterback Scott Mitchell, who made big bucks last year, but missed much of the year due to injury. Dave Krieg isn't around any more, so Mitchell must stay healthy and earn his money by throwing some accurate lobs to Herman Moore.

QUARTERBACK

When Scott Mitchell signed with the Lions last year, it looked like the perfect marriage. But for the second straight year for Mitchell, injuries put him in street clothes. Mitchell performed well as a relief man in Miami for Dan Marino in 1993, until a shoulder injury sidelined him. His short-term performance, though, was enough to get the big money from the Lions, until more injuries sidelined him again last year. Fortunately for the Lions, Dave Krieg was there, and he responded by putting up 17 TDs and helping the Lions make the playoffs. This year, Mitchell must remain the starter, as the only experienced backup Detroit has is Don Majkowski.

RUNNING BACK

Barry Sanders displaced Emmitt Smith atop the NFL rushing leaders in 1994, and his yardage enabled him to rack up 164 performance scoring points in the FFL, twice as many points in that category as any other NFL players. Additionally, his seven rushing touchdowns and one TD through the air helped rank Sanders 5th last year in total FFL points. Lions fans better hope that Sanders stays healthy. Not only was he the league's leading rusher last year, there also is no depth behind him. Reggie Rivers, a former practice squad player, is the backup right now, but a move could be made to bolster a position where Sanders is simply irreplaceable.

WIDE RECEIVER

There isn't a better leaper in football than Herman Moore. Height and hops help make Moore an extremely dangerous receiver in the red zone. If he could develop some chemistry with Scott Mitchell (a la Young-Rice, or Aikman-Irvin), Detroit's offense could take some pressure off of Barry Sanders. Last season, Moore pulled down eleven touchdown passes. To complement Moore, Detroit deploys Aubrey Mathews (3 TDs in 1994) and Brett Perriman (4 TDs in 1994). Tight end Ron Hall hopes to bounce back from an injury-plagued season, and might be challenged by rookie David Sloan from New Mexico.

DEFENSE/SPECIAL TEAMS

The Lions lost special teams sensation Mel Gray. They hope to get the same kind of production from Johnny Morton and Brett Perriman, but replacing Gray and his cat-quick moves is almost impossible. The overall Detroit defense should be helped by the free agent acquisition of the Vikings' Henry Thomas, who along with the spirited Chris Spielman, should make the Lions defense a more aggressive unit.

KICKER

When you play in a dome, the kicker needs to be consistent. No excuses will be accepted, and no excuses are being offered from Jason Hanson. After a 1993 season when he connected on 34 field goals, including seven attempts outside the 50, last year he dipped to just 18 field goals, and he missed all five tries outside the 50! If your FFL team needs a kicker, Hanson could be a steal late in your draft. He's too good a kicker to have another sub-par year.

★☆★☆GREEN BAY PACKERS★☆★☆

by Larry Michael
NFL Play-by Play Announcer
Mutual Radio Network

The clock is ticking for the Green Bay Packers. Sterling Sharpe's career as a Packer is over, age is setting in on defense, and they still are looking for a consistent ground game. Mike Holmgren got his troops into the playoffs, but the other contenders in the NFC Central have made significant moves during the offseason. Can Green Bay take it to the next level in '95, or will they regress? A disappointing playoff loss to Dallas showed Green Bay has a tough time coming from behind, and the offense at this point hasn't replaced their biggest contributor, Sterling Sharpe.

QUARTERBACK

Quarterback Brett Favre had a tremendous year in '94. Favre's 33 touchdown passes were second best to league MVP Steve Young. Favre also proved to be an effective scrambler, finishing the season as the team's third leading rusher with 202 yards and 2 touchdowns. Mark Brunell has been sent packing, so the back-up job belongs to two unproven commodities, former Heisman Trophy winner Ty Detmer, and rookie Jay Barker of Alabama.

RUNNING BACK

The fact that Brett Favre had the third most carries on the team last season is cerainly an indictment on the Packers punchless ground game. Edgar Bennett is a solid do-it-all back who had 5 touchdowns rushing and 4 receiving last season. He's not what you'd call a "game-breaker", and neither are any of the other Green

Bay running backs. 3rd round draft pick Willian Henderson of North Carolina is a big back, who'll do some blocking for Bennett, and Dorsey Levens was a pleasant surprise last year. This is a team which still is in need of some speed out of the backfield, and they might make a move before the start of the season to fill that gap.

WIDE RECEIVER

How do you replace Sterling Sharpe? How do you replace 94 receptions in '94? How do you replace a player who caught 18 touchdown passes last season, three better than the great Jerry Rice? How do you replace over 1,000 yards receiving? The obvious answer to these questions is YOU DON'T. Robert Brooks is a good complimentary receiver who caught 56 passes and 4 touchdowns last year. Rookie 3rd round draft pick Antonio Freeman out of Virginia Tech might lend a hand, but as the Packers need some help in the backfield, they need even more help outside, replacing the contributions of one of the NFL's great receivers in Sterling Sharpe. To further complicate the situation, Tight end Keith Jackson, acquired in a trade with the Miami Dolphins, says he won't play in Green Bay under any circumstances, and would rather retire than play for the Pack. It might get worked out by the start of the season, but don't expect the welcome wagon to meet Jackson at the airport

DEFENSE/SPECIAL TEAMS

Reggie White is another year older, Terrell Buckley is gone, Bryce Paup left as a free agent, the Packers defense is in need of some new blood. Rookie Craig Newsome of Arizona State is expected to compete immediately for a cornerback spot. Free agency and the expansion draft hurt the Packer's special teams.

KICKER

Chris Jacke's production fell in 1994, as he converted 19 of 26 field goals, 41-43 PATs for a total of 109 FFL points. The lack of offensive firepower could create a situation where the strong-legged Jacke gets some added cracks from long distance. Two years ago he drilled six field goals from outside the 50 yard line, last year converting just 1 of 3 attempts. He fell to 18th among FFL kickers in '94.

★☆★☆**HOUSTON OILERS**★☆★☆

By Dave Douglas
NFL Films

What a difference a year makes. The Oilers were 12-4 in 1993 and 2-14 last season. The reason was simple. The three headed quarterback mutation of "Bucky-Joe-Cody" couldn't get the job done when venerable Warren Moon took his 1994 season total of 4000 passing yards up to Viking land. Jack Pardee was fired and replaced by young defensive mind Jeff Fisher. Fisher has his work cut out for him in a division that includes Pittsburgh and Cleveland.

QUARTERBACK

Last season, injuries forced the Oilers to field three different signal callers and the result was chaos at the position and a never-ending struggle to put points on the board throughout the year. Cody Carlson had waited in the wings and was a solid backup to Moon for years but injuries limited his playing time and the result was a mere 59 completions and a lone touchdown pass. The Oilers thanked him for that merely adequate performance by releasing him.

Professional backup Billy Joe Tolliver is gone to the CFL (the Shreveport Tigers dealt for him in the NFL offseason) and Bucky Richardson (94 of 181 for 1,202 yds. and 6 TDs.) is simply not worthy of being drafted, although Tolliver was certainly the better and more experienced of the two. Adding more confusion to the mix is Chris Chandler, acquired from the Rams.

All eyes will be on Steve "Air" McNair, Alcorn State's flamethrower of a quarterback. Can this small-school standout make it in the NFL? Mississippi Valley State's Jerry Rice and Jackson State's Walter Payton did pretty well. Fisher will bring him along slowly but he'll start before too long. Don't pick him this year unless he's going to be your FFL backup.

RUNNING BACK

Injuries again struck the Oilers at the running back position as Gary Brown missed chunks of playing time, allowing Lorenzo White to pick up a lot of yards that would have belonged to Brown.

Brown is a great cutback runner who allows his blockers to set the table for him and one of those new blockers will be former Cowboy All Pro center Mark Stepnoski.

Brown (648 yards and 5 TDs.) should return to form and will challenge the 1,000 yard mark if the Oilers can use the pass to set up his cutback opportunities. White (757 yards and 4 TDs.) signed with the Cleveland Browns.

Fisher, like his mentor Buddy Ryan, loves to control the game with the ground attack so watch Brown in the preseason.

WIDE RECEIVER

Without the vaguest idea as to whom would throw the ball each Sunday, Houston's receivers actually did a yeoman's job week in and week out. Offensive coordinator Kevin Gilbride has taken his run-and-shoot attack to Jacksonville so don't look for the all-out passing game any more in the 'Dome. Still, Haywood Jeffires (68 for 783 yds. and six TDs.), Webster Slaughter (68 for 846 yds. and two TDs.), and veteran Ernest Givins (36 for 521 yds. and one TD.) are a talented group. Unfortunately, the rest of the league found out about them, so Givins is now a Jaguar, and Jeffires is a free agent who may or may not re-sign. Only Slaughter is a sure bet to return.

Gary Wellman and Pat Coleman were spot players last season and are not going to be on an FFL roster this year. Tight end Pat Carter caught only 11 passes in 1994 and he only scored once. In the draft, the Oilers picked up a tall target in Auburn's Chris Sanders. Second-year receivers Malcolm Seabron and Travis

Hannah should get good looks early, so they could easily be great sleeper picks. Watch them in the preseason.

DEFENSE/SPECIAL TEAMS

Fisher's forte is the 4-6 defense and it is precisely the gambling, turnover-driven, blitz-happy style that FFL'ers crave. The loss of Sean Jones to Green Bay and William Fuller to the Eagles in 1994 hurt them but it didn't kill them and there's more than meets the eye on the this unit for your FFL roster.

Sack leader Lamar Lathon (8.5) was lost to the Panthers but Ray Childress (6) and Kenny Davidson (6) can heat up the pass pocket and Cris Dishman is a true playmaker in the secondary. Free Safety Bo Orlando was sent to San Diego. Defensive tackle Anthony Cook was selected in the third round.

Fisher will unleash everybody and two games against the Jaguars are 2 more reasons to consider the Oilers as your defensive unit.

Punter Rich Camarillo averaged a solid 42.9 yards per punt and had none blocked. Return chores were handled by Ernest Givins, who took one the distance. Former Lion Mel Gray will be the man this year. He took three back all the way last season and he's the best in the league, period.

KICKER

Al Del Greco didn't get many opportunities because of Houston's offensive woes but he made the most of them, hitting on 16 of 20 attempts. 66 points last year...not much from your FFL kicker.

★☆★☆INDIANAPOLIS COLTS★☆★☆

By Dave Douglas
NFL Films

The Colts finished a respectable 8 an 8 last year thanks in large part to versatile rookie running back Marshall Faulk, who exploded onto the NFL scene in spectacular fashion. Ted Marchibroda's young Colts need to refine the defense and improve the passing game, however, if they are to challenge the Dolphins, Patriots and Bills in the AFC East. Faulk can't do it alone but with some support and a solid draft, the Colts could be a wild card contender. Wins over division rivals Miami and Buffalo in the final two weeks could be a springboard for success in 1995.

QUARTERBACK

Jim Harbaugh doesn't exactly strike fear in the hearts of NFL defenses now do they? Maybe Craig Erickson will. Harbaugh (125 of 202 for 1,440 yards and 9 TDs.) was the main man last year and he'll be in the pre-season battle of his life to keep the starting job. Don Majkowski (84 of 152 for 1,010 yards and 6 TDs.) took his magic to Detroit. Erickson (225 of 399 for 2,919 yds. and 16 TDs.) was acquired from Tampa Bay and when all the dust settles, I think he'll be the starter...but not for your FFL squad.

RUNNING BACK

I hate to brag...but this is what I wrote about Marshall Faulk when the Colts made him their #1 pick last year. "Faulk is the most explosive back to be drafted in years. He could be the next Barry Sanders. He'll go quickly although he's untested. I believe he'll rush for 1,200 yards and be named Rookie of the Year." Well, he rushed for 1,282 yards, caught passes for another 522 yards and scored 12 touchdowns so don't say I didn't tell you so.

I took a shot on him in the second round and he put me over the top. He'll go in the first round this year or very early second. Roosevelt Potts (336 yards and 2 TDs.) is tough inside the ten But #28 is the man now so Potts will be doing a lot of blocking. Seminole fullback Zack Crockett was taken in the fourth round.

WIDE RECEIVER

Former Saint Floyd Turner tied Faulk for the team receiving lead with 52 catches, good for 593 yards and 6 touchdowns. He's a solid third fantasy receiver. Six foot four Sean Dawkins is the best, however, and he grabbed 51 for a team high 742 yards and 5 touchdowns. Turner and Dawkins are close, but I give the edge this year to big Sean. Former Ram Flipper Anderson (46 catches -- 945 yards -- 5 TDs.) could become a starter, so see how he fares in the pre-season. Tight end Kerry Cash (16 -- 190 -- 1) took off for the Raiders but the Colts signed Green Bay's Ed West and drafted Illinois tight end Ken Dilger to shore up the position.

DEFENSE/SPECIAL TEAMS

The Colt defense is better than most think but not quite dominant enough to take over games yet. Check out all the "Tonys". Tony Bennett had 9 sacks and led the pass rush while Nose Tackle Tony McCoy added 6. Tony "The Goose" Siragusa put up five sacks and is the defensive line's emotional leader. Injury-free seasons from Steve Emtman and young talent Trev Alberts would obviously make the Colts a different unit entirely. The problem...only 29 total team sacks last year. Hopefully, top pick Ellis Johnson (DT Florida) can help turn up the heat.

There are two unknown great players on this defense...linebacker Jeff Herrod and defensive back Ray Buchanan. Herrod made a remarkable 200 tackles. He was everywhere.

Buchanan picked off eight passes. He was everywhere Herrod wasn't. If Marchibroda can find a new chemistry, the Colts will field a defense to be reckoned with.

One punter's gone. Another has arrived. Long time Colt Rohn Stark has been replaced by ex-Bear Chris Gardocki. Gardocki is a reliable left-footer who can drill it 40 yards or better consistently.

Punts were brought back by Dewell Brewer, who took one 75 yards for a score. Kick returns were handled by Ronald Humphrey, who raced all the way as well. Both are young guys who can fly.

KICKER
Kicker Dean Biasucci scored only 85 points last season and missed 8 of 24 field goals, but he hit two from 50 yards out and he still has a strong leg. Former Forty Niner place kicker Mike Cofer was brought in to challenge Biasucci.

★☆★☆JACKSONVILLE JAGUARS★☆★☆

by Dick Giebel

This season, folks will see rather quickly that Jacksonville will not be as good as the Carolina Panthers. Carolina's lineup actually appears to have some punch and some talented players that could make a bit of noise. Unfortunately Jacksonville appears to be starting off with a whimper. I just don't see them winning any games this season and I would be hard-pressed to enthusiastically predict success for any of their offensive players. The best part of this team may be the offensive line, starting with the highly acclaimed 325 lb. OT Tony Boselli. Joining Boselli is OG Eugene Chung, OG Shawn Bouwens and OG Dave Widell. But what is behind them? The good news is that several of the 1995 draft picks will blossom into solid players. QB Rob Johnson was a 4th round pick and could have easily been a first-rounder in the views of many experts. LB Bryan Schwartz is a little known but highly regarded player and should be a mainstay in that defense for the next decade.

QUARTERBACK

QB Steve Beuerlein is a solid QB, but look how much trouble he had moving the Arizona Cardinals over the last two seasons. At the very least , he had several reliable receivers to throw to (Ricky Proehl Gary Clark, Randal Hill etc.) Who is Beuerlein's favorite target--Desmond Howard? I visualize Beuerlein getting sack for a record amount this season...and unless he can throw from the prone position I can't predict over 10 TDs for 1995. Mark Brunell is a capable backup and I am sure that he and rookie Rob Johnson will be forced to play after Beuerlein goes down or wears out.

RUNNING BACK

Ex-Tampa Bay Buc Reggie Cobb has found another Florida home (he certainly was a bust in the frozen tundra of Green Bay) but unless a line suddenly forms around the super talented rookie lineman Boselli, Cobb will be a 2.5-yards-per-carry kind of guy. Now the back that *does* excite is the terrific James Stewart. While all this is fine if you are a casual fan of the game; if you are drafting for your franchise, however, you must take time to consider that Jacksonville has very few weapons and a ton of building to do. Even a talent like Stewart becomes a real question mark. Also joining in the backfield will be rookie fullback Ryan Christopherson (fifth round/Wyoming).

WIDE RECEIVER

Spare me the "Desmond Howard wasn't given a chance in Washington" speech. Three head coaches in Washington (Joe Gibbs, Richie Petitbon and Norv Turner) each gave Desmond a shot: Gibbs retired, Petitbon was fired and Turner doesn't want retirement or a firing...he'd seen enough. Personally I thought that the expansion draft pickups of Cedric Tillman and Kelvin Martin were nearly as good as Howard. Evidently Jacksonville didn't because they released Martin in early summer. Then, as if picking up Howard wasn't enough of a bust, TE Derek Brown gets tabbed by Jacksonville. If I am an opposing defensive coach I am licking my chops at the sight of thumping Howard at the line and working against an inexperienced receiver (Tillman), while the QB is running for his life and Derek Brown is trying to remember whether he is supposed to block or go out in the pattern.

DEFENSE/SPECIAL TEAMS

Two solid bookends at defensive end (Jeff Lageman and Kelvin Pritchett)...so the opposition will run up the middle for huge gains. Or the QBs will drop back and count "One Mississippi...two Mississippi...three Mississippi" and bomb downfield where

88

defensive confusion will abound. The MVP is likely to be punter Bryan Barker because he will be on the field probably more than anyone. As for a return man, I thought that would have been the elusive Kelvin Martin's job...but he was released.

KICKER

Jacksonville had no definite kicker at this writing. But even if they did have someone, you would be a fool to draft him. Field goals will be out; after all, the Jags will be getting smeared early in games. Touchdowns will not be plenty--just think of all those seasoned NFL squads that treat scoring across the goal line like Superman does Kryptonite. How do you expect the Jags to score? Don't even waste a pick for the Jags kicker...he'll work less than the terminally bored Maytag repairman.

★☆★☆KANSAS CITY CHIEFS★☆★☆

By Dave Douglas
NFL Films

Marty Schottenheimer's Kansas City Chiefs are the only NFL team to earn a playoff spot each of the last five seasons. None of those seasons ended with a Super Bowl trip though, so if Marty doesn't get them there soon...changes could be made in Chiefland. They are a very good team but far from a great one and, barring a blockbuster trade or draft picks that make an immediate impact, the Chiefs seem destined to be just the best of the rest and not a conference champion.

QUARTERBACK

Joe Montana (299 of 493 for 3283 and 16 TDs. last year) announced his retirement and soon he'll be off to Canton. Four Super Bowl rings...a lasting legacy of excellence and poise under pressure...he will be missed by FFL'ers and NFL'ers alike. In all likelihood Steve Bono will be the opening day starter. Last season he threw only 117 passes as Joe's caddie. Can he and will he take control of the team and put up some solid FFL numbers? I think he's an 18-touchdown pass kind of guy: good back up numbers...less than stellar starter numbers. Matt Blundin and Rich Gannon are also in the fold but only if you have to shore up a position during the season should you consider either. Stanford Quarterback Steve Stenstrom was picked in the fifth round and he'll watch and learn. Huge Michigan tackle Trezelle Jenkins was selected in the first round to aid in pass protection.

RUNNING BACK

How long can Marcus Allen keep finding the endzone? Maybe into the next century...maybe no more. He scored seven times last season but rushed for only 709 yards. Maybe a fifth rounder? The future seems to be in Greg Hill's legs. Marty pushed for him in last year's draft and he's committed to him. As a rookie, Hill started slowly and then came on, finishing up with 574 yards and a touchdown.

He has to prove that inside the five he can ram it in; otherwise, it could be "Marcus time" again. I think Hill will shine in the preseason and earn the job.

Kimble Anders plays in spurts and is best as a pass catcher. He won't get enough carries to make an FFL roster. Despite his team-high 67 catches, he only scored three touchdowns.

WIDE RECEIVER

J.J. Birden took off to catch passes from Jeff George down in Atlanta but Derrick Walker was resigned. The best of the bunch was Willie Davis, who snared 51 for 822 and five touchdowns. He's the perfect third receiver on your FFL team. He can score from long distance but he drops more than you'd like to see. Lake Dawson is a star on the rise in my opinion, and I believe he'll be the prime target. He caught 37 balls last year and scored twice, but I think this could be a breakthrough year for him Right now tight end Keith Cash (19 catches for 192 and two TDs.) is second on the depth chart behind Walker. Florida State's Tamarick Vanover was drafted to run deep routes while Victor Bailey was obtained through a draft day trade with the Eagles.

DEFENSE/SPECIAL TEAMS

Despite all the big names, the defense is a bit overrated and seems to always have trouble with a power running game. They make a ton of big plays but give up too many in return. Neil Smith (11.5 sacks) is still a dominant defensive end by any standards, leading a unit that allowed 18.6 points per game. In a year in which the Chiefs kept seven opponents under 14 points or less, linebacker Derrick Thomas sacked quarterbacks 11 times. Dale Carter made the Pro Bowl and picked off a pair of passes, while Charles Mincy (now a Viking) led the club with three. Tracy Simien paced the team with 99 tackles while veteran Mark Collins scored the only defensive touchdown on a 78 yard return against the Raiders. Smith and Thomas are clearly the studs of this unit. Veteran safety Ronnie Lott was signed.

The Chiefs special teams are always a force and last season they recovered 4 fumbles, blocked a field goal, and courtesy of Jon Vaughn, scored on a 91 yard kickoff return.

Greg Manusky's 22 tackles were the most by a special teamer while punter Louie Aguiar averaged 42.1 yards.

KICKER

Kicker Lin Elliott scored 105 points and was a solid 25 of 30 on field goals but made none of the 50-plus yard variety.

★☆★☆LOS ANGELES RAIDERS★☆★☆

By Larry Michael
NFL Play-by Play Announcer
Mutual Radio Network

LA Raiders managing general partner Al Davis made a coaching change at the end of last year, firing Art Shell and giving Mike White his first job as an NFL head coach. This team has talent. WHAT'S MISSING? Maybe White has the answer. Last season's disappointing loss at home to Kansas City with a playoff berth on the line hurt this always-proud team. I've been a student of the FFL since its inception, and the cornerstone of your franchise, just like in the NFL, is a prime-time quarterback. Last season Jeff Hostetler finished 11th in the FFL with 174 total points. His primary target, Tim Brown, was the 8th rated receiver, and Jeff Jaeger was the 8th rated kicker. Still, the question remains: WHAT'S MISSING?

QUARTERBACK

Now that Montana is gone, there isn't a quarterback in the NFL with more guts than Jeff Hostetler. The Raiders offensive line allowed over 40 sacks in 1994, and "Hoss" spent many a Sunday afternoon buried under defenders. Still, he managed 20 touchdown passes with four over 40 yards, and two rushing touchdowns. He's still a solid pick in the FFL. The back-up situation, though, is murky at best. Art Shell favorite Vince Evans is the NFL's oldest quarterback at 40 years old.

93

RUNNING BACK

Maybe the missing link here in the Raiders' playoff dreams is the fact that, basically, they have no ground game. Harvey Williams was supposed to help, and he did an admirable job, rushing for 935 yards and four touchdowns. Tom Rathman did not score last season, and Napolean McCallum suffered a devastating knee injury. Help is on the way, however, in the form of a lightning-quick bundle of muscle named Napoleon Kaufman out of the University of Washington. An extremely hard worker, Kaufman is a future star that would just as soon streak downfield to deliver a touchdown-helping block as he would dart through the middle carrying the ball. In case you haven't guessed it, I really like this guy. So will Raider fans.

The breakout guy for this year, though, could very well be Derrick Fenner. He didn't do a whole lot in Cincy, and Mike White wants to feature him in the offense. Look for this to be the year Fenner proves himself.

Also drafted was Joe Aska out of little Central State in Oklahoma. A third-round pick, Aska will get a chance to show what he's made of. The Raiders used two of their first three picks on running backs. Get the picture?

WIDE RECEIVER

Tim Brown will be back, which is good news for Hostetler. Brown has developed into one of the best receivers in the NFL, nine touchdown receptions, over 1,200 yards receiving in 1994 make Brown a top FFL pick. Rocket Ismail showed flashes last season pulling in five touchdown passes, but he still hasn't realized the potential which was displayed under the Golden Dome. Maybe this will be the year. (Note to LA coaching staff: Please get James Jett the ball. He can run real fast. Honest.)

DEFENSE/SPECIAL TEAMS

Defensive mistakes such as penalties and busted coverages caused the Raiders to sag at times last season. Chester McGlockton and Anthony Smith are strong inside, and Terry McDaniel had a great year with seven interceptions, returning three for touchdowns. Two former Notre Dame stars handle kick returns duties, with Tim Brown returning punts, and Rocket Ismail handling kickoffs. So, picking one of those two as your receivers could have some nice side benefits of they bust one loose.

KICKER

Jeff Jaeger has a strong leg and good accuracy. He will again this season be a high FFL draft pick. During the last fall campaign he connected on both of his attempts outside of 50 yards, and had ten field goals from 40 yards and out. Only seven kickers had more points than Jaeger last year.

★☆★☆MIAMI DOLPHINS★☆★☆

by Larry Weisman
Sports Columnist
USA TODAY

The Miami Dolphins considered it a huge disappointment to be knocked out of a chance of playing in Super Bowl XXIX in their home stadium. The theme for this year might be sending Don Shula out as a winner.

Shula has not indicated any plans to retire but there's a sense of impatience in south Florida. The Dolphins haven't been to the Super Bowl since the 1984 season, Dan Marino's second in the league, and Jimmy Johnson's spectre continues to hover.

The Dolphins were a very active club in free agency and trades, looking to shore up weak areas.

QUARTERBACK

Try to find a reason not to take Marino. There isn't one. Miami just doesn't figure to ever be a dominating running team, or a dominant defensive one. And that means Marino will throw, throw, throw.

He put it up 615 times last year, passed for 4,453 yards and 30 touchdowns. Do you have a problem with that?

True, he's gimpy. But that's not news. He might not be pretty running, but no one slides around in the pocket and finds an open guy the way he does.

Bernie Kosar is a good relief man but he can't carry the team the way Marino does. The other backup is Dan McGwire, a former No. 1 and occasional starter in Seattle. He is 6-8 and has an excellent chance of remaining tall.

RUNNING BACK

Terry Kirby, a superior pass-catcher coming off a knee injury, will have a tough time unseating rugged Bernie Parmalee. After becoming a starter in mid-season, Parmalee bruised for 868 yards and six touchdowns. In Miami's attack, no single back will get enough work to be the type of player fantasy GMs seek. Parmalee could well be the starter, with Kirby subbing on third downs.

Keith Byars is back from his injury as well, and figures to give you an occasional rushing touchdown, some good blocks and, most importantly, some big-time receptions out of the backfield. Byars might be a good third second or third running back, but watch how Shula uses him in camp. Will he block for the proven Miami ball carriers, be a decoy, or a veritable weapon?

Another guy who was sneaky good last year was Irving Spikes. Miami, though, only scored 13 rushing touchdowns, so this may not be the best place to shop.

WIDE RECEIVER

This is a changed group. Irving Fryar remains the standard bearer and he and Marino have good chemistry. Fryar caught 73 passes, seven for touchdowns, and averaged 17.4 yards per catch.

An infusion of speed comes from Randal Hill, once a high draft pick who was traded to the Cardinals from the 'Fins and now re-acquired. He'll replace Mark Ingram, who was traded to Green Bay. Hill is erratic but a true deep threat. Joining his ex-Cardinal teammate is Gary Clark, who signed with Miami in late spring. Clark is by no means the player he was in Washington, and he tends to get hurt a lot more these days, but he's a competitor, and as such you can never count him out.

Eric Green, the free agent, replaces Keith Jackson, the disgruntled, at tight end. (Jackson was traded to Green Bay, where he might just refuse to play.) Green is a massive target and excellent around the goal line. Grab him and hang on. He should be good for 8-10 touchdowns. Rookie Pete Mitchell really doesn't figure yet.

O.J. McDuffie continues to improve as a third receiver and should produce more than the three touchdowns he scored in '94.

DEFENSE/SPECIAL TEAMS

Miami's defensive numbers aren't bad. The Dolphins forced 32 turnovers, 23 on interceptions. They need more pass rush, as 29 sacks just won't get it done. The addition of Terrell Buckley, probably as a nickel back, puts more speed in the secondary.

Miami's return game was average. McDuffie averaged a paltry 7.6 yards on punt returns and coverage was only fair. The Dolphins did not score on punt or kickoff returns while allowing three return touchdowns.

KICKER

Pete Stoyanovich comes off one of his lesser years and I'd look for him to rebound. It's hard to explain it when a kicker hits 8 of 10 FGs from 40-49 yards and only 6 of 10 from 30-39. Only Indianapolis' Dean Biasucci had a worse percentage of FG conversion than Stoyanovich's .774 in the AFC last year. Nonetheless, he has a fine leg and is a good pick.

★☆★☆MINNESOTA VIKINGS★☆★☆

by Larry Michael
NFL Play-by Play Announcer
Mutual Radio Network

Classy Quarterback Warren Moon will turn 39 during the upcoming NFL season, and it might be his last chance to get to a Super Bowl. The Viking's ship sailed to their second NFC Central title over the last three years, but losses on the defense make the upcoming season a serious challenge to Coach Dennis Green. Green is only the seventh coach in NFL history to lead his team to a playoff berth in each of his first 3 seasons.

QUARTERBACK

Is there a player in the NFL who is liked as well as Warren Moon? Not only is he a nice guy, he's also sixth all time in history in passing yardage and completions. Last season he set team standards for completions with 345, and yardage with 3,912. He was the fifth-rated quarterback in the FFL, delivering 18 touchdowns, with four of those going for over 40 yards. A superb athlete who always keeps himself in tremendous shape, Moon's abilities don't seem to have diminished with age. A battle for the backup job is shaping up between incumbent Brad Johnson, and draft pick Chad May from Kansas State.

RUNNING BACK

The Vikings released their most productive back, Terry Allen, in the offseason. However, the running back position is still one of their deepest. Amp Lee comes in on passing situations, and the shifty Lee pulled in 45 receptions and 2 touchdowns. Look for him to carry the ball more this season. Robert Smith was slowed early by a knee injury, but if he returns to form he should play a big role in the running attack. Add to the mix the bruising Scottie Graham, and you have still have a crew of running backs who can give the team a ball control complement to Warren Moon.

WIDE RECEIVER

Another strong area of talent for the Vikings, the team now boasts the single season NFL reception record holder in Chris Carter. Last Season Carter collected 122 catches, the MOST EVER in a season! He and Jake Reed are the only Viking receiver tandem in history to each top the 1,000 yard mark in receiving in a single season. Carter had seven touchdown receptions while Reed added four. When Moon deploys three receivers in a formation, Qadry Ismail brings the jet fuel, and last year he grabbed five touchdowns including a nifty 65 yard catch-and-run. With all this talent, the tight end doesn't get many looks; witness Adrian Cooper's 32 receptions last year with no touchdowns. Last year's rookie scatback David Palmer saw limited action, but his talent will give Dennis Green an ace in the hole in '95.

DEFENSE/SPECIAL TEAMS

If you concentrated on the offensive talent of the Vikings, you'd think this team was headed for the Super Bowl. Unfortunately, the defense needs some rebuilding. Henry Thomas has left as a free agent, and last year's sub par secondary has been completely dismantled. First Round pick Derrick Alexander should help the team cope with the loss of Thomas. The kick return chores are in good hands with both Qadry Ismail and David Palmer capable of breaking one at any time.

KICKER

You don't get much more consistent than Fuad Reveiz. He drilled nine of 13 field goals from 40 yards and out, was a perfect 30-30 in PATs, and overall scored 155 FFL points. He was the second-rated FFL kicker last season behind John Carney. Once again, a dome might be a little antiseptic for some football purists, but for kickers it's the best. Reveiz won't last long in any FFL draft.

★☆☆☆NEW ENGLAND PATRIOTS★☆★☆

By Dave Douglas
NFL Films

Last year I wrote that the Patriots would make the playoffs. Who's laughing now? Of course after they were off to a shaky 3-6 start I was a bit worried but by winning their last seven in a row they proved me right. They'll win 10 or 11 this year as well because Bill Parcells is a superior coach and Drew Bledsoe is the best young quarterback to hit the NFL since Dan Marino. They believe in themselves and the system and the AFC East title should be theirs this season. They have more balance than the Dolphins and the Bills are starting to rebuild.

QUARTERBACK

Drew Bledsoe will be the number one overall pick in many FFL drafts this year and with good reason. He's the rocket man who Parcells has unleashed and there seems to be no turning back. I don't believe that Bill will become conservative with his young prodigy and will ride that big right arm as far as it will take him. Bledsoe overcame some midseason doldrums to post astronomical numbers for a second year player. He threw the ball an amazing 691 times, completing an even 400 passes for 4555 yards and 25 touchdowns. The heck with the 27 interceptions...you want a guy who just keeps on puttin' it up. He'll go right away. Grab him if you can.

RUNNING BACK

Marion Butts was a disappointment last season, rushing for 703 yards and eight touchdowns. They're solid numbers but Butts seemed capable of much more. Former Steeler Leroy Thompson only carried the ball 102 times in Bill Parcell's committee-of-backs system. Kevin Turner was snatched up by the Eagles and Sam Gash gained only 86 yards. Corey Croom is a young speedster who could make a move.

The biggest development in the running game could be the reunion of Dave Meggett with Coach Parcells. I still don't think that Meggett will get the carries required for FFL consideration but Bill may decide to feature him. Watch and find out.

WIDE RECEIVER

The main target is man mountain tight end Ben Coates. Coates caught a phenomenal 96 passes for 1,174 yards and seven touchdowns. He's the best tight end in the league by a wide margin. He'll go fast and if you have Bledsoe, what a great duo that would be. Michael Timpson (74 catches and three TDs.) is a Chicago Bear but Bledsoe still has a lot of reliable weapons left. Vincent Brisby (59 for 904 yds. and five TDs.) is a sure-handed receiver and Ray Crittenden (28 catches and three TDs.) could step up his level of play. None are high picks but each could round out your FFL receiving corps quite nicely.

DEFENSE/SPECIAL TEAMS

If anybody knows defense it's Parcells, who along with defensive coordinator Al Groh, has forged an emerging power. The Patriot defense is young and superbly coached and this season the group could really take charge. They don't rely on one man. They got sacks from everywhere but the leader was cat-quick linebacker Chris Slade who logged 9.5. For the fourth straight year, Vincent Brown cracked the 100 tackle barrier. Second-year man Willie McGinest will thrive under Parcells and the secondary could be one of the best. Maurice Hurst led the defensive backfield with seven interceptions but Harlon Barnett and Ricky Reynolds are playmakers in their own right. The Patriots grabbed a league-high

40 takeaways. In the draft, Parcells spent his first two picks on defense...no surprise there. Michigan defensive back Ty Law and Colorado linebacker Ted Johnson will make a good "D" even better.

Troy Brown and Ray Crittenden split time handling punt returns while Crittenden was the primary kick returner, although having a Dave Meggett in their lineup means this position could be wide open.

KICKER

Punter Pat O'Neill averaged 41.2 yards per boot while Matt Bahr made good on 27 of 34 field goals along the way to 117 points. Bahr can't hit from over 45 anymore so Parcells is in the market for more consistent long-range guy.

★☆★☆NEW ORLEANS SAINTS★☆★☆

by Larry Michael
NFL Play-by Play Announcer
Mutual Radio Network

The New Orleans Saints took a step backward last season, but last season, but make no mistake about it, Jim Mora is still in charge and he promises the Saints will bounce back in '95. A disappointing 7-9 record after a 1-3 start has Mora motivated. To make matters worse, a fire devastated the team's practice facility in Metairie, and work is underway on a new facility which won't be ready until 1996. On the bright side, Jim Everett had a fine year, ranking seventh among FFL signal-callers. If Mora's work ethic is any indication, the Saints appear headed back above .500 with a playoff berth within their reach.

QUARTERBACK

The much-maligned Jim Everett hoped to get a fresh start in New Orleans, and he definitely did. He finished fourth in the NFL with 3,855 yards, completed 64% of his passes and fired 22 touchdowns. He finished the year in the top seven in the NFL in completions, completion percentage, passing yards, and touchdowns. Wade Wilson is no longer the backup, with relief chores left to Tom Hodson and Doug Nussmeier, and Timm Rosenbach. Saints fans better hope William Roaf and the rest of the offensive line can keep Everett safe.

RUNNING BACK

Rookie running back Mario Bates became the fourth straight rookie to lead the team in rushing. He had six touchdowns in 1994, the longest being a 40-yard scamper. Lorenzo Neal and Derek Brown combined on 4 touchdowns. A man to watch will be second-round draft pick Ray Zellars from Notre Dame, who could see loads of playing time if he can stay healthy. Size and speed make him an explosive package. He was nicked up last year, but could be a real second-round steal for the Saints.

WIDE RECEIVER

The Saints got good production last season from Michael Haynes and Quinn Early as they combined for 159 catches and 1,879 yards. Haynes had five touchdown catches while Early hauled in four. It's worth noting that Haynes has great deep speed, with one of last year's scoring receptions traveling 78 yards. Torrence Small is a restricted free agent, and if he departs Jim Mora will have to find a way of replacing five touchdown catches from his number-three receiver. The Saints offense went to the tight end with more frequency with Jim Everett at the controls. Irv Smith had a fine year with three TDs, while former 49er Wesley Walls grabbed four.

DEFENSE/SPECIAL TEAMS

The defense has lost some serious punch due to free agency. New Orleans did re-sign free safety Vince Buck, but this is a team in need of some new blood defensively. First round pick Mark Fields out of Washington State could get a look as a replacement for Sam Mills. New Orleans' special teams are led by a real special player: Tyrone Hughes. In 1994, Hughes set or tied six kick return records! He brought two kickoffs back for touchdowns, with one going 98 yards! He might just be the best return man in all of football, and certainly deserves major consideration on your FFL draft.

KICKER

Morten Andersen continues to be one of the elite kickers on all of football. For the ninth time in 13 years he kicked for over 100 points in the NFL, good for an FFL total of 134 points, tying him fifth among all FFL kickers. For the first time in a while, though, Andersen failed to connect outside of 50 yards. His 0-6 record from this distance could be a sign of diminishing leg strength, but give me Morten Andersen with the ballgame on the line, anytime. His 8-10 record from 40-49 yards tells me this man still has lots of leg left.

★☆★☆NEW YORK GIANTS★☆★☆

by Larry Weisman
Sports Columnist
USA TODAY

The New York Giants twisted an expression from another sport to describe their 9-7 record and playoff absence -- three streaks and you're out.

They won their first three games, spiraled downward through a seven-game losing streak, then won their last six.

Expect the Giants to look for a little more consistency.

Dave Brown, who replaced Phil Simms at quarterback, showed good poise and some physical skills while struggling with his reads and decisions. He'll improve and the Giants should not rank last in the NFL in passing again.

The defense, settling into a 4-3 with some new talent on the line and at linebacker, needs to produce a lot more pressure and that should lead to more than the 16 interceptions made in 1994.

QUARTERBACK

Brown played poorly during the losing streak and gave way to Kent Graham before regaining the job and his confidence. He has fine size, a good arm, and a good head.

Dan Reeves' offense requires great mental effort and Brown is up to it. He'll do a better job picking receivers. He threw 12 TD passes against 16 interceptions and ought to be able to reverse that ratio or at least even it up. But don't look for the Giants to be playing wide-open football, especially with their strong backfield.

Graham is strong-armed and a capable backup.

RUNNING BACK

The Giants averaged a meager 3.3 yards per carry and scored just 12 rushing touchdowns. They'll do better with more depth.

Rodney Hampton struggled through injuries and a heavy workload to gain 1,075 yards and score six touchdowns. He's not a breakaway threat who will reward fantasy GMs with long TD dashes. But he will get his carries and get his fair share of goal-line attempts.

Herschel Walker could be an interesting play. He'll see time at fullback, he'll spell Hampton, and he'll fill David Meggett's third-down role as a receiver. Walker will have good numbers for combined yardage, can still explode for the big play, and ought to have a few touchdowns in the mix. Reeves has talked about putting in some I-formation tosses from a two-back set for Walker.

Tyrone Wheatley, the No. 1 pick, probably will get garbage time in the early going and doesn't look like a big-time contributor as a rookie. Neither Gary Downs nor Kenyon Rasheed figures to get much playing time in the backfield.

WIDE RECEIVER

Mike Sherrard is the standout of the group. He can get deep and probably will with a more confident Brown standing in the pocket. Six of his 53 catches went for touchdowns. Durability has always been his problem but he stayed healthy for the most part in '94.

Chris Calloway lacks the great breakaway speed but makes some big plays. He hasn't been a big factor around the end zone, though.

When the Giants hit the red zone, they look to the tight end Howard Cross and H-back Aaron Pierce. Cross doesn't catch many balls but four of his 31 receptions were for touchdowns. Pierce turned four of 20 catches into scores. In leagues where yardage counts, they won't be big plusses but they'll get some touchdowns.

The wild card is Thomas Lewis. Knee problems shortened his rookie year and his recovery period was uneven. He's fast and can stretch a defense but caught only four passes in 1994. He'll do more but not enough to make him a big fantasy league star.

DEFENSE/SPECIAL TEAMS
The Giants recorded only 26 sacks and 16 interceptions, so they're not a devastating force. Nor did they score any defensive touchdowns.

They hope free agent defensive end Robert Harris will help the pass rush from the left side with Keith Hamilton, who had 6.5 sacks, moving inside to defensive tackle. Mike Croel will rush from the weakside. Mike Strahan needs to come on at right end but has raw pass-rushing skills.

Thomas Randolph could become a top cover corner but the Giants have questions at safety. Vencie Glenn should help. They cannot risk being too aggressive in coverage and can't really ball-hawk unless the pass rush comes on.

KICKER
Brad Daluiso and his thunderous leg booted David Treadwell out of the kicker's job. Never very accurate before in limited placekicking tries, Daluiso, a kickoff specialist, blossomed last year. He hit 11 of 11 FG tries, including a game-winning 52-yarder. He's a gamble because he has very little track record but he should get opportunities.

★☆★☆NEW YORK JETS★☆★☆

by Larry Weisman
Sports Columnist
USA TODAY

The New York Jets give a whole new meaning to the expression "Coach of the Year."

Every year, they have a new coach.

Bruce Coslet couldn't get the Jets past an 8-8 record and was let go after the '93 season. Pete Carroll oversaw a 6-10 debacle in '94 and won't get a second chance.

The new neck on the chopping block belongs to Rich Kotite, late of Philadelphia. His immediate goal is to bring the Jets' their first winning season since 1988, which could be a tall order. He needs to restore confidence to a club shaken by its season-ending five game losing streak and to improve the overall talent.

QUARTERBACK

Boomer Esiason remains a clever ball-handler whose season tends to look better on paper than on the field. He just cannot carry a club any longer.

Kotite has promised to put in more of the play-action passes Esiason loves and the Jets may set up their limited running game with more short tosses. It's an open question whether Esiason has enough oomph left to fling the deep ball. Esiason's TD-INT ratio will be positive, but he won't throw enough of those scoring passes to warrant his being a high fantasy pick.

Glenn Foley moves into the No. 2 spot. He threw only eight passes last year as the No. 3 behind Jack Trudeau (gone to Carolina). His potential remains that and nothing more. During the spring, the Jets also brought in perennial backup Bubby Brister from Philadelphia.

RUNNING BACK

There's an old saying in the NFL: "A team with three running backs doesn't have one running back." For fantasy players, the "running back by committee" philosophy stinks. Nor had it worked too well for the Jets.

So, in a trade the day before the draft, they acquired Ronald Moore from Arizona as part of their shift to a one-back, two tight end offense. The bullish Moore had a great season in '93 but slipped last year as Arizona's offense never really jelled. In a one-back, as the featured performer, he could do well if the Jets get some offensive line help.

Johnny Johnson is capable but a journeyman. He gained 931 yards but scored only three touchdowns and won't really figure in the goal-line sets.

Kotite likes the outside speed of Adrian Murrell, who began to show signs of some skills last year before suffering a knee injury. He figures mostly as a spot performer.

If anyone will score on the ground -- and the Jets only did that eight times in '94 -- it could be smash-mouth fullback Brad Baxter. He faded from the scheme last year but still led the team with four touchdowns. Kotite favors two-back sets so Baxter will be on the field and is the player to watch. Richie Anderson could also challenge for time.

WIDE RECEIVER

The go-to guy was Rob Moore, but he went to Arizona in a trade. As the Jets had previously released Art Monk, they were, at presstime, without an established wideout.

Erratic tight end Johnny Mitchell could be a big producer in a play-action offense, running seam routes. He needs to be more disciplined and mature but could be a sneaky pick. In the double tight scheme, he'll play H-back and the motion involved could really free him up.

No. 1 pick Kyle Brady will also start at tight end but may pick up more of the blocking assignments. He's not polished as a receiver but he's big and NFL teams that scouted him tended to like him more and more as they watched films and analyzed his play. He's a good learner but his true impact is probably a year away.

The Jets seem certain to try to get more speed on the field in the persons of Ryan Yarborough and Orlando Parker, two second-year players who saw very little game action in 1994. Their lack of experience, coupled with learning their second offensive system in two years, limits the possibility of them being big contributors, at least early on.

DEFENSE/SPECIAL TEAMS

The Jets seem strong at linebacker, less so elsewhere. They dumped safeties Ronnie Lott and Brian Washington for youngsters Gary Jones and Todd Scott They need to replace cornerback James Hasty, who, with Washington, signed with Kansas City. The only returning starter in the secondary is second-year cornerback Aaron Glenn. This should all make for very interesting combination coverages and breakdowns.

Linebacker Mo Lewis is the best defensive player. He had six sacks last year and four interceptions (two returned for scores). The Jets want him to rush the passer more and he could be worth nine sacks or more.

The Jets' best pass rusher, Jeff Lageman, went to Jacksonville as a free agent. He led the club with 6.5 sacks and no other lineman had more than three. Erik Howard is a good add at defensive tackle against the run. Donald Evans, who moves outside to DE, has a history of being a fair rusher.

Glenn did a decent job returning kickoffs but might cede that role to free agent signee (and world champion) Dexter Carter. The Jets anticipated using Glenn last year primarily on punt returns but rookie jitters in the preseason scuttled that. Look for Carter on kickoffs, the talented Glenn on punts. The Jets did not score last year on any kick returns.

KICKER

Nick Lowery no longer has the booming leg but he's still very accurate and made 20 of 23 FG tries. The Jets' limited offense held down his opportunities and they don't show the signs of emerging as some sort of dominating offensive juggernaut.

★☆★☆PHILADELPHIA EAGLES★☆★☆

By Dave Douglas
NFL Films

After a 7-2 start, including a crushing of the 49ers in San Francisco, the Eagles limped home, losing their last seven in a row. As a result, head coach Rich Kotite was fired and former Forty Niner and Packer coach Ray Rhodes was hired. The Eagles also brought in 31-year-old Packer coach Jon Gruden to be their offensive coordinator. The Eagles hope to install the West Coast offense that has spearheaded the Niners to their five Super Bowl victories and upgrade their defense in the hopes of overtaking the Cowboys in the NFC East.

QUARTERBACK

Randall Cunningham has been named as Rhodes' starter in perhaps the most critical season in his career. Last year, Randall joined Ron Jaworski as the only Eagle to throw for 20,000 career yards. This season he'll get a chance to learn and execute the 49er system of quick slants and throwing to backs. He could flourish or he could fail. Behind a line that allowed 48 sacks, Cunningham played well in the beginning of the season and poorly toward season's end. He threw a ton of crippling picks down the stretch but he seems ready for the new approach. Cunningham completed 265 of 490 for 3229 yards and 16 touchdowns...very solid numbers.

Bubby Brister was the back up and this year he'll rejoin Kotite with the Jets so the new insurance policy will be Rodney Peete. California quarterback Dave Barr was picked in the seventh round of the draft and is years away.

RUNNING BACK

One of the biggest free agent signings was that of Ricky Watters from San Francisco. Watters will be a vital cog in the new offense and could rush for 1200 yards and score 10 touchdowns this season.

He's from the Harrisburg area and will play well in front of his friends and family. He'll run and catch and touch the ball on every series. He's a second-round FFL steal and if you take him in the first round you're not out of your mind.

Blocking for Watters and catching balls out of the backfield is former Patriot Kevin Turner. Turner will play the Tom Rathman spot for Rhodes and last season he rushed for only 111 yards but caught 52 passes and scored three touchdowns. He was signed primarily for his receiving skills. Herschel Walker and James Joseph were sent to the Giants and Bengals, respectively. The wild card is speedster Charlie Garner. Garner (399 yards and three TDs.) is an Eric Metcalf type who, when not sidelined by injury, can turn heads. Watters is the main man, obviously, so Garner would be a real luxury pick. Vaughn Hebron will not play a major role.

Kansas State tackle Barrett Brooks was picked in the third round to help protect Randall and open holes for Watters.

WIDE RECEIVER

The early word from the new staff is that they believe Fred Barnett and Calvin Williams will excel in the new system. Last year Barnett rebounded from his knee injury to post big numbers (78 catches for 1,127 yards and five TDs.). He'll run some routes over the middle, unlike years past, and at least duplicate those stats in the west coast style offense. Williams is a solid second or third FFL receiver. His performance dipped toward the end of the season but he still caught 58 passes for 813 yards and three scores.

Victor Bailey (20 catches for 311 yards and one TD.) was traded to the Chiefs on draft day. Tight end Reggie Johnson was obtained from Green Bay and will start. Tight end Mark Bavaro

(17-215-3) is gone and Maurice Johnson (21-204-2) will be the likely backup.

DEFENSE/SPECIAL TEAMS

It's no coincidence that after linebacker Byron Evans went down against the Browns that the Eagles began their seven-game skid. Whether he returns or not is still uncertain.

One thing for sure is that their best corner, Eric Allen, is off to play for the Saints. Rhodes has a bright defensive mind and he'll find a way to mold a tough unit by mid-season. William Fuller had a great season (9.5), edging out unsung star Andy Harmon (9) for the team sack lead.

Defensive tackle Rhett Hall was imported from the Niners and that more than likely means that William Perry's days as an Eagle are · numbered. Greg Jackson led the team with six interceptions, while Michael Zordich added four.

Mike Mamula, a Charles Haley-like speed rusher, was picked seventh overall in the draft and he will be an instant starter and an instant impact player. Notre Dame's Bobby Taylor was snatched up in the second round and will provide speed in the secondary.

The special teams star last season was Herschel but now he's a Giant. Rhodes will look at Jeff Sydner, Vaughn Hebron and the draft for his punt and kick returners. Punting has been a problem in Philly since the departure of Jeff Feagles. Mitch Berger didn't pan out but things improved a bit with Brian Barker. Now Barker is a Jaguar so who knows.

KICKER

Kicker Eddie Murray was good on 21 of 25 field goals and totalled 96 points, but Rhodes is looking for a kicker with a much stronger leg.

★☆★☆PITTSBURGH STEELERS★☆★☆

By Dave Douglas
NFL Films

It's the 1994 AFC championship game...San Diego 17...Pittsburgh 13...4th down...seconds remaining on the clock. Neil O'Donnell's pass is batted away from Barry Foster in the endzone, and the Chargers, not the Steelers, fly down to Miami for Super Bowl 29. What a way for it to end for Steeler fans. But what a season it was.

Head coach Bill Cowher finished up his third season the way he ended his first...as division champion. The Steelers won an AFC-high 12 games for only the fourth time in their history. They won seven of their last eight, sparked by a ferocious defense and an opportunistic offense. This season, another division title is a near-certainty unless the Browns can make some noise.

QUARTERBACK

The Steelers will only go as far as Neil O'Donnell can take them. It was true in both the '93 and '94 seasons and little has changed. His numbers (212 of 370 for 2443 yds. and 13 TDs.) were solid but not spectacular. He threw only nine interceptions but he doesn't go deep and challenge defensive backs enough. He must stretch the field more in 1995 and throw ten more touchdown passes if the Steelers are to go to the proverbial "next level".

O'Donnell is near the top of the second tier of fantasy quarterbacks. He is certainly not a Young, Marino or Bledsoe, especially if Pittsburgh continues to grind it out and let their defense win games.

Backup Mike Tomczak (54 of 93 for 804 yds. and four TDs.) barely played and it's doubtful he'll see much action this season. Pittsburgh grabbed Colorado quarterback Kordell Stewart in the draft, but he needs a lot of reps to polish his passing skills. Could he be another Randall Cunningham?

RUNNING BACK

Barry Foster is not as precious a commodity as he was going into the '94 season, and the Steelers evinced that by trading him to Carolina in late May. He seems to miss key stretches of the fantasy season when you need him the most.

Byron "Bam" Morris is the real deal and he's the perfect battering ram of a back for Ron Erhardt's trapping, power running game. Once he got over a bout of "fumble-itis", the rookie settled in to be a relied-upon ball carrier. He finished with 836 yards, only 15 short of Foster, and the Steeler need his seven TDs in 1994 to become 12 to 14 this season. Although Foster rushed for about 400 yards short of what most FFL'ers thought he'd get, he did add 10 touchdowns rushing and receiving combined.

Veteran John L. Williams only carried the ball 68 times last year and, despite his team-high 51 catches, he should go undrafted. In the FFL, limited carries mean limited points.

The Steelers also signed Erric Pegram away from the Falcons, so the only thing certain in the Steel City is that their 1995 backfield is really wide open.

WIDE RECEIVER

All you need to know about Pittsburgh's wideouts is that none caught 50 balls. Is that what you're looking for on your FFL squad? I think not. However, I believe one is worthy of consideration as your second or third receiver. He's Charles Johnson, a rookie last season who got hit hard and often but it was just the punishing initiation he needed. Johnson caught 38 passes and scored three times. He loves to go over the middle and I think that this year it'll be more like 65 catches and 10 TDs. Yancey Thigpen (36 catches and four TDs.) and Andre Hastings (20 catches and two TDs.) will battle it out in the preseason for the other starting spot. Tight end Eric Green signed with Miami so the Steelers made Washington Huskies tight end Mark Bruener their first pick in the draft.

DEFENSE/SPECIAL TEAMS

Defensive coordinator Dom Capers took off to take the head coaching job in Carolina...be patient, Dom. Despite his exit, there will be little change in the effectiveness and intensity of the Blitzburgh defense. Linebackers Kevin Greene and Greg Lloyd simply won't allow any let down. Last year the "Steel Trap" defense ranked first overall in the conference.

Greene (14) and Lloyd (10) combined for 24 sacks as the Steelers dropped enemy quarterbacks 55 times. As well, Pittsburgh picked off 17 passes, led by Darren Perry's seven. Rod Woodson and Carnell Lake are the best safety/corner combination in the league. The Steeler defense is a top notch fantasy defense and two meetings a year with the struggling Oilers and Bengals and a pair with newcomer Jacksonville are another big reason to draft this solid unit.

Punter Mark Royals was picked up by Detroit so former Colt Rohn Stark will be booming them for Pittsburgh. Rod Woodson (8.2 per return, no TDs.) will more than likely continue to return punts while Charles Johnson (21.6 per return) handles most of the kickoff return duties.

KICKER

Kicker Gary Anderson ranked second in the NFL for efficiency and his solid 104 points placed him ninth in the AFC. Last season he also nailed one from 50 yards out.

★☆★☆SAN DIEGO CHARGERS★☆★☆

By John Weiss
NFL Films

One would be tempted to dismiss the Chargers' Super Bowl season as nothing more than a streak of good luck that smiled on them at just the right times and places. They had their Cinderella season, and they won't be back for a while, right? Don't be so sure. Power running and tough defense makes champions, and the Chargers have both. Plus, head coach Bobby Ross had the NFL's youngest team last season, and another year together should only help San Diego improve. And even if you don't think the Chargers are the best team in the AFC, they are the best team in their division. And if they win the AFC West like they should, anything can happen in the playoffs. They proved that last season.

QUARTERBACK

If toughness was a fantasy category, Stan Humphries would be its top point producer. Once again, the gutty Humphries proved his mettle by playing through a variety of aches and pains, including a sprained knee and a dislocated elbow.

But stats are what count for you, and while the numbers Humphries produces are decent, they don't put him among the elite of fantasy quarterbacks. Last season, Humphries completed 264-of-453 passes (58.3%) for 3,209 yards, with 17 touchdowns and 12 interceptions. His receivers aren't great, and that holds him back. Plus, when the Chargers can, they like to plug away with the ground game. Overall, Humphries should be ranked around 10th on your quarterback draft board.

121

RUNNING BACK

Other than Emmitt Smith and Barry Sanders, you'd be hard-pressed to find as sure a thing for your fantasy backfield as Natrone Means.

Last season, his second in the league, Means broke out to rush for a team-record 1,350 yards, second in the AFC. He had six 100-yard rushing games, and a whopping 12 touchdowns. When the Chargers got in close, they didn't give the ball to anyone other than Means to pound it in for the score. It's nice to have that kind of certainty in your fantasy backfield.

The versatile Ronnie Harmon keeps going strong as a pass catcher, tying for the team lead with 58 catches for 615 yards last season.

WIDE RECEIVER

Three different Charger receivers posted career highs for catches and yardage last season, but none of the totals were very impressive.

Mark Seay was the team's co-leader with 58 catches for 645 yards and six scores. Tony Martin added 50 catches for 885 yards and seven touchdowns, and Shawn Jefferson had 43 catches for 627 yards and three touchdowns. None of the three stands out as a top-notch point producer. Seay and Martin would be worth looking at in the late rounds to fill out your receiving corps.

H-back Alfred Pupunu had 21 catches for 214 yards and two touchdowns, while tight end Duane Young had 17 catches for 217 yards and one score.

DEFENSE/SPECIAL TEAMS

The area the team must improve most is pass defense, which ranked 22nd in the league last season. The Chargers lost their two starting safeties, Darren Carrington (Jacksonville), and Stanley Richard (Washington), but they signed safety Shaun Gayle away from the Bears to help fill the gap.

Pro Bowl linebacker Junior Seau remains the heart of the defense, as he led the team with 155 tackles (124 solo) despite playing hurt the latter part of the year. It was the fourth straight season he led the Chargers in tackles. He was also fourth on the team with 5.5 sacks.

San Diego has a terrific pair of pass rushers up front in defensive ends Leslie O'Neal (12.5 sacks) and Chris Mims (11 sacks). They were the main reasons the Chargers improved their sack total to 43 last season. Defensive tackle Shawn Lee was third on the team with 6.5.

On special teams, the Chargers have two explosive return men. Darrien Gordon led the AFC and finished second in the NFL with a 13.2-yard punt return average. He ran two back for touchdowns, 90 yards against the raiders and 75 yards against the Rams. Andre Coleman was second in the AFC and fifth in the NFL with a 26.4-yard kickoff return average. He returned three for touchdowns, including a 98-yarder in the Super Bowl.

KICKER

You can't rate any kicker higher than John Carney, who led the NFL in scoring last season with a club-record 135 points. He connected on 34-of-38 field goals, including 21 in a row, and fell just one shy of the NFL record of 35 field goals in a season. He's now ranked as the third most accurate kicker in NFL history. If the Chargers keep getting him into position, he'll continue to provide big points for a lucky fantasy owner.

★☆★☆SAN FRANCISCO 49ERS★☆★☆

by Larry Weisman
Sports Columnist
USA TODAY

The San Francisco 49ers went into the '94 season expecting to win the Super Bowl. Anything less, they said as time went on, would be a tragedy.

No tragedy in the Bay Area. A revamped and revitalized defense stood firm against Dallas in a regular-season victory and the NFC championship game and the offense continued its mechanized assault on scoreboards.

Free agency has since taken its toll. Offensive coordinator Mike Shanahan returned to Denver as head coach and Ray Rhodes, who masterminded the resurgent defense, is now Philadelphia's coach. Rhodes promptly lured free agent running back Ricky Watters, a dangerous rusher and receiver.

QUARTERBACK

The number one pick in any draft has to be Steve Young. We've said it before and we'll say it again. Young threw 35 touchdown passes and ran for seven scores. He keeps the interceptions down. He passed for almost 4,000 yards and ran for almost 300. He is the single most dominant fantasy player out there. Don't blow the chance to getting him.

Backing Young is Elvis Grbac. He showed good accuracy in limited play but is untested in real battle. The 49ers are unsettled at No. 3, losing Bill Musgrave to Denver (and Shanahan) as a free agent.

RUNNING BACK

Once a deep area, now a deep concern. Watters took a lot of explosion out of the lineup with his departure and he accounted for 11 touchdowns (six rushing, five receiving).

The 49ers won a bidding war with Denver (and Shanahan) to keep Derek Loville, a journeyman who had only 99 yards rushing. The 49ers like him but he's not Watters. They also traded with Detroit for Derrick Moore, a solid inside runner who had some big games subbing for Barry Sanders in '93. He may be the guy to watch.

More focus could be on William Floyd, the cocky and powerful fullback who just kept getting better as his rookie season wore on. He scored six touchdowns but could emerge much more as both a rusher and receiver, much in the mold of Tom Rathman.

The 49ers released Marc Logan and mostly like Adam Walker for his special teams play. Dexter Carter signed with the New York Jets. The 49ers need to find a marquee back.

WIDE RECEIVER

Clearly the 49ers' strength. There's no reason to expect any drop-off from Jerry Rice, who caught 112 passes for 1,499 yards and 13 touchdowns. In fact, with Watters (66 catches) gone, Rice may figure more in the attack.

Brent Jones scored nine touchdowns on 49 catches after a slow start due to surgery the season before. He's sneaky good, working the middle of the field and the seams of the zones and a strong pick for leagues that mandate a tight end.

John Taylor was less explosive but still dangerous and should have a better season. Rice, Jones, and Taylor, however, are all on the wrong side of 30.

Depth was a problem that rookie J.J. Stokes should solve. The big UCLA receiver was considered a Rice clone and now gets to learn from the master. He should be the No. 3 receiver and good for 20 catches. Nate Singleton has speed and moves but not much experience. He's a good sleeper pick. The 49ers lost Ed McCaffrey to Denver.

DEFENSE/SPECIAL TEAMS

Without Deion Sanders, the 49ers can't and won't do many of the pass-coverage tricks they employed last year. Second-year cornerback Tyronne Drakeford, who emerged as a solid nickel back, should replace Sanders. Sanders returned three of his six interceptions for touchdowns, including one of 93 yards. Drakeford won't do that.

The 49ers need a pass-rushing end, having got most of their pressure from sturdy defensive tackles Dana Stubblefield and Bryant Young. The 49ers lost Rhett Hall (four sacks), Richard Dent (two sacks), and probably won't bring aging Rickey Jackson (3 1/2 sacks) and Tim Harris (two sacks). New defensive coordinator Pete Carroll has some interesting times ahead.

The lost Carter handled punt and kickoff returns adequately and must be replaced. Singleton might be the guy but he's relatively untested.

KICKER

Rookie Doug Brien never had to win a game with a kick. He scored 105 points, 60 on PATs. He only attempted 20 field goals and made 15, with a long of 47. Four of his five misses were from 40 yards or longer (one of 55). Range and the loose turf at Candlestick Park hurt his stock. Still, 105 points is 105 points.

★☆★☆SEATTLE SEAHAWKS★☆★☆

By John Weiss
NFL Films

Just when it looked like the Seahawks might be turning the corner last year, they collapsed after a 3-1 start and once again finished in fifth place at 6-10. Of course, Seattle was riddled with injuries throughout the season, with players missing a total of 213 games, and 16 players ending the year on injured reserve.

So just what kind of team has former University of Miami head coach Dennis Erickson inherited in Seattle? With the right breaks, and some good health, the Seahawks look like a legitimate playoff contender. At the very least they should be able to move up the AFC West ladder and avoid a fourth straight last-place finish. Erickson has some legitimate stars to help take the Seahawks back to contention, some stars that would also make nice additions to your fantasy lineup.

QUARTERBACK

Rick Mirer didn't show as much improvement as expected in his second season, and he's still not a quarterback you can count on to consistently put up big fantasy numbers.

Last season, Mirer missed the final three games with a broken left thumb, and finished the year 195-of-381 (51.2%) for 2,151 yards and 11 touchdowns. His seven interceptions tied for the league low among starters. He's not the type of quarterback who can carry your fantasy team, but you could do worse. He should be somewhere in the middle of your quarterback draft board.

Former Redskin John Friesz was signed as a backup, but he's only there as insurance.

RUNNING BACK

It's hard to believe Seattle finished second in the NFL in rushing offense despite winning just six games. The main reason was the outstanding performance of Chris Warren, who should certainly be one of the top backs you consider on draft day.

Warren put up phenomenal numbers last year, including 1,545 yards rushing to lead the AFC. He posted a 4.6-yard average, had seven 100-yard rushing games, and scored nine touchdowns. He also caught 41 passes for 323 yards and two scores. He did all this despite playing the last four games with two fractured ribs, sustained in the car accident that left teammate Mike Frier paralyzed.

Warren now has three straight 1,000-yard seasons, and there's no reason to believe he won't be just as productive this season. He'd be a terrific no. 1 back in any fantasy lineup.

Fullback Tracy Johnson carried just 12 times for 44 yards and two touchdowns.

WIDE RECEIVER

Brian Blades is once again Seattle's main target to look at for big numbers this season. Last year, Blades had a career-high 81 catches for 1,086 yards and four touchdowns. However, he didn't catch a touchdown pass over the last nine games.

Seattle hopes it has added another big-play man with no. 1 Draft pick Joey Galloway out of Ohio State. Galloway is only 5-10, but he flat-out flies with 4.18 speed. He'll be a future playmaker, but you shouldn't look for too much from him this season. Rookie receivers rarely put up big numbers.

The Seahawks also bolstered their receiving corps by adding former Cardinal Ricky Proehl. Tight end Paul Green caught 30 passes for 208 yards and one score.

DEFENSE/SPECIAL TEAMS

Seattle lost two of its top tacklers to free agency when Rod Stephens signed with Washington and Rufus Porter with New Orleans. Stephens was the Seahawks' leading tackler a year ago, while Porter was fourth.

Cortez Kennedy is still a Pro Bowl force up front, but with opponents keying on him he had just four sacks and 70 total tackles (54 solo). Defensive end Michael Sinclair led the team with 4.5 sacks.

An emerging force is linebacker Terry Wooden, second on the team with 127 tackles (94 solo). Wooden had five double-figure tackle games, and also was a team co-leader with three interceptions. Playing opposite wooden will be former Raider Winston Moss.

Safety Eugene Robinson missed the final two games of last season with a torn Achilles' tendon, and finished third on the team with 80 tackles (65 solo), and tied for the team lead with Three interceptions. Seattle is hoping to have former Bills' All-Pro cornerback Nate Odomes healthy this season, after he missed all of last year with a knee injury.

On special teams, Michael Bates led Seattle in kick return yardage, but Terrence Warren led with a 25-yard average. The Seahawks must replace leading punt returner Kelvin Martin, who was lost to Jacksonville in the expansion draft.

KICKER

The Seahawks must fill the shoes of John Kasay, who signed with Carolina. If last year is any indication, whoever gets the job probably won't get a lot of scoring opportunities. Kasay was one of the lowest scoring kickers in the league, totaling just 85 points.

★☆★☆ST. LOUIS RAMS★☆★☆

by John Weiss
NFL Films

The Rams hope to keep fans in St. Louis more interested than the ones they left behind in Anaheim. It won't be easy if they don't turn this lost franchise around in the next few seasons. The challenge this year lies with new head coach Rich Brooks, who is fresh off a Rose Bowl berth at the University of Oregon. Brooks inherits one of football's most anonymous teams, one which finished 4-12 last season. He has a long road ahead of him to get the Rams back to respectability.

QUARTERBACK

Chris Miller is the starter, but only by default. The Rams left him unprotected in the expansion draft and there were no takers. Chris Chandler, who replaced Miller on and off last season, has signed with Houston.

Miller missed three games with a pinched nerve in his right shoulder last season, and also suffered three concussions, furthering his reputation as one of the league's most injury-prone quarterbacks. He finished the year completing 173-of-317 (54.6%) for 16 touchdowns and 14 interceptions. If he can stay healthy, he's a middle-of-the-road fantasy starter or a solid backup. But that's a big "if."

Tommy Maddox was signed from Denver in the offseason, so he's the likely backup to Miller. The simple answer: don't look for a whole lot from the St. Louis QB depth chart this season. Former Super Bowl MVP Mark Rypien was signed late in the spring to back up all these guys, so the preseason should be interesting.

RUNNING BACK

After a terrific rookie year, a lot more was expected of Jerome Bettis in 1994. But injuries to the Rams' offensive line contributed to a frustrating season for Bettis, who finished with 1,025 yards rushing but only three touchdowns. And his 3.2-yard average was among the league's lowest. Bettis also added 31 catches for 293 yards and one score.

Don't be too discouraged by his numbers last season. Remember, he's the team's only legitimate offensive weapon and he's guaranteed to get a ton of carries. If the line gives him a little more help, his yardage and touchdown total should improve. He's one of the top 10 backs to look at on draft day.

WIDE RECEIVER

The Rams lost their best receiver, Flipper Anderson, to the Colts. That leaves Jessie Hester, Alexander Wright and Isaac Bruce as the big receiving threats. In other words, it doesn't leave much.

Hester had 45 catches for 644 yards and three touchdowns last season. Maybe his production will pick up this year due to the loss of Anderson. But certainly he's not worth counting on as a fantasy go-to guy.

Bruce had 21 catches for 272 yards and three touchdowns before going on IR with a knee injury in week 15. Wright can fly, but his hands are average.

If you need a tight end, Troy Drayton is a solid pick. In his second season, Drayton caught 32 passes for 276 yards and six touchdowns.

DEFENSE/SPECIAL TEAMS

The Rams finished 16th in total defense a year ago, and 20th against the run. But they have the makings of a pretty decent unit, especially up front. Robert Young continued to emerge at defensive end and led the team with six sacks. Jimmie Jones has become a big run stuffer in the middle and added five sacks. Sean

Gilbert was bothered by shoulder problems and finished with just three sacks, but he can be a force when he's at full strength. The Rams added more help up front with no. 1 draft choice Kevin Carter out of Florida. Carter is an excellent pass rusher to add to an already-solid defensive line.

Middle linebacker Shane Conlan was the team's MVP last season, leading the club with 106 tackles (82 solo). He had double-digit tackle games four times. Outside linebacker Roman Phifer added 96 tackles (78 solo). Carlos Jenkins was signed away from Minnesota and will play opposite Phifer.

Safety Marquez Pope tied for second on the team with 96 tackles (72 solo), and tied for the team lead with three interceptions. Cornerback Todd Lyght was fourth on the team with 84 tackles (72 solo), and one interception last year. Safety Anthony Newman had two interceptions, including a 22-yard return for a score.

On special teams, David Lang led the Rams in kick return yardage, but Todd Kinchen led in average with 24.3. Kinchen also had a 9.9-yard average on punt returns.

KICKER

Last season, Tony Zendejas connected on 18-of-23 field goals, including 12 straight, but he finished with only 82 points, one of the lowest totals among kickers. The Rams drafted Steve McLaughlin out of Arizona in the third round to vie for the job. As long as the Rams struggle on offense, whoever is kicking won't be given enough chances to put up substantial numbers.

★☆★☆TAMPA BAY BUCCANEERS★☆★☆

by Larry Michael
NFL Play-by Play Announcer
Mutual Radio Network

As usual, it's going to be another year of surprises for the Tampa Bay Bucs. Though the Buccaneers are being touted as a team on the upswing, Tampa fans have had their hearts broken many times, and proving it on the field is what counts this year for head coach Sam Wyche. The offense certainly has some good second year studs in QB Trent Dilfer and RB Erricht Rhett, but consistency and chemistry will be needed--two qualities that this team has sorely lacked for quite some time. Maybe the addition of a proven winner like former Dallas receiver Alvin Harper is the needed ingredient for this team to make a run at the playoffs.

QUARTERBACK

With Craig Erickson having moved on to Indianapolis, Trent Dilfer gets a shot at starting in the NFL without having to look over his shoulder. Dilfer tossed only one solitary TD pass his rookie year, while Erickson overshadowed the highly-paid, high-profile rookie with 16 scoring strikes. When drafting for your FFL team, do you take a flyer on Trent Dilfer? The backups of record at press time are Casey Weldon, Todd Philcox and Peter Tom Willis--overall, not an impressive group.

RUNNING BACK

It looks like the Buccaneers have finally found a running back with all the right moves in Erricht Rhett. The former Florida Gator start will be the featured back for Sam Wyche this season, on the heels of a rookie year that occasionally showed flashes of brilliance. Unfortunately for Tampa Bay, if Rhett can't carry the load, there's no Plan B. Vince Workman and Anthony McDowell are competent backs, but FFL teams are sure to look elsewhere for a late round running back pickup.

WIDE RECEIVER

Former Cowboy Alvin Harper had plenty of options when pursuing free agency, and he opted for a team which has a tradition diametrically opposite to his former squad. Harper is looking to escape the shadow of Michael Irvin, and if he can help get the Bucs to the playoffs he will have accomplished that. With Troy Aikman firing the football, Harper had eight touchdowns last year, with two going for over 40 yards. Can Trent Dilfer deliver the ball the same way? Harper is sure to get double coverage, so Charles Wilson (six TDs in 1994) and Lawrence Dawsey (one TD) will have to step up and make sure Dilfer has someplace else to go. Tight end Jackie Harris is solid, solid, solid. And you can never forget about Courtney Hawkins, although he might get overshadowed by Harper. Wathc how this drama is played out in the preseason.

DEFENSE/SPECIAL TEAMS

Return man Vernon Turner is gone, but there's optimism on the defensive side of the ball with first round pick Warren Sapp hoping to prove to the football world that he is a quality defensive lineman as well as a quality person. Hardy Nickerson hopes to regain the form he showed in 1993; last season he missed three games due to injury.

KICKER

The Bucs return Michael Husted for the place-kicking duties. Last season Husted moved up statistically from 24th to 20th among FFL kickers. The leg man connected on 23 field goals and

20 PATs in 1994, and his outlook for this year is about the same. Unless the Bucs can move the ball and score, though, his numbers will never be among the league's best.

★☆★☆WASHINGTON REDSKINS★☆★☆

by Larry Weisman
Sports Columnist
USA TODAY

Washington lost a club-record 13 games last season in Norv Turner's first year as head coach.

It's very nice that seven of those defeats were by 21 combined points, meaning the Redskins were at least competitive against a fifth-place schedule.

Quarterback Heath Shuler, after the rookie year from hell, should be more solid. He'll get the benefit of a full training camp and won't have the first-year jitters. The defense ought to be a bit more sound. Beyond that, questions and more questions for Turner and his once-proud club.

Who's the running back? Who's the fullback? Who's the tight end? Who are the offensive and defensive linemen? These are hard questions.

QUARTERBACK

Shuler's holdout retarded his development and Turner's strange handling of the rookie didn't help. He yanked him for John Friesz (gone to Seattle), let Gus Frerotte play himself into and out of the lineup, allowed a flu-ridden Shuler (also with a sprained ankle) to throw five interceptions in giving away a game to Arizona, then retreaded him for a late, more successful run.

Shuler won only one of his eight starts (the last one at the Los Angeles Rams) and threw ten touchdown passes and 12 interceptions. In his last four games, however, he averaged 7.94 yards per pass attempt and threw six touchdown passes to three picks. That's encouraging. But not enough to make him a real factor for fantasy GMs.

With Friesz gone, Frerotte is No. 2. Washington could stand an experienced hand around to tutor the two second-year passers.

RUNNING BACK

With the signing of free agents Terry Allen and Marc Logan, the Redskins now seem to have an embarrasment of riches at RBs that could turn this team's dismal 1994 rushing performance around. (Last season's 1,415 rushing yards was the club's worst since 1968.)

Allen brings some big-time speed, and big play capabilities with him. Unfortunately, he also brings a long history of major knee injuries. Watch him in camp to see how they use him.

Reggie Brooks came to 1994 training camp with hamstring problems and never got himself right. He was benched after five games and finished with 297 yards, 92 in one game. He must return to his 1,000-yard form of the season before. He doesn't seem all that comfortable in a two-back set, so it remains to be seen how well he will fit in with all the rest of the runners in camp.

Versatile Brian Mitchell is a good pick because of all the things he can do and all the money the Redskins invested in him. He could be a bit of a sleeper kick as a running back, having scored only one touchdown from scrimmage last season. He'll definitely get more work rushing and receiving.

Logan looks to be the Gerald Riggs-type rusher that may cruise for a few under-5-yard Tds. He could be the go-to guy around the goalline.

With the signing of Allen, Ricky Ervins, who led the club with 650 yards, will not be back.

WIDE RECEIVER

Henry Ellard had a splendid year, with 74 catches for 1,397 yards and six touchdowns (including one of 73 yards). He's clearly the go-to guy but he's also 34 and apt to slow down at some point.

The Redskins expect second-year Tydus Winans to emerge and fill Desmond Howard's role. Howard went to Jacksonville in the veteran allocation draft. Winans averaged 18.1 yards a catch and scored twice on 19 receptions. The Redskins need another receiver, failing in its attempts to sign free agents Alvin Harper and Jake Reed.

Look for instant impact from Michael Westbrook, the fourth player selected in the NFL draft. The Redskins debated for about a minute before picking him. He's good enough to step in and start.

Ethan Horton bombed at tight end and will not return, and Washington missed out on signing Eric Green. Perhaps Frank Wycheck, who has been tried at fullback, will emerge as a Jay Novacek type. James Jenkins is the sleeper here. He caught only eight passes but four were for touchdowns and almost no one knows who he is. Rookie Jamie Asher could surprise.

DEFENSE/SPECIAL TEAMS

If your fantasy league penalizes defenses that give up plenty of points, put Washington on the bottom of your list. The defensive line is a mess and the Redskins allowed 24 rushing touchdowns in 1994.

The linebackers are much better, with the addition of Marvcus Patton and Rod Stephens to go with Ken Harvey (13 1/2 sacks). James Washington and Stanley Richard provide an instant upgrade at safety. Still, that shaky line means these guys will have to make a lot of tackles.

The Redskins created only 21 turnovers last season. Their leading interceptor was linebacker Andre Collins and he's gone.

Mitchell is a superior special teams player. He returned two punts for touchdowns last season and set or tied six club records. He returned 58 kickoffs last season, though none for touchdowns. The odds are in his favor.

KICKER

Chip Lohmiller rebounded a bit and scored 90 points, hitting on 20 of 28 on field goals. He missed twice from 29 yards or shorter and twice from 50-plus. From 40-49 yards he was five of eight. He is not the kicker he once was and only got signed to a contract in late April.

★5★

Quarterbacks

Talk to me, guys: when was the last time you or anyone in your league won with a stiff at the QB controls? If you take a quick glimpse at the franchise from your league that sported STEVE YOUNG and I betcha he or she finished near the top. What other position can decisively spark your team with double digit point totals? A top QB can tally 3-4 TDs in any given game, week in week out.

The only running back with the ability to pop in 20 TDs a season right now is Emmitt Smith. Jerry Rice and the injured Sterling Sharpe have been receivers with the knack to challenge the 20 TD mark. A great QB can really make your franchise a winner. There is nothing worse than suffering a season with a slack-armed QB who never musters big performances. How exciting it is to be watching your local regional telecast and have the network cut in with a update highlighting your QB tossing a 65 yard TD bomb! Or to watch ESPN Sunday Night highlights show and witness your QB running a keeper over the one yard line for a score...oh, ain't the beer cold now! Besides an Emmitt Smith, Marshall Faulk, Jerry Rice or Andre Rison, you should always draft a quarterback in the first round. The QB is really the heart and soul of the team. Check out a team with a scatter-armed, injury-prone quarterback and you've discovered a team that stinks. Even Madison Avenue is aware of this--after all, who gets most of the commercials on TV? QBs!

140

When was the last time you saw McDonald's chase down a pulling guard or an offensive tackle and make them a commercial star success?!? Fantasy football mirrors real life...or is that vice versa? So don't be a chump and bypass on someone who can get you 25-40 TDs. Remember, in this game you receive zero points for style...ya gotta score!

DRAFTING STARTING QUARTERBACKS

Simple rule of thumb: always try to draft a quarterback that is entrenched in an offense that is dynamite and centered around a talented QB. I like a QB that has an arsenel of receivers and an offensive game plan that is aggressive and explosive. QBs on teams that play for field advantage so that they can kick field goals and win on defense are not the guys you want to draft. It is a terrible feeling to see the score of your starting QB's game and it is 10-6 with two minutes remaining. Teams like the Niners, Dolphins, Browns, Raiders, Patriots, etc. tend to be explosive clubs that can score in the blink of an eye.

QB

DRAFTING BACKUP QBs

For those of you familiar with my backup quarterback theory, this may be a bit redundant but I maintain it is a key strategy for a winning franchise. I *always* stick to this adage: if you draft an explosive QB from an explosive, offensive-minded team, draft his backup as well. For years I have pursued this philosophy and slept well knowing that when I drafted Joe Montana...I had Steve Young as backup. When I drafted Steve Young...I had Steve Bono as backup. When I drafted Mark Rypien several years back...I had Stan Humphries as backup. When I drafted Jim Kelly...I had Frank Reich as backup. The idea is structured so that if your hot-shot QB goes done with an injury, his replacement would have the ability to step in and perform nearly as well. This theory worked and in fact always protected me from being in the unenviable position of perhaps having no starting QBs or being forced to play a dweeb QB from a lousy team. One year I went so far as to draft Joe Montana, Steve Young *and* Steve Bono in order to protect me from suffering QB injuries and being forced to trade with one of the many despicable, blood-sucking franchises in my league. You know how that story goes: everyone realizes your pathetic position and they toss you the dregs of their franchise for some twinkling gem running back or receiver.

Unfortunately this season, there is a major dropoff in the talent level from starters to the backup. Why? I feel that due to the salary cap implemented, teams are now forced to release the high-priced backup QBs and gamble with younger or simply less talented players. Therefore my suggestion is to hedge just a wee bit. For example in a 10 - 12 team league, if I selected John Elway, perhaps I would draft a player like Rick Mirer, Craig Erickson, Jeff Blake or Scott Mitchell since many folks will underestimate these players and one or all could be available in later rounds. If they are still there, grab 'em! Then, in the late, late rounds, draft Elway's backup, Bill Musgrave.

As for the backups, I have really done the homework here. A tip is to keep an eye out for injuries and player moves. For example, in Houston don't expect a battle beween Cody Carlson and Chris Chandler. Something to remember here is that Cody Carlson had signed last season for a good salary and as per the norm of the NFL...Carlson has been released. Steve McNair is obviously the heir apparent but Chris Chandler will probably get the opportunity to start so the pressure will not be on McNair. Also in Arizona, we may see ex-Saint Mike Buck hook on and replace Jay Schroeder. Also expect someone to be in a desperate situation and sign the balding blondes of the southwest, Schroeder and Carlson.

TEAM	STARTER	2ND STRING	3RD STRING
Arizona	Dave Krieg	Jay Schroeder	Stoney Case
Atlanta	Jeff George	Bobby Hebert	Perry Klein
Buffalo	Jim Kelly	Todd Collins	Rick Strom
Carolina	Frank Reich	Jack Trudeau	Kerry Collins

TEAM	STARTER	2ND STRING	3RD STRING
Chicago	Erik Kramer*	Steve Walsh*	Shane Matthews
Cincinnati	Jeff Blake	David Klingler	John Walsh
Cleveland	Vinny Testaverde	Eric Zeier	Brad Goebel
Dallas	Troy Aikman	Wade Wilson	Jason Garrett
Denver	John Elway	Bill Musgrave	Hugh Millen
Detroit	Scott Mitchell	Don Majkowski	Gino Torretta
Green Bay	Brett Favre	Ty Detmer	Jay Barker
Houston	Chris Chandler	Steve McNair	Bucky Richardson
Indianapolis	Craig Erickson	Jim Harbaugh	Paul Justin
Jacksonville	Steve Beuerlein	Mark Brunell	Rob Johnson
Kansas City	Steve Bono	Matt Blundin	Steve Stenstrom
Los Angeles	Jeff Hostetler	Vince Evans	Billy Joe Hobert
Miami	Dan Marino	Bernie Kosar	Dan McGwire
Minnesota	Warren Moon	Brad Johnson	Chad May
New England	Drew Bledsoe	Scott Zolak	Jay Walker
New Orleans	Jim Everett	Doug Nussmeier	Timm Rosenbach
NY Giants	Dave Brown	Kent Graham	Stan White
NY Jets	Boomer Esiason	Bubby Brister	Glen Foley
Philadelphia	Randall Cunningham	Rodney Peete	Dave Barr
Pittsburgh	Neil O'Donnell	Mike Tomczak	Kordell Stewart
San Diego	Stan Humphries	Gale Gilbert	
San Francisco	Steve Young	Elvis Grbac	
St. Louis	Chris Miller	Mark Rypien	Tommy Maddox
Seattle	Rick Mirer	John Friesz	Stan Gelbaugh
Tampa Bay	Trent Dilfer	Casey Weldon	P.T. Willis
Washington	Heath Shuler	Gus Frerotte	Trent Green

QB

* This may be the most highly controversial starting position in the NFL--pay close attention to who gets the job in the preseason.

AIR CONTROL TO THE BOMB PATROL

Quick, name the rookie QB that was tied with Steve Young with five bombs? No fair peeking below for the answer, trivia schmoe. The answer: Heath Shuler! Not bad, considering that Shuler only tossed a total of 10 TDs. So what does the "Bombing

TD" stat mean to you, my intrigued FFL'er? Well, if your league gives double points for TDs over 40 yards...then it matters greatly to you. In a league that gives six points for a TD pass and twelve points for a TD pass over 40 yards, the difference adds up quickly! The tip here is to find a QB that hooks up with a receiver or receivers that go long downfield. That is why QBs who perhaps are not near the skill levels of a Steve Young, Dan Marino, Jeff George, John Elway etc., several like Jeff Hostetler, Craig Erickson, Jeff Blake or Heath Shuler look like good FFL picks because of the bomb factor.

1994 OFFICIAL TD BOMBERS (2 or more OVER 40 Yds.)

PLAYER	TEAM	TDs
Stan Humphries	San Diego Chargers	6
Steve Young	San Francisco 49ers	5
Craig Erickson	Tampa Bay Buccaneers	5
Heath Shuler	Washington Redskins	5
Jeff Hostetler	LA Raiders	4
Jeff George	Atlanta Falcons	4
Warren Moon	Minnesota Vikings	4
Jeff Blake	Cincinnati Bengals	4
John Elway	Denver Broncos	3
Vinny Testaverde	Cleveland Browns	3
Jim Kelly	Buffalo Bills	2
Jim Everett	New Orleans Saints	2
Chris Miller	St. Louis Rams	2
Neil O'Donnell	Pittsburgh Steelers	2
Dave Brown	New York Giants	2
Erik Kramer	Chicago Bears	2
Chris Chandler	Houston Oilers	2
John Friesz	Seattle Seahawks	2

QB

BEAT THE BYE WEEK BLUES

The three-QBs-from-one-team scenario I mentioned earlier does not work quite so well, however, now that the NFL has instituted bye weeks. Nowadays when you are drafting, you must ensure that all your QBs are from at least two *different* divisions. Having Randall Cunningham and Troy Aikman on your franchise is of course a real scoring gold mine, until that dreadful week when both Dallas and Philly have a bye and you are left without a starting quarterback. If that won't impress your league, nothing will. (Of course, only a knucklehead would go into a draft unaware of bye weeks, and which divisions have byes in which weeks. See the 1995 NFL Schedule in the Appendix for more information on bye weeks.) If you pay careful attention to the bye weeks, you won't have the Bye Week Blues.

QBs DANCING INTO ENDZONES FOR SCORES

QB

How truly enjoyable it must have been for you FFL'ers that owned Steve Young in 1994. Although he tossed 35 TDs, right now I am more interested in discussing his running prowess. In 1994, Young crossed the goal on seven occasions. *Seven* TD rushes! Once again, that is worth double points in most leagues...talk about your proverbial backbreaker! So when you are selecting a QB, check out his running ability and incorporate this knowledge into your drafting schemes. As a tip, I would caution you not to draft solely on escapability and running potential...but if the QB can throw and run...think of the possibilities. Although Steve McNair hasn't taken his first snap yet in the NFL...this guy is *both* a runner and passer! As a footnote, several months prior to the NFL collegiate draft, BYU's John Walsh was expected by many experts to be the number one QB drafted. However, after witnessing his lack of foot speed at the scouting combines, his stock dropped and he was a number seven round draft selection. Speed counts!

FAST FEET FEATS: 1994 QB RUSHING STATS

PLAYER	TEAM	RUSHING YDS	RUSHING AVG.	TDs
Steve Young	SF	293	5.1	7
Randall Cunningham	PHI	288	4.4	3
John Elway	DEN	235	4.1	4
Bucky Richardson	HOU	217	7.2	1
Jeff Blake	CIN	204	5.5	1
Brett Favre	GB	202	4.8	2
Jeff Hostetler	RAI	159	3.5	2
Rick Mirer	SEA	153	4.5	0
Chris Miller	STL	100	5.0	0

QB

QUARTERBACK REVIEW

1. Steve Young, San Francisco 49ers

Passing TDs	35
Rushing TDs	7
Total TDs	42
TDs over 40 Yds.	5
Total Passing Yds.	2,969
Interceptions	10

It will be interesting to see how the 49er offense will operate without offensive guru Steve Shanahan and running back Ricky Watters. The weight of a Super Bowl win and the shadow of Joe Montana are now both gone in Steve Young's life, and the chances of him repeating his 1994 season are overwhelming. Young's durability, talent and 49er attitude still make him the number one fantasy QB selection.

2. Dan Marino, Miami Dolphins

Passing TDs	30
Rushing TDs	1
Total TDs	31
TDs over 40 Yds.	4
Total Passing Yds.	4,453
Interceptions	17

At the start of the 1994 season, everyone was questioning the health of Dan Marino after and the true healing process of his Achilles' heel. In other words, would he play the entire season or go off limping? The only limping was done by the opposing defenses as Marino silenced all doubters with 30 TDs. This season, Miami has added Eric Green, Randal Hill and Gary Clark to his firepower-- watch out for the super-serious Super Bowl-bound Marino!

3. Drew Bledsoe, New England Patriots

Passing TDs	25
Rushing TDs	0
Total TDS	25
TDs over 40 Yds.	1
Total Passing Yds.	4,555
Interceptions	27

To me, Bledsoe is another Dan Marino. Like Marino in his early career, he reflects that confident posture and a whip arm. Bledsoe still throws into the throat of the defenses, thinking that he can outgun defenders or thread the needle on every pass; this cockiness will soon grow into experience. This is the season for the Bledsoe-Brisby combination--we will be talking about these guys well into the next decade.

4. Brett Favre, Green Bay Packers

Passing TDs	33
Rushing TDs	2
Total TDs	35
TDs over 40 Yds.	1
Total Passing Yds.	3,882
Interceptions	14

What will life without Sterling Sharpe be like for Brett Favre? For the last two seasons Favre grew as a QB but he survived mostly because of Sharpe's on-the-line ability to make great plays and scores. Just when Favre has grown into a Steve Young type, Sharpe is forced to retire with a serious neck injury. Now Favre must be the take-charge guy and take over Sharpe's job as the leader--I think he can and will!

5. Jeff George, Atlanta Falcons

Passing TDs	23
Rushing TDs	0
Total TDs	23
TDs over 40 Yds.	4
Total Passing Yds.	3,734
Interceptions	18

Jeff George took the necessary steps last season to prove that he has grown up and yes that he can deliver with his awesome talent. Last season was a bit wacky with the Andre Rison situation but George kept in focus and developed a great feel for secondary receiver Terance Mathis. Add underrated but solid J.J. Birden to the offensive mix and George should have a great season.

6. John Elway, Denver Broncos

Passing TDs	16
Rushing TDs	4
Total TDs	20
TDs over 40 Yds.	3
Total Passing Yds.	3,490
Interceptions	10

Last season on paper appeared to be John Elway's season. The paper crumbled as key offensive injuries and the addition of so many new players cost Elway his glorious year. Elway is no longer the dodge-baller he was, but he managed four TD rushing scores and he still has that "I'm-in-charge-here" persona. Now with his close friend and now head coach Steve Shanahan back, expect the offense and Elway to fly high in the Denver thin air.

QB

7. Vinny Testaverde, Cleveland Browns

Passing TDs	16
Rushing TDs	2
Total TDs	18
TDs over 40 Yds.	3
Total Passing Yds.	2,575
Interceptions	18

Seeing Vinny Testaverde ranked as high as number seven will surely cause whiplash to the craning necks of many skeptical fantasy experts, but listen to reason--Andre Rison! Yes, anytime you add the brash, nimble receiver to a roster, one can expect that the QB will see an increase in productivity. Add in the fact that Cleveland has great offensive weapons and is very balanced, and we could see Vinny elevate his game to the potential that experts belived that he would reach when he entered the NFL. Pass out those "I like Vinny" buttons!

8. Jeff Hostetler, LA Raiders

Passing TDs	20
Rushing TDs	2
Total TDs	22
TDs over 40 Yds.	4
Total Passing Yds.	3,334
Interceptions	16

OK, let's throw out last season and start over again. The Raiders will be a much better team offensively and adding Derrick Fenner and Napoleon Kaufman to the backfield will keep defenses honest. Plus, expect White to design more offensive schemes to stretch out the playing field and take advantage of the blazing wide receiver speed with Tim Brown, Raghib Ismail and James Jett. Plus add the threatening running ability of Hostetler and now you have an exciting QB pick for your fantasy team.

QB

9. Randall Cunningham, Philadelphia Eagles

Passing TDs	16
Rushing TDs	3
Total TDs	19
TDs over 40 Yds.	4
Total Passing Yds.	3,229
Interceptions	13

"Earth to Randall...Earth to Randall" Hey pal, time to wake up that incredible talent and actually utilize it for an entire season! If not, Rodney Peete will be ready to replace you. By adding Ricky Watters to the mix, Randall now has a multi-dimension running back that will pump life into the offense and hopefully the unusually stoic Cunningham. This is a key season for Randall and I expect him to turn it back on under the wise and sure-handed tutelage of Ray Rhodes.

10. Craig Erickson, Indianapolis Colts

Passing TDs	16
Rushing TDs	1
Total TDs	17
TDs over 40 Yds.	5
Total Passing Yds.	2,919
Interceptions	10

Look, I know that Trent Dilfer is the rising sun in Tampa but with the artillery that they have put together there--Craig Erickson would have led them deep into the playoffs. But now that won't happen because he was traded to the newly wise and shrewd Indy Colts (when did you ever think you'd hear wise and shrewd in a Colts description?) Erickson is going to love throwing to Floyd Turner, Willie Anderson, Sean Dawkins and the versatile Marshall Faulk. Expect a big season for Erickson and playoffs for the Colts!

QB

11. Stan Humphries, San Diego Chargers

Passing TDs	17
Rushing TDs	0
Total TDs	17
TDs over 40 Yds.	6
Total Passing Yds.	3,209
Interceptions	12

One of the best features of Stan Humphries' game is his prowess for the bomb. Last season he had a young, inexperienced receiving corps and many experts figured he'd falter. He didn't, despite battling injuries and a young group of wideouts. Now he will go into this season with a healthier body and some seasoned receivers that will enable Humphries to put up sizeable numbers and perform effectively.

12. Rick Mirer, Seattle Seahawks

Passing TDs	11
Rushing TDs	0
Total TDs	11
TDs over 40 Yds.	1
Total Passing Yds.	2,151
Interceptions	7

In this book I have been repeatedly discussing Rick Mirer and my belief that under Dennis Erickson, Mirer and the Seahawks will be much more explosive and victorious in 1995. Adding reliable veteran Ricky Proehl, and rookie standouts Joey Galloway and Christian Fauria will give Mirer an opportunity to expand his game. Mirer should easily double his TD output in 1995 under Erickson's direction.

13. Jeff Blake, Cincinnati Bengals

Passing TDs	14
Rushing TDs	1
Total TDs	15
TDs over 40 Yds.	4
Total Passing Yds.	2,154
Interceptions	9

Now here is a guy that went from the outhouse to the penthouse! I love it. No one expected Jeff Blake to do more than grab a Gatorade and a clipboard when he joined the Bengals after getting released by the Jets during the exhibition season. Yet the guy jumps into the Bengal lineup and plays like Joe "Willie" Namath! Blake charged up the meek Striped Cats and immediately developed a touch with Carl Pickens and Darnay Scott. The Cincy gang will be exciting this season and I expect Blake to keep former number one pick (and ex-starter) David Klingler in plenty of Gatorade and pencils for that clipboard.

14. Troy Aikman, Dallas Cowboys

Passing TDs	13
Rushing TDs	1
Total TDs	14
TDs over 40 Yds.	1
Total Passing Yds.	2,676
Interceptions	12

Cowboy Troy really needs a healthy season. If Dallas is to challenge for that Super Bowl, they can't lose any of their keys (Aikman, Emmitt Smith or Michael Irvin). Because a big part of his job is dumping the ball off to Smith, FFL'ers tend shy away from Aikman, but he is due!

QB

15. Trent Dilfer, Tampa Bay Buccaneers

Passing TDs	1
Rushing TDs	0
Total TDs	1
TDs over 40 Yds.	0
Total Passing Yds.	433
Interceptions	6

Last year was a real disaster for Dilfer. He held out in a contract dispute during the preseason, and squandered away his few opportunities during the preseason by being just plain terrible! Enough said, Tampa traded away Craig Erickson and now Dilfer has the job. Plus Sam Wyche has brilliantly set him up with a solid offensive unit that should score and score often.

16. Jim Everett, New Orleans Saints

Passing Tds	22
Rushing TDs	0
Total TDs	22
TDs over 40 Yds.	2
Total Passing Yds.	3,855
Interceptions	18

Crazy Jimmy's a joke no longer. In 1994, Everett looked like the Jim Everett of five years ago. It is difficult to throw all your eggs in Everett's fickle basket but I gotta expect similar numbers in 1995.

17. Warren Moon, Minnesota Vikings

QB

Passing TDs	18
Rushing TDs	0
Total TDs	18
TDs over 40 Yds.	4
Total Passing Yds.	4,264
Interceptions	19

I would love to be wrong for rating a class quarterback like Warren Moon so low in the pack, but he no longer possesses that monster arm. Still, I like his receivers (Cris Carter and Jake Reed) and having an Amp Lee scooting out of the backfield for pass routes could pump up his offensive numbers. On the whole, though, I think 20 short-range TDs is the maximum for '95.

18. Jim Kelly, Buffalo Bills

Passing TDs	22
Rushing TDs	1

Total TDs	23
TDs over 40 YDs	2
Total Passing Yds.	3,114
Interceptions	17

I have a real concern over gritty Jim Kelly lasting the entire season. I am hoping that the loss of Don Beebe, Bill Brooks and Pete Metzelaars doesn't take a big chunk out of Buffalo's offense (but it must). I think 18-20 TDs is a push here.

19. Scott Mitchell, Detroit Lions

Passing TDs	10
Rushing TDs	1
Total TDs	11
TDs over 40 Yds.	0
Total Passing Yds.	1,456
Interceptions	11

QB

I am still in the "Show Me" mode with Scott Mitchell. He signs a big contract, and promptly fades into oblivion. Last season even prior to getting injured he fared poorly. Sure Mitchell can be a steal. Sure Mitchell can be a star. But for now he is just another big maybe--he *needs* to produce.

20. Heath Shuler, Washington Redskins

Passing TDs	10
Rushing TDs	0
Total TDs	10
TDs over 40 Yds.	5
Total Passing Yds	1,658.
Interceptions	12

155

Completely blew it last season with his holdout--who's his agent, Chuck Woolery? Expect Shuler to be more in rythmn this season with a full camp and exhibition season. Great arm strength and a solid offensive coaching structure to teach him. He could really develop into a gem this season, and may surprise.

21. Chris Miller, St. Louis Rams

Passing TDs	16
Rushing TDs	0
Total TDs	16
TDs over 40 Yds.	2
Total Passing Yds.	2,104
Interceptions	14

QB

Shoulda...if he coulda. Unfortunately, Miller's injuries are getting to be an annual occurrence. He's got great talent, but how can you build around a guy that gets hurt watching the TV show *ER*! But if for some reason he could survive a full year--the mind will boggle over his numbers!

22. Erik Kramer, Chicago Bears

Passing TDs	8
Rushing TDs	0
Total TDs	8
TDs over 40 Yds	2
Total Passing Yds.	1,129
Interceptions	8

Nothing worked out for Kramer last season. In fact, he must have felt like the Kramer on TV sitcom *Seinfeld*. Steve Walsh is a great guy and hustles hard, but Kramer (Erik, not Cosmo) should be the starting QB. Expect a better season and an improved receiving corps with Michael Timpson and Curtis Conway.

23. David Krieg, Arizona Cardinals

Passing TDs	14
Rushing TDs	0
Total TDs	14
TDs over 40 Yds.	1
Total Passing Yds.	1,629
Interceptions	14

Mr. Fantasy! David Krieg never will be recalled as a great NFL QB, but as a fantasy QB...the guy's an All Pro! Age is becoming a factor and he still can fumble the ball with the best of them, but I like his chances in Arizona. Heck, he is almost as old as Buddy and will ignore the Budster's shenanigans and he will like throwing to Rob Moore deep!

24. Steve Bono, Kansas City Chiefs

Passing Tds	4
Rushing TDs	0
Total TDs	4
TDs over 40 Yds.	1
Total Passing Yds.	796
Interceptions	4

Steve Bono has been a solid backup player to Steve Young and Joe Montana...but can he actually be a solid starter? When he did play last season he didn't look very good, so I am still on the fence on whether Bono can be Pro Bono.

25. David Brown, New York Giants

Passing Tds	12
Rushing TDs	2
Total TDs	14
TDs over 40 yds.	2
Total Passing Yds.	2,536
Interceptions	16

A bit low-keyed for a quarterback--in fact, he looks like just a goofy kid neighbor that is suddenly grown up. But hey, the guy *does* squeeze points out of a very conservative offense. Plus he is one of those awkward runners that manages to mess up the defense and score.

QB

QUARTERBACK RATING

1. Steve Young — San Francisco 49ers
2. Dan Marino — Miami Dolphins
3. Brett Favre — Green Bay Packers
4. Drew Bledsoe — New England Patriots
5. John Elway — Denver Broncos
6. Jeff George — Atlanta Falcons
7. Vinny Testaverde — Cleveland Browns
8. Jeff Hostetler — LA Raiders
9. Randall Cunningham — Philadelphia Eagles
10. Craig Erickson — Indianapolis Colts
11. Troy Aikman — Dallas Cowboys
12. Rick Mirer — Seattle Seahawks
13. Stan Humphries — San Diego Chargers
14. Jim Everett — New Orleans Saints
15. Warren Moon — Minnesota Vikings
16. Scott Mitchell — Detroit Lions
17. Jeff Blake — Cincinnati Bengals
18. Jim Kelly — Buffalo Bills

19.	Chris Miller	St. Louis Rams
20.	Trent Dilfer	Tampa Bay Buccaneers
21.	Heath Shuler	Washington Redskins
22.	Erik Kramer	Chicago Bears
23.	Neil O'Donnell	Pittsburgh Steelers
24.	Steve Bono	Kansas City Chiefs
25.	Dave Krieg	Arizona Cardinals
26.	Dave Brown	New York Giants
27.	Frank Reich	Carolina Panthers
28.	Boomer Esiason	New York Jets
29.	Steve Beuerlein	Jacksonville Jaguars
30.	Steve McNair	Houston Oilers
31.	Chris Chandler	Houston Oilers
32.	Bernie Kosar	Miami Dolphins
33.	Elvis Grbac	San Francisco 49ers
34.	Rodney Peete	Philadelphia Eagles
35.	David Klingler	Cincinnati Bengals
36.	Bill Musgrave	Denver Broncos
37.	Bobby Hebert	Atlanta Falcons
38.	Wade Wilson	Dallas Cowboys
39.	Mark Rypien	St. Louis Rams
40.	Steve Walsh	Chicago Bears
41.	John Friesz	Seattle Seahawks
42.	Jim Harbaugh	Indianapolis Colts
43.	Don Majkowski	Detroit Lions
44.	Gale Gilbert	San Diego Chargers
45.	Mike Tomczak	Pittsburgh Steelers
46.	Casey Weldon	Tampa Bay Buccaneers
47.	Gus Frerotte	Washington Redskins
48.	Mark Brunell	Jacksonville Jaguars
49.	Jack Trudeau	Carolina Panthers
50.	Matt Blundin	Kansas City Chiefs

QB

Running Backs

Ooooohhhh, to have the talent and luck to draft a pair of starting running backs that can push the point button and score! After selecting a great QB, I really like to make sure that I have running backs that get full-time opportunities. Depending on your league's scoring format you must be sharp on this pick. If your league just utilizes a scoring system based strictly on TD scoring, then yardage stats will not concern you. However, if you play in a format where performance points are involved (i.e. yardage, number of receptions, etc.) than you want to select runners who carry a major load of the offense. For example, in a league that just gives points to scoring TDs, a Barry Sanders is not as valuable as a Keith Byars (an RB who receives limited use but catches TD passes). But if your league counts TDs *and* yardage...hey, Barry's 1,883 rushing yardage sure looks appealing.

It used to be that running backs took several years to develop before they would get the opportunity to start in the NFL. Now, however, rookies seem to be starting and doing well. Two years ago, Jerome Bettis steamrolled over the opposition and scored well. Last season Marshall Faulk and Errict Rhett played extremely well. Faulk is now a premiere player and a sure shot early number one draft pick. This season we will see two additional rookie backs break onto the scene: Ki-Jana Carter (Cincinnati) and Rashaan Salaam (Chicago). Both will played huge roles on their teams and I believe Ki-Jana has the opportunity to join Emmitt Smith, Marshall Faulk, Chris Warren, and Barry Sanders in that high-stepping superstar club.

BONUS SCORING

In most FFL leagues, policy allows for bonus scoring. The bonus is based on distance scoring. The FFL suggests 40 yards as a distance barometer. Therefore, if a running back romps off for a 40-yard-plus TD run, he would receive double points. Another bonus comes when a running back catches a pass and scores a TD. If the yardage distance was 39 yards or under, the running back gets double points. If the pass play TD was 40 yards or more, the running back gets the famous "DOUBLE/DOUBLE!" The DOUBLE/DOUBLE is a rarity, but when it occurs...it is *sooo* sweet

EXAMPLE POINT SYSTEM:

RB scores on a TD run 39 yards or less: 6 points
RB scores on a TD pass 39 yards or less: 12 points
RB scores on a TD run 40 yards or more: 12 points
RB scores on a TD pass 40 yards or more: 24 points

DOUBLE/DOUBLE GUYS (40+ YD TD)

PLAYER	TEAM	40+ YD TD
Ricky Watters	SF	1
Marshall Faulk	IND	1
Leroy Hoard	CLE	1
Eric Metcalf	ATL	1
Brian Mitchell	WAS	1

1994 TOP RECEIVING RBs

PLAYER	TEAM	REC	YDS.	TDs
Edgar Bennett	GB	78	546	4
Larry Centers	AZ	77	647	2

PLAYER	TEAM	REC	YDS.	TDs
Glyn Milburn	DEN	77	549	3
Ricky Watters	PHI	66	719	5
Leroy Thompson	NE	65	465	5
Ronnie Harmon	SD	58	615	1
Johnny Bailey	STL	58	516	0
Marshall Faulk	IND	52	593	1
Kevin Turner	PHI	52	471	2
J.L. Williams	PIT	51	378	2
Ricky Ervins	F/A	51	293	1
Thurman Thomas	BUF	50	349	2
Emmitt Smith	DAL	50	341	1
Herschel Walker	NYG	50	500	2
Keith Byars	MIA	48	418	5
Harvey Williams	RAI	47	391	3
Eric Metcalf	ATL	47	436	2
Leroy Hoard	CLE	45	445	4
Amp Lee	MIN	45	368	2
Daryl Johnston	DAL	44	325	2
Barry Sanders	DET	44	283	1
Derek Brown	NO	44	428	1
James Joseph	CIN	43	344	2
Johnny Johnson	NYJ	42	303	2
Marcus Allen	KAN	42	349	0
Chris Warren	SEA	41	323	2
Raymont Harris	CHI	39	236	0
Natrone Means	SD	39	235	0
Reggie Cobb	JAX	38	299	1
Leonard Russell	DEN	38	227	0
Derrick Fenner	RAI	36	276	1
Bernie Parmalee	MIA	34	249	1
Ironhead Heyward	ATL	32	335	1
David Meggett	NE	32	293	0

RB

RUNNING BACK REVIEW

1. Emmitt Smith, Dallas Cowboys

Rushing TDs	21
Receiving TDs	1
Total TDs	22
Rushing Yds.	1,484
Receiving Yds	341

There is no reason not to think that Emmitt won't score another 20 rushing TDs in '95. But a word of caution is that Emmitt needs to realize that he is no longer bruise-free and will need a few more breathers in order to stay fresh legged and healthy. This season expect Emmitt, Michael and Troy to step up and play the pivotal roles to bring the Cowboys eye level with the San Francisco 49ers.

2. Marshall Faulk, Indianapolis Colts

Rushing TDs	11
Receiving TDs	1
Total TDs	12
Rushing Yds.	1,282
Receiving Yds	522

I call him Emmitt Jr., although he doesn't really have the muscle and thighs of Mr. Smith. What Marshall does better than Emmitt is receive passes out of the backfield, and he can really step up the jets when necessary. I expect QB Craig Erickson to dump off 65-70 passes to The Marshall. As for running, I anticipate 1,400-1,500 yards but around the goal line we may see big rookie Zack Crockett being used for the plunges.

3. Natrone Means, San Diego Chargers

Rushing TDs	12
Receiving TDs	0
Total TDs	12
Rushing Yds.	1,350
Receiving Yds.	235

Natrone is not much of a distance runner but he can pound and pound away on defenses and he can score a lot, too! Means will never be a toedancer but who cares when the guy is a solid 1,400-1,500 yard ground gainer and a cinch for 12-15 TDs.

4. Chris Warren, Seattle Seahawks

Rushing TDs	9
Receiving TDs	2
Total TDs	11
Rushing Yds.	1,545
Receiving Yds.	323

RB

With the new style Seattle offense going into effect under Dennis Erickson, expect Chris Warren to play a rather major role. Remember when Chris Warren was a late round backup fantasy pick? No more, huh, gang?!?

5. Barry Sanders, Detroit Lions

Rushing TDs	7
Receiving TDs	1
Total TDs	8
Rushing Yds.	1,883
Receiving Yds.	283

It is difficult to argue with such quality rushing yardage, but for us fantasy players, we sure would like to see Barry get more cracks at the goal line. And for the life of me, I will never understand why Detroit refuses to put him into the passing game (e.g. Thurman Thomas, Emmitt Smith and Marshall Faulk)? Maybe with Derrick Moore shoving off to San Francisco, we will finally see more of Barry in the endzone.

6. Ki-Jana Carter, Cincinnati Bengals

Rushing TDs	Rookie
Receiving TDs	
Total TDs	
Rushing Yds.	
Receiving Yds.	

Now, don't be giving me any of that "This is just Giebel going out on his 'I saw that rookie first' binge." I'll admit that I have a tendency to leap at certain players that have all the potential, the talent and the look. Right now the look is all over Ki-Jana Carter. I am telling you that Carter and the Bengals will be the fun team of the NFL. Carter rules, baby!

RB

7. Ricky Watters, Philadelphia Eagles

Rushing TDs	6
Receiving TDs	5
Total TDs	11
Rushing Yds.	877
Receiving Yds.	719

Sometimes I get up in the air over Ricky Watters. Will he explode to stardom or will he miss the 49ers magic? I believe that Ricky will add pizzazz, yardage and points to the staid Eagles.

165

Personally, I'd like to see Ricky run the ball more, with that quick-stepping, slashing, bob-and-burst-style. Whatever, you won't go wrong with Runnin' Watters.

8. Jerome Bettis, St. Louis Rams

Rushing TDs	3
Receiving TDs	1
Total TDs	4
Rushing Yds.	1,025
Receiving Yds.	293

What a major disappointment last season. A big mass of power like Bettis should gain 1,500 yards and 12-15 TDs not that puny showing in 1994. The move to St. Louis will help Bettis shake out that "I'm a pretty cool dude" attitude and hopefully get him back on track. I predict that he will get closer to the 12-15 TDs and the 1,500 yards I think he's capable of.

9. William Floyd, San Francisco 49ers

Rushing TDs	6
Receiving TDs	0
Total TDs	6
Rushing Yds.	305
Receiving Yds.	145

One of the reasons that I kid about why the 49ers allowed Ricky Watters to scoot is because William Floyd is just as jive and hip as the Rickster, yet works cheaper. Actually Floyd's talent really began to show near the end of the season. The guy is a goal line terror and if given the ball 20-25 times he will amass 1,200-1,300 yards and 12-14 TDs. One thing to watch is how the Niners intend to utilize Derrick Moore (who can also slam the goal line).

10. Erricht Rhett, Tampa Bay Buccaneers

Rushing TDs	7
Receiving TDs	0
Total TDs	7
Rushing Yds.	1,011
Receiving Yds.	119

Dig the Pearl...Erricht Rhett is worth drafting this high. Why? The kid wants the ball and he makes things happen. Last year he reported late and started late, but he finished fast and strong. He is the lone runner of note in Tampa Bay so I say don't overlook this pearl.

11. Bam Morris, Pittsburgh Steelers

Rushing TDs	7
Receiving TDs	0
Total TDs	7
Rushing Yds.	836
Receiving Yds.	204

RB

How can you not like anyone named BAM? Despite the acquisition of Erric Pegram and the loss of Barry Foster, I think that Bam is a player I would want on my team. Bam had only played about half the season (in Foster's place) and still gained 836 yards and 7 TDs. Give him a full season and we can project at least 12 TDs and 1,200 yards.

12. Ironhead Heyward, Atlanta Falcons

Rushing TDs	7
Receiving TDs	1
Total TDs	8

Rushing Yds.   779
Receiving Yds.   335

IRONHEAD! Hey that gives any fantasy team and "all-nickname" backfield...Bam Morris and Ironhead Heyward toting the pigskin. Now, if I could only get Bum Phillips out of retirement for my coach! When I look at the Falcon offense I only see one running back in a one back offense. I also see a big year on the horizon for the hard-headed Ironhead!

13. Leroy Hoard, Cleveland Browns

Rushing TDs   5
Receiving TDs   4
Total TDs   9
Rushing Yds.   890
Receiving Yds.   445

RB

Hey, Leroy! If you followed my advice two years ago, you would remember that I predicted a great season for Leroy Hoard. Unfortunately my advice was not heard by the Browns and he disappeared off the fantasy radar into oblivion. Finally last season (after I received a year of heckling), Leroy got his due. Solid player...solid pick.

14. Rashaan Salaam, Chicago Bears

Rushing TDs   Rookie
Receiving TDs
Total TDs
Rushing Yds.
Receiving Yds.

All right, here is my word of advice to Salaam: Don't screw up or you will forever be nicknamed Salami. Pass on the mustard and the pizza and keep in shape. Potential is huge with Salaam...but if he doesn't pan out it will be because he doesn't come to play in shape mentally and physically. You've been warned, but what a steal he will be if he plays with an Emmitt Smith mindset.

15. Gary Brown, Houston Oilers

Rushing TDs	4
Receiving TDs	1
Total TDs	5
Rushing Yds.	648
Receiving Yds.	194

Whoa, what happen to Gary in 1995? What a flop of a pick, after such a solid 1993 season. Well this season the door is wide open again for Gary as Lorenzo White has signed with Cleveland. The only downer and question is whether the Oilers will be offensive-minded or just *offensive*! I like Brown this season...but not the Oilers.

RB

16. Thurman Thomas, Buffalo Bills

Rushing TDs	7
Receiving TDs	2
Total TDs	9
Rushing Yds.	1,093
Receiving Yds.	349

Thurman ain't Thermal no more...but he still can notch the score, catch the pass, and gain the yardage. I have a theory here: With the Bills no longer a contender, maybe Thurman can relax and bust loose. It would be nice to see Thurman Thomas finally enjoy

himself and shake off the ghosts of the past. By the way Thurman...
four Super Bowl appearances is better action than most of these
stiffs have seen!

17. Rodney Hampton, New York Giants

Rushing TDs	6
Receiving TDs	0
Total TDs	6
Rushing Yds.	1,075
Receiving Yds.	546

Last season really hurt Rodney (and you, if he was a first
or second round pick for your squad.) Now suddenly we hear
reports that the Giants have been attempting to trade him and they
drafted future phenom Tyrone Wheatley. Add to that pile of talent
Herschel Walker and man-oh-man we have a quagmire. Still, my
point...how do you bench a Rodney Hampton?

RB

18. Mario Bates, New Orleans Saints

Rushing TDs	6
Receiving TDs	0
Total TDs	6
Rushing Yds.	579
Receiving Yds,	N/A

If we can keep fellow Naarlins' backfield mates from
breaking his jaw, I feel Mario will be a solid pick. After all he
gained all his yards and scored all his TDs in about a quarter and a
half. My only hesitation here is that the Saints march out about 4-5
super stud running backs (their latest acquisition is Notre Dame
standout Ray Zellars). Bates is all they really need.

19. Ron Moore, New York Jets

Rushing TDs	4
Receiving TDs	1
Total TDs	5
Rushing Yds.	780
Receiving Yds.	N/A

Here is a guy that should welcome leaving Buddy's roost and land in New York with the Jets. Two years ago he was "Who?" and "Wow!" Last season his face appeared on milk cartons ("Have you seen me?") and the only offense he saw was the opposition's. Moore should thrive with the Jets, but he may share with Johnny Johnson.

20. Edgar Bennett, Green Bay Packers

Rushing TDs	5
Receiving TDs	4
Total TDs	9
Rushing Yds.	623
Receiving Yds.	546

RB

Without Sterling Sharpe for 1995, Edgar Bennett's value has to rise even more. I would like to see if Bennett could be a premiere rusher (1,000 yards). My one question here is will the Packers give LeShon Johnson a crack or will Bennett be the full time offensive backfield weapon?

21. Barry Foster, Carolina Panthers

Rushing TDs	5
Receiving TDs	0
Total TDs	5

171

Rushing Yds.	851
Receiving Yds.	124

Great move by the Panthers   Hopefully all that funky "Is he injured or is he not?" garbage that kept surrounding Foster and the Steeler brass, is gone. No doubt that Foster will be an integral component for Carolina and he should do well.

22. Derrick Fenner, Los Angeles Raiders

Rushing TDs	1
Receiving TDs	1
Total TDs	2
Rushing Yds.	468
Receiving Yds.	276

I know you are thinking "Whaddya nuts...Derrick Fenner?" Yep. The Raiders have been searching for a nimble, big runner. Derrick fits this description and he has the ability to be a surprise player in 1995.

23. Terry Allen, Washington Redskins

Rushing TDs	8
Receiving TDs	0
Total TDs	8
Rushing Yds.	1,031
Receiving Yds.	148

I always felt that Terry Allen was too good not to get picked up, and at press time, the Redskins signed him to a deal. The key here is to see where he ends up--starting or backing up Reggie Brooks or Marc Logan. Right now, the Redskins have three **backs** capable of causing some damage, and it will be interesting to see how Allen fits into the mix. Plus, you got to give Allen points for tenacity since he has recovered from two separate knee operations.

24. Terry Kirby, Miami Dolphins

Rushing TDs	2
Receiving TDs	0
Total TDs	2
Rushing Yds.	233
Receiving Yds.	154

I have total belief that Terry Kirby was on his way for a great season until he suffered a season-ending injury. Kirby is a better receiving than runner and he could see some competition from Bernie Parmalee. Check into this status in August. I like Terry Kirby!

25. Leonard Russell, Denver Broncos

RB

Rushing TDs	9
Receiving TDs	0
Total TDs	9
Rushing Yds.	620
Receiving Yds.	227

Leonard Russell suffered an injury and *still* scored nine TDs. Russell has double-digit scoring potential and can gain over 1,000 yards. This pick won't make or break your franchise but he will be consistent and plays on a John Elway offense that moves downfield and attacks.The only question here on this pick is where does oft-injured Rod Bernstine fit into the equation?

RUNNING BACK RATING

1.	Emmitt Smith	Dallas Cowboys
2.	Marshall Faulk	Indianapolis Colts
3.	Natrone Means	San Diego Chargers
4.	Chris Warren	Seattle Seahawks
5.	Barry Sanders	Detroit Lions
6.	Ki-Jana Carter	Cincinnati Bengals
7.	Ricky Watters	Philadelphia Eagles
8.	Jerome Bettis	St. Louis Rams
9.	William Floyd	San Francisco 49ers
10.	Erricht Rhett	Tampa Bay Buccaneers
11.	Bam Morris	Pittsburgh Steelers
12.	Ironhead Heyward	Atlanta Falcons
13.	Leroy Hoard	Cleveland Browns
14.	Rashaan Salaam	Chicago Bears
15.	Gary Brown	Houston Oilers
16.	Thurman Thomas	Buffalo Bills
17.	Rodney Hampton	New York Giants
18.	Mario Bates	New Orleans Saints
19.	Ron Moore	New York Jets
20.	Edgar Bennett	Green Bay Packers
21.	Barry Foster	Carolina Panthers
22.	Derrick Fenner	Los Angeles Raiders
23.	Terry Allen	Washington Redskins
24.	Terry Kirby	Miami Dolphins
25.	Leonard Russell	Denver Broncos
26.	Garrison Hearst	Arizona Cardinals
27.	Eric Metcalf	Atlanta Falcons
28.	David Meggett	New England Patriots
29.	Curtis Martin	New England Patriots
30.	Herschel Walker	New York Giants
31.	Harvey Williams	Los Angeles Raiders
32.	Glyn Milburn	Denver Broncos
33.	Amp Lee	Minnesota Vikings

RB

34. Ken Davis	Buffalo Bills
35. Reggie Brooks	Washington Redskins
36. Greg Hill	Kansas City Chiefs
37. James Stewart	Jacksonville Jaguars
38. Keith Byars	Miami Dolphins
39. Bernie Parmalee	Miami Dolphins
40. Derrick Moore	San Francisco 49ers
41. Lorenzo White	Cleveland Browns
42. Johnny Johnson	New York Jets
43. Napoleon Kaufman	LA Raiders
44. Marcus Allen	Kansas City Chiefs
45. Lewis Tillman	Chicago Bears
46. Kevin Turner	Philadelphia Eagles
47. Erric Pegram	Pittsburgh Steelers
48. Rod Bernstine	Denver Broncos
49. Leroy Thompson	New England Patriots
50. Larry Centers	Arizona Cardinals
51. Brian Mitchell	Washington Redskins
52. Ray Zellars	New Orleans Saints
53. LeShon Johnson	Green Bay Packers
54. Tyrone Wheatley	New York Giants
55. Sherman Williams	Dallas Cowboys
56. Marc Logan	Washington Redskins
57. Robert Smith	Minnesota Vikings
58. Tommy Vardell	Cleveland Browns
59. Dexter Carter	New York Jets
60. Ronnie Harmon	San Diego Chargers
61. John L. Williams	Pittsburgh Steelers
62. Reggie Cobb	Jacksonville Jaguars
63. David Lang	Dallas Cowboys
64. Derek Brown	New Orleans Saints
65. Chuck Levy	Arizona Cardinals
66. Terrell Fletcher	San Diego Chargers
67. James Stewart II	Minnesota Vikings
68. Mack Strong	Seattle Seahawks
69. James Joseph	Cincinnati Bengals

RB

175

70.	Johnny Bailey	St. Louis Rams
71.	Brad Baxter	New York Jets
72.	Zack Crockett	Indianapolis Colts
73.	Carwell Gardner	Buffalo Bills
74.	Larry Jones	Washington Redskins
75.	Kimble Anders	Kansas City Chiefs
76.	Corey Croom	New England Patriots
77.	Lorenzo Neal	New Orleans Saints
78.	Derrick Lassic	Jacksonville Jaguars
79.	Reggie Rivers	Denver Broncos
80.	Charlie Garner	Philadelphia Eagles
81.	Ricky Ervins	Free Agent
82.	Vince Workman	Tampa Bay Buccaneers
83.	Raymont Harris	Chicago Bears
84.	Calvin Jones	Los Angeles Raiders
85.	Scottie Graham	Minnesota Vikings
86.	Eric Bienemy	Cincinnati Bengals
87.	Cleveland Gary	St. Louis Rams
88.	Sean Jackson	Houston Oilers
89.	Jeff Cothran	Cincinnati Bengals
90.	Joe Aska	Los Angeles Raiders
91.	Roosevelt Potts	Indianapolis Colts
92.	Butler By'note'	Denver Broncos
93.	Tony Vinson	San Diego Chargers
94.	William Henderson	Green Bay Packers
95.	Cory Schlesinger	Detroit Lions
96.	Chuck Evans	Minnesota Vikings
97.	Eric Lynch	Detroit Lions
98.	Adrian Murrell	New York Jets
99.	Blair Thomas	Dallas Cowboys
100.	Darrell Thompson	Chicago Bears

RB

★7★

Wide Receivers

This position can drive you *crazy* if you have any intention of winning. Wide receivers are the glamour boys. For example, if you wanted to borrow some cool threads, you wouldn't want to schlep around in the hand-me-down, could-be-a-farmer clothes of an offensive lineman. No...no...but you'd be strut-steppin' happy to trip the light fantastic wearing a wide receiver's chic hip-hop garb.

Wide receivers also always have hot-looking women riding in their Jaguars or Mercedes, whereas tight ends are always tooling around in Jeeps or wide-bodied pickup trucks. Also, if you notice, instead of leaving the ballpark with a Cindy Crawford look-a-like (as wide receivers normally do), tight ends amble off alone, or share their vehicle with a hounddog affectionately named Rusty or Shane. Big difference in the cool factor rating system, huh?! Lately wide receivers are finding out that they have perhaps outpriced themselves in the marketplace with those strapping salaries. In fact many a wide receiver may soon be selling the cool Jags and real estate (their own) if they don't watch out. The salary cap has taken a big bite out of many NFL clubs and the receivers are feeling it.

A word to the wise when drafting make sure that the receivers you are drafting play a major role with this year's team. It's easy to say that Jerry Rice, Andre Rison, Tim Brown, Herman Moore, etc., are going to be hooking up for big seasons in 1995...but what about the question marks? I for one like Gary Clark's chances

WR

in Miami with Dan Marino...but by the end of exhibition season maybe Clark will have worn out his welcome and we could be seeing Randal Hill being the Marino deep threat.

My advice with this position is to select receivers that play with a QB that is solid, like Steve Young, Dan Marino, etc. Select a receiver on an offense that will throw deep and often (i.e. Raiders, Patriots, Browns, etc.) Select a receiver on a team prone to head for the playoffs. This season, with so much parity and coaching job insecurity, coaches will be forced to stick with their starters and light up the skies. Stay away from gambles and remember that rookie receivers have difficulty breaking into starting lineups and making big splashes in the first season

MAJOR TIP: KNOW THE QB & THE RECEIVERS

I really believe in knowing not just the starting #1 quarterback and receiver...I think it is paramount to also know who are the second and third receivers. The more you know, the more effective a drafter you will be. So don't be a chump--study the QB/WRs breakdown below and keep track of these rascals for your draft preparation. See if there are any injuries, any roster or depth chart moves, or any released players. Also keep an eye on a rookie like Jack Jackson in Chicago. This little receiver is a very dangerous runner once he gets the ball. How about Tamarick Vanover (whom I rated as the #3 receiver for KC)? This guy left school after his second year in college and played last season in Canada--this cat can play! How about that exciting Cleveland team...they've also added two super fast receivers in the draft: Mike Miller and A.C. Tellison. I feel that Miller could be a real steal. Miller's small--but a real burner. The problem is being a real knucklehead at Notre Dame really cost him. Gee, maybe Andre Rison can help him GROW UP!

WR

QUARTERBACK/WIDE RECEIVERS LISTING

TEAM	QB	1ST REC	2ND REC	3RD REC
SF	Steve Young	Jerry Rice	John Taylor	J.J. Stokes
MIA	Dan Marino	Irving Fryar	Randal Hill	Gary Clark
NE	Drew Bledsoe	Vincent Brisby	Ray Crittenden	Kevin Lee
GB	Brett Favre	Robert Brooks	Mark Ingram	Anthony Morgan
ATL	Jeff George	Terance Mathis	J.J. Birden	Bert Emanuel
DEN	John Elway	Anthony Miller	Mike Pritchard	Ed McCaffrey
CLE	Vinny Testaverde	Andre Rison	Michael Jackson	Derrick Alexander
RAI	Jeff Hostetler	Tim Brown	Raghib Ismail	James Jett
PHI	R. Cunningham	Fred Barnett	Calvin Williams	Chris T. Jones
IND	Craig Erickson	Floyd Turner	Willie Anderson	Sean Dawkins
SD	Stan Humphries	Tony Martin	Mark Seay	Shawn Jefferson
DAL	Troy Aikman	Michael Irvin	Kevin Williams	Willie Jackson
DET	Scott Mitchell	Herman Moore	Brett Perriman	Johnnie Morton
CIN	Jeff Blake	Carl Pickens	Darnay Scott	David Dunn
SEA	Rick Mirer	Brian Blades	Ricky Proehl	Joey Galloway
TB	Trent Dilfer	Alvin Harper	Courtney Hawkins	Lawrence Dawsey
WAS	Heath Shuler	Henry Ellard	Michael Westbrook	Tydus Winans
MIN	Warren Moon	Cris Carter	Jake Reed	Qadry Ismail
NO	Jim Everett	Michael Haynes	Quinn Early	Torrance Small
BUF	Jim Kelly	Andre Reed	Bucky Brooks	Billy Brooks
KAN	Steve Bono	Willie Davis	Lake Dawson	Tamarick Vanover
ARZ	Dave Krieg	Rob Moore	Anthony Edwards	Frank Sanders
STL	Chris Miller	Alexander Wright	Isaac Bruce	Todd Kinchen
CHI	Erik Kramer	Michael Timpson	Curtis Conway	Jeff Graham
NYG	Dave Brown	Mike Sherrad	Thomas Lewis	Chris Calloway
CAR	Frank Reich	Don Beebe	Mark Carrier	Dwight Stone
PIT	Neil O'Donnell	Charles Johnson	Yancey Thigpen	Andre Hastings
NYJ	Boomer Esiason	Ryan Yarbough	Orlando Parker	Tyrone Davis
JAX	Steve Beuerlein	Ernest Givins	Desmond Howard	Cedric Tillman
HOU	Steve McNair	Pat Coleman	Chris Sanders	Malcolm Seabron

WR

179

WIDE RECEIVER REVIEW

1. Jerry Rice, San Francisco 49ers

Receptions	112
Touchdowns	15
TDs +40 Yds.	2
Total Rec. Yds.	1,499

Still the best ever at the receiver position. Any of the young receivers entering the NFL should look at Rice's work ethic and decide whether they want to reach the pinnacle of greatness or just grab the cash and run. Rice has not shown any drop off in skills or stats, as clearly noted in that total of 112 receptions--that's 7 receptions per game! This guys always good for 18 TDs and 100-plus receptions.

2. Andre Rison, Cleveland Browns

Receptions	81
Touchdowns	8
TDs +40 Yds	1
Total Rec. Yds	1,088

If Andre can refrain from mouthing off, getting his home burned up or worrying about the latest fashion trends in the hip music scene, this guy could have a record-breaking season. Rison is the key to Vinny Testaverde becoming a top echelon quarterback and the Browns to challenge for a run at the Super Bowl. Rison could easily score 16 TDs in '95.

3. Tim Brown, Los Angeles Raiders

Receptions	89
Touchdowns	9
TDs +40 Yds.	2
Total Rec. Yds.	1,309

Listen up, Tim Brown will hook up more often (and on deeper pass patterns) now that Mike White has taken over the Raiders. Brown is one of the class acts in the NFL and his durabilty, versatility and solid work ethic makes him always a great fantasy pick. I think this season we will see Hostetler to Brown long and often. 14 TDs and 100 receptions is not a far cry for this burner.

4. Carl Pickens, Cincinnati Bengals

Receptions	71
Touchdowns	11
TDs +40 Yds.	2
Total Rec. Yds.	1,127

WR

Carl Pickens is ready for stardom and I think that Jeff Blake and Pickens will be effective and very similar to Hoss and Brown. This guy is a flyer and plays for an exciting offense. Watch how exciting *and* fun the Bengals will be in '95! Including Pickens in the 14 TD category is a reality, but he tends not to get as many receptions. Look for 85-90 receptions out of this guy--he *will* score!

5. Herman Moore, Detroit Lions

Receptions	72
Touchdowns	11
TDs +40 Yds.	1
Total Rec. Yds.	1,173

Another great pick! Man, am I excited over the prospects of some truly talented receivers that are now popping up throughout the NFL. Moore really isn't a downfield bomb-type receiver, but catch him inside the ten yard line and he is a sure thing. No one can out jump Moore on those alley-oop type of plays. Good for 14-15 TDs for this season.

6. Michael Irvin, Dallas Cowboys

Receptions	79
Touchdowns	6
TDs +40 Yds.	1
Total Rec. Yds.	1,241

Just like Jerry Rice, Irvin is a real battler and pure professional. With Alvin Harper gone (whose success was due purely to Irvin getting doubled team every play...every game.), Irvin will be the point man once again. This season in particular the Cowboys must strap their Super Bowl hopes on the backs of Irvin, Emmitt Smith and Troy Aikman. Aikman needs to open his game up and hit Irvin with 100 receptions and a dozen TDs in '95.

7. Terance Mathis, Atlanta Falcons

Receptions	111
Touchdowns	11
TDs +40 Yds.	2
Total Rec. Yds.	1,342

From the outhouse to the penthouse! What a fine, fine season 1994 was for Mathis. With the addition of J.J. Birden, the Falcons will continue to open up and improve through the bullet arm

WR

of Jeff George. In '95, Mathis should put up similar stats and be George's primary receiver.

8. Anthony Miller, Denver Broncos

Receptions	60
Touchdowns	5
TDs +40 Yds.	1
Total Rec. Yds.	1,107

I'll equate last season as a learning experience for Anthony Miller. However, he should have no excuse this season and John Elway should take advantage of his speed. With Steve Shanahan taking over the team, I would expect a more spread-the-ball-around type offense and even more isolated attention to the primary receiver (Miller). Expect 80 receptions and 10 TDs.

9. Andre Reed, Buffalo Bills

Receptions	90
Touchdowns	8
TDs +40 Yds.	1
Total Rec. Yds.	1,303

WR

The Bills this season have got to let loose the offense this season! Jim Kelly is nearing the end of a fine career, but this team lost too many starters (Don Beebe, Billy Brooks and Pete Metzelaars). Therefore expect Kelly to really concentrate on Andre Reed and Thurman Thomas. Reed should hit stride for 90-100 receptions and 10 TDs.

10. Cris Carter, Minnesota Vikings

Receptions	122
Touchdowns	7
TDs +40 Yds	2
Total Rec. Yds.	1,256

Cris Carter finally has earned the respect of the NFL after turning in season after season of solid football. In 1995 he only had 122 receptions! It is unlikely that he will put up those reception numbers again, since Warren Moon is ever nearer the end of his career, and Jake Reed is developing into a fine receiver in his own right. However, Carter is still Moon's go-to clutch receiver so I expect 90 receptions and 9-10 TDs.

11. Alvin Harper, Tampa Bay Buccaneers

Receptions	33
Touchdowns	8
TDs +40 Yds.	2
Total Rec. Yds.	821

WR

This is a tough pick for me. Alvin Harper has been a truly talented player that frankly has not produced as large as he should. Harper would occasionally disappear during critical times in games and he never had to be a leader (with Aikman, Smith and Irvin in charge.) So will Harper take over in Tampa and become a tough receiver (like Rice, Irvin, Brown, etc.) or will he take the money and disappear in the Ol' Sombrero? With this offense (as long as Trent Dilfer doesn't become a bust) he should be explosive. Harper should be a cinch for 80 receptions and 10 TDs.

12. Robert Brooks, Green Bay Packers

Receptions   58
Touchdowns   4
TDs +40 Yds.   0
Total Rec. Yds.   648

Life without Sterling Sharpe begins now and Robert Brooks is the fellow who needs to pick up the team with a solid performance. The question here has been whether Brooks was successful due to Sharpe being double-teamed or successful due to being a solid receiver? Brett Favre will be searching for Brooks and he could notch 80 receptions and 9-10 TDs.

13. Irving Fryar, Miami Dolphins

Receptions   73
Touchdowns   7
TDs +40 Yds.   3
Total Rec. Yds.   1,270

Irving Fryar has finally hit his potential with great strides after a solid 1994 season. With the addition of Eric Green, Randal Hill and Gary Clark into this potent offense I feel that Fryar's numbers will not diminish and he can nail 80 receptions and 10 TDs. Remember that Dan Marino likes to spread the ball around and he likes to keep his receivers happy. Here's to a smiling Irving Fryar!

WR

14. Vincent Brisby, New England Patriots

Receptions   58
Touchdowns   5
TDs +40 Yds.   0
Total Rec. Yds.   904

Bledsoe to Brisby will be the combo to remember! This could become the battle cry of New England for the next decade. Although Michael Timpson and his 74 receptions will be missed, Brisby is much more talented and has the potential to become a top echelon receiver soon! I think Brisby could achieve 75-80 receptions and 10 TDs quite easily.

15. Henry Ellard, Washington Redskins

Receptions	74
Touchdowns	6
TDs +40 Yds.	3
Total Rec. Yds.	1,397

Although he may be getting older (who among us isn't, genius?), Ellard is still a fantastic receiver that can slip away from a defender with a burst of speed. Ellard should really be valuable in developing both Heath Shuler and rookie wide receiver Michael Westbrook. Ellard is on course for 80 receptions and 10 TDs.

WR

16. Brian Blades, Seattle Seahawks

Receptions	81
Touchdowns	1,086
TDs +40 Yds.	0
Total Rec. Yds.	4

Look up underrated receiver in the dictionary and you will see a picture of Brian Blades' smiling mug. With the arrival of an offense in Seattle, we will all soon be treated to a great season by Blades. Projected 80 receptions and 9-10 TDs.

17. Rob Moore, Arizona Cardinals

Receptions	78
Touchdowns	6
TDs +40 Yds	1
Total Rec. Yds	1,010

My only hesitation here is if Rob Moore had problems with the New York Jets' coaching staff questioning his dedication, what's going to happen when Buddy Ryan says BOO? One thing I do like is the fact that Dave Krieg is a decent bomber who could hook up well with Rob Moore. I project Moore (if he stays out of doghouse) to hit the field running with 80 receptions and 9-10 TDs.

18. Floyd Turner, Indianapolis Colts

Receptions	52
Touchdowns	6
TDs +40 Yds.	3
Total Rec. Yds.	593

"Turner the Burner" will really like new QB Craig Erickson in Indy (and vice versa.) The Colts will join the Bengals as much improved and exciting ballclubs and Turner will be the primary receiver (even with the newly acquired Flipper Anderson.) I project Turner will latch onto 70-75 receptions and 9 TDs.

WR

19. Jake Reed, Minnesota Vikings

Receptions	85
Touchdowns	4
TDs +40 Yds.	0
Total Rec. Yds.	1,175

Jake Reed really improved in 1994, and should still catch close to 80-85 passes and scoring should increase to 8 TDs.

20. Randal Hill, Miami Dolphins

Receptions	38
Touchdowns	0
TDs +40 Yds.	0
Total Rec. Yds.	544

Will Thrill Hill finally live up to his self-confident views of his own ability? He should be happy to be finally back in Miami and having Dan Marino as a QB (after Jay Schroeder last year) should really test that talent. I feel either Hill or Gary Clark will emerge with a solid season (maybe both will?) I project Hill will catch 70 passes and 8-9 TDs.

WIDE RECEIVER RATING

WR

1. Jerry Rice   San Francisco 49ers
2. Andre Rison   Cleveland Browns
3. Tim Brown   Los Angeles Raiders
4. Carl Pickens   Cincinnati Bengals
5. Herman Moore   Detroit Lions
6. Michael Irvin   Dallas Cowboys
7. Terance Mathis   Atlanta Falcons
8. Anthony Miller   Denver Broncos
9. Andre Reed   Buffalo Bills
10. Cris Carter   Minnesota Vikings
11. Alvin Harper   Tampa Bay Buccaneers
12. Robert Brooks   Green Bay Packers
13. Irving Fryar   Miami Dolphins
14. Vincent Brisby   New England Patriots

15.	Henry Ellard	Washington Redskins
16.	Brian Blades	Seattle Seahawks
17.	Rob Moore	Arizona Cardinals
18.	Floyd Turner	Indianapolis Colts
19.	Jake Reed	Minnesota Vikings
20.	Randal Hill	Miami Dolphins
21.	Fred Barnett	Philadelphia Eagles
22.	Willie Davis	Kansas City Chiefs
23.	Kevin Williams	Dallas Cowboys
24.	J.J. Birden	Atlanta Falcons
25.	Tony Martin	San Diego Chargers
26.	Floyd Turner	Indianapolis Colts
27.	Darnay Scott	Cincinnati Bengals
28.	Courtney Hawkins	Tampa Bay Buccaneers
29.	Michael Jackson	Cleveland Browns
30.	Gary Clark	Miami Dolphins
31.	Jake Reed	Minnesota Vikings
32.	Michael Haynes	New Orleans Saints
33.	Calvin Williams	Philadelphia Eagles
34.	Flipper Anderson	Indianapolis Colts
35.	Ernest Givins	Jacksonville Jaguars
36.	Quinn Early	New Orleans Saints
37.	John Taylor	San Francisco 49ers
38.	Don Beebe	Carolina Panthers
39.	Michael Westbrook	Washington Redskins
40.	Michael Timpson	Chicago Bears
41.	Raghib Ismail	Los Angeles Raiders
42.	Charles Johnson	Pittsburgh Steelers
43.	Alexander Wright	St. Louis Rams
44.	J.J. Stokes	San Francisco 49ers
45.	Joey Galloway	Seattle Seahawks
46.	Mike Pritchard	Denver Broncos
47.	Mark Seay	San Diego Chargers
48.	Derrick Alexander	Cleveland Browns
49.	Lawrence Dawsey	Tampa Bay Buccaneers
50.	Haywood Jeffires	Free Agent

WR

189

51. Webster Slaughter Free Agent
52. Mark Carrier Carolina Panthers
53. Mike Sherrard New York Giants
54. Brett Perriman Detroit Lions
55. Ricky Proehl Seattle Seahawks
56. Ryan Yarborough New York Jets
57. Curtis Conway Chicago Bears
58. James Jett Los Angeles Raiders
59. Mark Ingram Green Bay Packers
60. Pat Coleman Houston Oilers
61. Bucky Brooks Buffalo Bills
62. Shawn Jefferson San Diego Chargers
63. Qadry Ismail Minnesota Vikings
64. Desmond Howard Jacksonville Jaguars
65. Bert Emanuel Atlanta Falcons
66. Ray Crittenden New England Patriots
67. Sean Dawkins Indianapolis Colts
68. Orlando Parker New York Jets
69. Lake Dawson Kansas City Chiefs
70. Thomas Lewis New York Giants
71. Frank Sanders Arizona Cardinals
72. Tydus Winans Washington Redskins

WR

73. Yancey Thigpen Pittsburgh Steelers
74 Torrance Small New Orleans Saints
75. Johnnie Morton Detroit Lions
76. Ed McCaffrey Denver Broncos
77. Chris Sanders Houston Oilers
78. Anthony Morgan Green Bay Packers
79. Chris Calloway New York Giants
80. Dwight Stone Carolina Panthers
81. Victor Bailey Kansas City Chiefs
82. Willie Jackson Dallas Cowboys
83. Vance Johnson Denver Broncos
84. Anthony Carter Detroit Lions
85. Kevin Lee New England Patriots
86. Billy Brooks Buffalo Bills

87.	Art Monk	New York Jets
88.	Eric Martin	Kansas City Chiefs
89.	David Palmer	Minnesota Vikings
90.	Chris T. Jones	Philadelphia Eagles
91.	Horace Copeland	Tampa Bay Buccaneers
92.	Andre Hastings	Pittsburgh Steelers
93.	Kevin Knox	Buffalo Bills
94.	Cedric Tillman	Jacksonville Jaguars
95.	Gary Wellman	Free Agent
96.	Charles Wilson	Tampa Bay Buccaneers
97.	Kelvin Martin	Philadelphia Eagles
98.	Andre Coleman	San Diego Chargers
99.	Michael Bates	Seattle Seahawks
100.	Steve Hawkins	New England Patriots

WR

★8★

Tight Ends

There are two things that keep me awake at night: First, what *are* the lyrics to Louie Louie? Second, where, oh where does the Tight End position fit into the fantasy football scheme of things?! Stop the presses! Tight Ends just may play a much bigger role in 1995.

Eric Green, Shannon Sharpe, Ben Coates, Brent Jones, Johnny Mitchell and Keith Jackson are as important to their teams as are the wide receivers. Therefore, as more NFL teams realize that a tight end can do more than just block, more and more will start drafting quality TEs. In this past draft the Jets outleaped the Cleveland Browns for Kyle Brady. Brady is a stud and will see immediate opportunities and will be a force with Johnny Mitchell. Seattle tabbed Chris Fauria as their number two draft pick and this guy will not disappoint. He will fill a glaring need in Seattle and help with blocking (for Chris Warren) and help open up the passing game (with fellow rookie Joey Galloway).

With some of the new rules implemented by the league in 1994, especially the two-point conversion, this season could be a record year for tight ends, and maybe, just maybe, we can once and for all get rid of those stupid tackle-eligible, my-hands-are-made-of-stone TD receptions.

TE

TIGHT END REVIEW

1. Eric Green, Miami Dolphins

Receptions	46
Touchdowns	4
Rec. Yds.	618

Here is the tester for Eric Green. Take stardom and live up to his vast potential or be a real knucklehead and blow it. I don't think Dan Marino will allow Green the opportunity to screw up and Green will have a superb season. Project: 70 receptions and 10-12 TDs.

2. Shannon Sharpe, Denver Broncos

Receptions	87
Touchdowns	4
Rec. Yds.	1,010

Now *here* is a guy that Green should emulate. Sharpe is a well-conditioned athlete and he's oh-so-reliable. Sharpe will like the fact that his tight end spot will still be geared for action under Steve Shanahan. Project: 90 receptions and 10 TDs.

TE

3. Ben Coates, New England Patriots

Receptions	96
Touchdowns	7
Rec. Yds.	1,174

Ben Coates could easily be the number one TE when the 1995 season is over. Just like Shannon Sharpe, he is an aggressive hard worker who has achieved much without a lot of fanfare. He's self made and reliable. Project: 90 receptions and 9-10 TDs.

4. Keith Jackson, Green Bay Packers

Receptions	59
Touchdowns	7
Rec. Yds.	673

Definitely needed by Green Bay in order to pick up the slack of Sterling Sharpe. Still a rumble tumble tough guy. Project: 75 receptions and 9-10 TDs

5. Brent Jones, San Francisco 49ers

Receptions	49
Touchdowns	9
Rec. Yds.	670

Brent Jones really picked up his production by the end of the season and he became a major component in the offense. If it's not broke don't fix it! Project: 60 receptions and 9 TDs.

6. Johnny Mitchell, New York Jets

Receptions	58
Touchdowns	4
Rec. Yds.	749

Offense will be geared around Mitchell and rookie tight end Kyle Brady. Project: 70 receptions and 8-9 TDs.

TE

7. Troy Drayton, St. Louis Rams

Receptions	32
Touchdowns	6
Rec. Yds.	276

Great talent but he needs a healthy QB. Project: 60 receptions and 8-9 TDs.

8. Pete Metzelaars, Carolina Panthers

Receptions	49
Touchdowns	5
Rec. Yds.	428

A very reliable tight end as a Buffalo Bill will now hook up with ex-Bill backup QB Frank Reich. Should have success in Carolina. Project: 55 receptions and 7 TDs.

9. Jackie Harris, Tampa Bay Buccaneers

Receptions	26
Touchdowns	3
Rec. Yds.	337

Harris should fare well with the spruced-up offense. Project: 50 receptions and 6-7 TDs.

10. Jay Novacek, Dallas Cowboys

Receptions	47
Touchdowns	2
Rec. Yds.	475

TE

Spent most of 1994 nicked up--needs a healthy season this year. Project: 60 receptions and 6 TDs.

11. Tony McGee, Cincinnati Bengals

Receptions	40
Touchdowns	1
Rec. Yds.	492

Remember things will be hot in Cincy this year--McGee will benefit. Project: 55 receptions and 5-6 TDs.

12. Kyle Brady, New York Jets

Receptions	ROOKIE
Touchdowns	
Rec. Yds	

Kyle Brady is a solid and terrific addition to the Jets. He will make Johnny Mitchell work! Project 50 receptions and 5 TDs.

TE

13. Howard Cross, New York Giants

Receptions	31
Touchdowns	4
Rec. Yds.	364

Howard Cross is never going to rewrite the record books but he is a consistent player in a very conservative offense. Project: 40 receptions and 5 TDs.

14. Wesley Walls, New Orleans Saints

Receptions   38
Touchdowns   4
Rec. Yds.   406

      Personally I would expect Irving Smith to be the primary tight end, but to date Walls is the man. Project: 40 receptions and 5 TDs.

15. Christian Fauria, Seattle Seahawks

ROOKIE
Receptions
Touchdowns
Rec. Yds.

      I like this kid's potential and his hands! Look for Seattle to include him into their offensive scheme. Project: 40 receptions and 5 TDs.

TIGHT END RATING

1. Eric Green   Miami Dolphins
2. Shannon Sharpe   Denver Broncos
3. Ben Coates   New England Patriots
4. Keith Jackson   Green Bay Packers
5. Brent Jones   San Francisco 49ers
6. Johnny Mitchell   New York Jets
7. Troy Drayton   St. Louis Rams
8. Pete Metzelaars   Carolina Panthers
9. Jackie Harris   Tampa Bay Buccaneers
10. Jay Novacek   Dallas Cowboys

TE

197

11. Tony McGee	Cincinnati Bengals
12. Kyle Brady	New York Jets
13. Wesley Walls	New Orleans Saints
14. Howard Cross	New York Giants
15. Christian Fauria	Seattle Seahawks
16. Adrian Cooper	Minnesota Vikings
17. James Jenkins	Washington Redskins
18. Mark Bruener	Pittsburgh Steelers
19. Aaron Pierce	New York Giants
20. Keith Cash	Kansas City Chiefs
21. Chris Gedney	Chicago Bears
22. Ron Hall	Detroit Lions
23. Irv Smith	New Orleans Saints
24. Kerry Cash	Los Angeles Raiders
25. Alfred Pupunu	San Diego Chargers
26. Jerry Evans	Denver Broncos
27. Derrick Walker	Kansas City Chiefs
28. Ed West	Indianapolis Colts
29. Mark Bavaro	Philadelphia Eagles
30. Marv Cook	Houston Oilers
31. Derek Ware	Arizona Cardinals
32. Lonnie Johnson	Buffalo Bills
33. Frank Wycheck	Washington Redskins
34. Andrew Glover	Los Angeles Raiders
35. Jon Hayes	Pittsburgh Steelers
36. Brian Kinchen	Cleveland Browns
37. Tygi Armstrong	Tampa Bay Buccaneers
38. Pete Mitchell	Miami Dolphins
39. Tracy Greene	Kansas City Chiefs
40. David Sloan	Detroit Lions
41. Jim Thornton	New York Jets
42. Ken Dilger	Indianapolis Colts
43. Ethan Horton	Free Agent
44. Ryan Wetnight	Chicago Bears
45. Jamie Williams	San Francisco 49ers
46. Reggie Johnson	Denver Broncos

TE

47. Pat Carter	Houston Oilers
48. A.J. Ofodile	Buffalo Bills
49. Paul Green	Seattle Seahawks
50. Fred Baxter	New York Jets

TE

★9★

Kickers and Punters

Earlier in this book I proclaimed that selecting kickers in the first three rounds was a big mistake. Now don't get me wrong, I have a healthy All-American cheeseburger respect for kickers; it's just that I'd rather pluck out a Drew Bledsoe, a William Floyd and a Carl Pickens in the first three rounds. (This example was taken from a simulated draft from a 10-team league). I would then proceed to think about a kicker in the 4th, 5th or 6th round.

One of the best thinkers in my own league is a fellow by the name of Mark C. (whose last name we shall not disclose because he is sure to receive a rash of phone calls inquiring on strategy of fantasy football, knowledge of astrology and his vast collection of Kenny G. tapes). Mark has a sincere disdain for drafting kickers before the 11th or 12th round. To me, waiting so long like this is a huge gamble, but somehow he manages to pick up a kicker that ends up having a good season. In the last dozen or so years, I can remember him getting burnt only once.

Personally I think that you would want to draft earlier and pick a Pete Stoyanovich, Jason Elam, Jeff Jaeger, Chris Boniol, or John Carney. You could hang out a little later and probably select my favorite sleeper player (Matt Stover), who is still relatively unknown and should get plenty of kicks. Other sleeper picks include Fuad Reveiz, Chris Jacke, Doug Brien, Jason Hanson, Doug Pelfrey, Morten Andersen, Norm Johnson, Michel Husted and Steve Christie.

That makes 15 kickers that have the potential for a superb scoring year. That also means that you don't have to blindly leap in the early rounds and draft a kicker too early

1994 FIELD GOAL LEADERS & 50-YARD BUSTERS

The 50 yard Buster Club is technically no longer in existence. Why? The new rules concerning the spotting of the ball and the fact that the NFL now penalizes the offense on missed kicks, certainly has taken the "Oooomphh" out of the field goal kickers.

Also, the two point conversion, although not yet a truly crucial part of the game, does exist and does take the automatic one-pointer out of the game. I can't tell you how many times I would check the score of a game that my kicker was involved and would see his team scored 12 points and I would automatically assume FOUR FIELD GOALS! Wrong!!! How about two touchdowns and two missed two-point conversions

As I wrote above, don't confuse the multitude of points from kickers of the past and don't get hung up on the long booming kickers...because frankly we aren't going to see 55-yard field goals unless it's two seconds before halftime or the game is on the line.

KEEP AN EYE ON:

As of this writing the Seattle Seahawks do not have a kicker. Whoever it is will be worth drafting because the Seahawks should move the ball well in 1995. Losing John Kasay to the Carolina Panthers was a major faux pas on Seattle's part. As discussed earlier, Carolina will also be moving the ball well with an effective offense led by Frank Reich and an arsenel including Barry Foster, Mark Carrier, Don Beebe and Pete Metzelaars. Also, watch out for whom the Indy Colts trot out...I can't believe it will be Mike Cofer...but check it out. Also wherever Dean Biasucci ends up (what happened in Indy?) he should be solid (how about Seattle?!). As much as I like Steve Christie (BUF), I really think that the offense will begin to head into the tank and kicking opportunities may fade. Keep an eye out as to where Gary Anderson ends up if he doesn't sign with Pittsburgh. Anderson is convinced he is worth

K/P

more money than the Steelers have wanted to spend. The problem that Anderson should consider is that he is getting older and no team is spitting out major bucks to kickers because of the salary cap.

This is also make it or break it year for the once dominant kicker Chip Lohmiller (WAS). This is a talented booter that for some reason has really developed a case of the yips I still envision him one day kicking in a dome and launching 60-yarders through the uprights--but for now Norv Turner would appreciate his undivided attention on Sundays!

PLAYER	TEAM	THE INSIDE SKINNY/FAT
Pete Stoyanovich	Miami	Points-a-plenty in Dolphin-land
Jason Elam	Denver	Tighter offensive feel with Shanahan
John Carney	San Diego	Continues to greatness
Chris Boniol	Dallas	More 'n' more opportunities
Jeff Jaeger	Los Angeles	Trust me the Raiders will roll
Matt Stover	Cleveland	Unknown...'til now...Big Potential
Fuad Reveiz	Minnesota	Loves the loud Metrodome
Doug Pelfrey	Cincinnati	See above on Stover..Ditto!
Doug Brien	San Francisco	Rookie jitters over...bright future
Morten Andersen	New Orleans	Feets never fail the Dutchman
Michael Husted	Tampa Bay	The Ol' Sombrero will be pumpin'
Norm Johnson	Atlanta	Second good kicker Seattle lost
Jason Hanson	Detroit	Talented enough to be in top three
Chris Jacke	Green Bay	Needs to pickup for Sterling Sharpe
Steve Christie	Buffalo	Offense is in question for '95

KICKER RATINGS

PLAYER	TEAM	FGs	MADE 50+	EXTRA Pts
Pete Stoyanovich	Miami	24	1	35
Jason Elam	Denver	30	1	29
John Carney	San Diego	34	2	33
Chris Boniol	Dallas	22	0	48
Jeff Jaeger	Raiders	22	2	31
Matt Stover	Cleveland	26	0	32

PLAYER	TEAM	FGs	MADE 50+	EXTRA Pts
Fuad Reveiz	Minnesota	34	1	30
Doug Pelfrey	Cincinnati	28	2	24
Doug Brien	San Francisco	15	0	60
Morten Andersen	New Orleans	28	2	24
Michael Husted	Tampa Bay	23	1	20
Norm Johnson	Atlanta	21	1	32
Jason Hanson	Detroit	18	0	39
Chris Jacke	Green Bay	19	1	41
Steve Christie	Buffalo	24	2	38
Matt Bahr	New England	27	0	36
Kevin Butler	Chicago	25	0	30
Chip Lohmiller	Washington	20	1	30
Gary Anderson	Pittsburgh	23	1	32
John Kasay	Carolina	20	0	25
Tony Zendejas	St. Louis	18	0	28
Nick Lowery	NY Jets	20	0	26
Lin Elliott	Kansas City	25	0	30
Eddie Murray	Philadelphia	21	0	33
Greg Davis	Arizona	20	1	17
Brad Daluiso	NY Giants	11	1	5
Al Del Greco	Houston	16	1	18
Dean Biasucci	Free Agent	16	2	37
Mike Cofer	Indianapolis	Did Not Play In 1994		

K/P

★10★

Defense and Special Teams

DEFENSIVE TEAMS RUSH/PASS EFFICIENCY RATINGS

Now in many fantasy football circles defensive scoring is thought of as a point potpourri. In other leagues, defensive points are not tallied. I firmly believe your league should operate in the comfort zone that you like. Just like my Uncle Jack use to say, "Some like whiskey, some like tea. Others like whiskey in their tea." Okay...okay sometimes Uncle Jack didn't make a lot of sense, but it sounded good.

When the FFL first came about, we would actually draft individual players on defense. We would be allowed to start one linebacker and two defensive backs. In theory it looked like a smart idea, but in reality these players rarely scored. If you took a closer look at the majority of defensive TD returns, it's always some guy no one has ever heard of. Last season Minnesota's defense scored practically every week and nearly a dozen (OK, so I exaggerate) TDs were scored by Anthony Parker. Who? Heck, someone in St. Louis was paying attention, because he was signed as a free agent and earned some bucks!

Anyway, with all that being said and done--we at the FFL resoundedly recommend drafting an entire defensive and special team unit, rather than hassling with the individual defensive and special team players. This is done so that each franchise owner has a

DT/ST

204

greater chance to score each week. This is especially true if your league counts interceptions, sacks and fumbles for points. And for you unaware of this type of scoring...you should hang around the harried FFL crew as they compile all of these stats. Boy-oh-boy do they get batty after tabulating the bazillion point breakdowns that some leagues utilize. With all of this in mind, it is with extremely great pleasure that I unveil the 1995 top defensive teams. Good luck and may an opposing team's miscue be sucked up by your defensive team and may the scoring barrage be plenty!

THE SACKMEISTERS

Depending on your league, generally sacks are credited specifically to a team Some leagues like to draft a defensive player and give points for sacks. So with that in mind, I will list the primo sackleaders from 1994.

PLAYER	TEAM	SACKS
Kevin Greene	Pittsburgh	14.0
Ken Harvey	Washington	13.5
John Randle	Minnesota	13.5
Leslie O'Neal	San Diego	12.5
Charles Haley	Dallas	12.5
Neil Smith	Kansas City	11.5
Chris Mims	San Diego	11
Darion Conner	Carolina	10.5
Sean Jones	Green Bay	10.5
William Fuller	Philadelphia	10.5
Bruce Smith	Buffalo	10
Rob Burnett	Cleveland	10
Greg Lloyd	Pittsburgh	10
Wayne Martin	New Orleans	10
Alfred Williams	Cincinnati	9.5
Jeff Cross	Miami	9.5
C. McGlockton	Los Angeles	9.5
Chris Slade	New England	9.5

DT/ST

205

PLAYER	TEAM	SACKS
Andy Harmon	Philadelphia	9
Tony Bennett	Indianapolis	9
Lamar Lathon	Carolina	8.5
Dana Stubblefield	San Francisco	8.5
Reggie White	Green Bay	8.0
Jim Jeffcoat	Buffalo	8.0
Bryce Paup	Buffalo	7.5

THE QUICK-HANDED INTERCEPTORS

When I work on a draft plan and I begin to decide just which defensive team I want to select, I *always* check for the squad with aggressive fleet-footed defensive backs. I still stick to my belief that the sweetest defensive score is when that little DB zones...reads the QBs darting eyes...cuts in front of the receiver...rips the pass off while in full gallop...and streaks down the sideline untouched for a 60-70 yard TD interception! Eric Allen, Rod Woodson, Cris Dishman, Darrell Green, Albert Lewis and Terry McDaniel have made great careers doing so. In fact two years ago Eric Allen scored four TDs on returns!

The most exciting DB of all, of course, is without a doubt Deion Sanders. Last season Deion stepped off the baseball diamond and slid into the 49er team apparel and immediately dissed his old Falcon team by taking an interception down the sideline right past the Atlanta bench. Deion got his wish for a Super Bowl win and also scored three TDs last season. Keep a watch for him...I think he will end up in Miami and try for back-to-back Super Bowls.

1994 LEADING INTERCEPTORS

DT/ST

PLAYER	TEAM	INTs	TDs
Eric Turner	Cleveland	9	1
Aenias Williams	Arizona	9	0
Ray Buchanan	Indianapolis	8	3
Terry McDaniel	Los Angeles	7	2

206

PLAYER	TEAM	INTs	TDs
Darren Perry	Pittsburgh	7	0
Maurice Hurst	New England	7	0
Merton Hanks	San Francisco	7	0
Deion Sanders	Free Agent	6	3
Greg Jackson	Philadelphia	6	1
Troy Vincent	Miami	5	1
Marcus Turner	NY Jets	5	1
Darren Woodson	Dallas	5	1
James Washington	Washington	5	0
Darryl Lewis	Houston	5	0
Terrell Buckley	Green Bay	5	0
D.J. Johnson	Atlanta	5	0
Donnell Woolford	Chicago	5	0
Jimmy Spencer	Washington	5	0
Andre Collins	Cincinnati	4	2
Anthony Parker	St. Louis	4	2
Rod Woodson	Pittsburgh	4	2
Stanley Richard	Washington	4	2
Cris Dishman	Houston	4	0
Larry Brown	Dallas	4	0
James Williams	Carolina	4	0
Robert Massey	Detroit	4	0
Vinnie Clark	Jacksonville	4	0
D. Washington	Minnesota	3	2
Darrell Green	Washington	3	1
Lionel Washington	Denver	3	1
Willie Clay	Detroit	3	1
Darnell Walker	Atlanta	3	1
Eric Allen	Philadelphia	3	0
J.B. Brown	Miami	3	0
Gene Atkins	Miami	3	0
Louis Oliver	Miami	3	0

DT/ST

DEFENSIVE TEAM TAKEAWAYS

By now your eyes are probably getting blurry and you may not be very pumped up over picking a defensive team. Most franchises virtually ignore this area and count any scores here as plain dumb luck. True, luck plays a part here, but it is stupid to not review each team's defensive tendencies and speed in the skill positions. Last season my team was going belly-up, but I literally qualified for my league's Head-to-Head playoffs due to the extremely good fortune of selecting the Minnesota Vikings defense!

When choosing a defensive team, be sure to use panache and most of all some sense. Luck plays a major role in selecting the correct defensive team that will get hot, but common sense dictates that we should also be aware of the team's takeaway abilities. Teams that converge on the ball like an angry pitbull after a bone usually show that scoring potential we all have come to know and love (ahem...Minnesota). My advice and tip here is to study the 1994 takeaway list below, and hopefully this information will help you visualize where your defensive scoring will come from.

DEFENSIVE TAKEAWAYS

TEAM	FUMBLES	INTs	TOTAL
New England	18	22	40
NY Giants	21	17	38
Kansas City	26	12	38
Arizona	13	23	36
San Francisco	12	23	35
Philadelphia	14	21	35
Minnesota	16	18	34
Green Bay	12	21	33
Atlanta	11	22	33
Miami	9	23	32
San Diego	15	17	32
NY Jets	16	16	32
Dallas	9	22	31

DT/ST

TEAM	FUMBLE	INTs	TOTAL
New Orleans	14	17	31
Cleveland	13	18	31
Pittsburgh	14	17	31
Seattle	11	19	30
Indianapolis	10	18	28
Buffalo	12	16	28
Denver	14	12	26
Houston	12	14	26
Los Angeles	13	12	25
Detroit	11	12	23
Washington	6	17	23
Chicago	10	12	22
Tampa Bay	12	9	21
St. Louis	6	14	20
Cincinnati	8	10	18

DEFENSIVE TEAM	RUSHING YARDS AGAINST AVG	PASSING YARDS AGAINST AVG	TOTAL YARDS AGAINST AVG
Dallas	97.6	172.0	269.6
Pittsburgh	90.8	179.6	270.4
Arizona	85.6	189.9	275.5
Philadelphia	101.0	193.4	294.4
Minnesota	68.1	228.3	296.4
Green Bay	85.2	212.6	297.8
Cleveland	104.3	197.3	301.6
San Francisco	83.6	218.8	302.4
Houston	132.5	174.7	307.2
LA Raiders	96.4	212.5	308.9
New York Giants	108.0	201.4	309.4
Kansas City	108.4	204.1	312.5
Chicago	120.1	192.9	313.1
San Diego	87.8	228.6	316.4
Cincinnati	119.1	203.0	322.1

DT/ST

DEFENSIVE TEAM	RUSHING YARDS AGAINST AVG	PASSING YARDS AGAINST AVG	TOTAL YARDS AGAINST AVG
St. Louis	111.3	211.8	323.1
Buffalo	94.7	228.8	323.4
New England	110.0	215.4	325.4
Miami	89.4	237.1	326.5
Indianapolis	102.9	229.9	332.8
Tampa Bay	122.8	210.8	333.5
New York Jets	113.1	220.6	333.6
Seattle	122.0	212.3	334.3
Detroit	116.2	221.6	337.8
New Orleans	109.9	238.2	348.1
Washington	123.4	227.1	350.6
Atlanta	105.8	258.5	364.3
Denver	109.5	259.7	369.2

DEFENSIVE TEAM RANKING

1. Minnesota Vikings
2. Arizona Cardinals
3. Cleveland Browns
4. Miami Dolphins
5. Philadelphia Eagles
6. Pittsburgh Steelers
7. Washington Redskins
8. San Diego Chargers
9. New England Patriots
10. New Orleans Saints
11. Cincinnati Bengals
12. San Francisco 49ers
13. Indianapolis Colts
14. Los Angeles Raiders
15. Dallas Cowboys
16. Tampa Bay Buccaneers

DT/ST

17. New York Jets
18. Buffalo Bills
19. Green Bay Packers
20. Atlanta Falcons
21. St. Louis Rams
22. Seattle Seahawks
23. Kansas City Chiefs
24. Carolina Panthers
25. Detroit Lions
26. Denver Broncos
27. New York Giants
28. Chicago Bears
29. Houston Oilers
30. Jacksonville Jaguars

SPECIAL TEAMS PLAYERS

Choosing a player or special team takes an equal mixture of research and good old-fashioned luck. When your player does return the ball for a TD, the feeling is electric! Lighting up the scoreboard is the name of our quaint little game, so when your returner streaks down field with a punt or kickoff you feel like getting down and celebrating because your franchise just got a beautiful boost.

I lost to a franchise last season in a head-to-head contest because of two (count 'em, two) Tyrone Hughes TD returns. In fact, it was a doubly tragic scene since the FFL's own Pat Hughes (no relation to Tyrone) had the great fortune of drafting the New Orleans returner and starting him that week. As Pat liked to tell me directly to my blank face "Hey, Dick, thanks for the tip...I see you rated Tyrone (No Relation) Hughes...#1!" To make matters worse, in 1994 Pat and his teammate Chris wiped up and had a sickeningly successful season. Whenever one of his minions would score, I would get a breathless phone call from Pat, "Hey did you see Marino's zillion TDs in the last 45 seconds of the game? Unbelieveable, huh?" Oh yeah, just ducky!

DT/ST

211

The real kicker to me and my dismal finish was when Pat made a concerted effort to thank me for writing such a good book and enabling him to exact a top finish. I can still hear him chortling in the crowd "Hey, all I did was use Dick's Picks and I won!" Unfortunately for me, I used the Dick's Picks that quickly became Injured Reserve Nicked Picks.

TIPS ON HOW I RANK THESE RETURNERS

1. When drafting a special team: If your league takes the approach of drafting a complete team, make sure it is a team with top-ranked return-men. The team concept gives you the opportunity for multiple scores from multiple players.

2. When drafting a return specialist (individual players): Select a full-time kick or punt returner. It simply makes more sense (and points) to select a player who will get many opportunities to "touch" the ball. Also, as long as your returner is healthy, do not develop the bad habit of flip-flopping specialists. As a rule of thumb, you will get burned as the player you benched will seemingly *always* score!

3. Select a double-duty returner: A player like this has awesome value since he returns both kickoffs and punts--he becomes a double threat to score. Need I remind you gang: the more opportunities, the more scores.

4. Select a speedster: Sure, there are returners who lack burning speed and do score, but your best bet for a return is with a player who can flat-out speed by everyone--feets don't fail me now! Keep in mind that a kickoff or punt return for a touchdown is still a rarity. I still believe that the guy with the best shot to break the crease and leave would-be tacklers in his wake is the returner with lightning speed.

1994 PUNT RETURN STAT LEADERS

PLAYER	TEAM	NO.	AVG. RET.	TDs
Eric Metcalf	ATL	35	9.9	2
Darrien Gordon	SD	36	13.2	2
Brian Mitchell	WAS	32	14.1	2
Tyrone Hughes	NO	21	6.8	0
Mel Gray	HOU	21	11.1	0
David Meggett	NE	26	12.4	2
Kevin Williams	DAL	39	8.9	1
Rod Woodson	PIT	39	8.2	0
Glyn Milburn	DEN	41	9.2	0
David Palmer	MIN	30	6.4	0
Dexter Carter	NYJ	38	8.4	0
O.J. McDuffie	MIA	32	7.1	0
Ernest Givins	JAX	37	5.7	1
Tim Brown	RAI	40	12.2	0
Jeff Sydner	PHI	40	9.5	0
Corey Sawyer	CIN	26	11.8	1
Pat Robinson	AZ	41	7.0	0
Tony Burris	BUF	32	10.4	0
Robert Brooks	GB	40	8.8	1
Dewey Brewer	CAR	42	8.1	1
Vernon Turner	CAR	21	10.4	1
Clarence Verdin	TB	23	4.9	0
Jeff Graham	CHI	15	9.3	1
Cliff Hicks	SF	38	9.0	0
Troy Brown	NE	24	8.4	0
Johnny Bailey	STL	19	8.1	0
Dale Carter	KC	16	7.8	0
Todd Kinchen	STL	16	9.9	0

DT/ST

1994 KICK RETURN LEADERS

PLAYER	TEAM	NO.	AVG. RET.	TDs
Tyrone Hughes	NO	63	24.7	2
Mel Gray	HOU	45	28.4	3
Andre Coleman	SD	49	26.4	2
Brian Mitchell	WAS	58	25.5	0
Kevin Williams	DAL	43	26.7	1
Dexter Carter	NYJ	48	23.0	1
Randy Baldwin	CAR	28	26.9	1
Glyn Milburn	DEN	37	21.4	0
Raghib Ismail	RAI	43	21.5	0
Qadry Ismail	MIN	35	23.1	0
David Meggett	NE	29	18.9	0
Herschel Walker	NYG	21	27.7	1
Vernon Turner	CAR	43	20.6	0
Charles Jourdain	BUF	27	22.3	0
Ronnie Humphrey	IND	35	22.4	1
Aaron Glenn	NYJ	27	21.6	0
O.J. McDuffie	MIA	36	21.3	0
Chuck Levy	AZ	26	19.7	0
Clarence Verdin	TB	44	23.3	0
Nate Lewis	SD	35	25.0	0
Michael Bates	SEA	26	19.5	0
Darnay Scott	CIN	15	22.8	0
Corey Harris	GB	29	21.3	0
Jon Vaughn	SEA	18	24.6	1
Charles Johnson	PIT	16	21.6	0
Ray Crittenden	NE	24	19.2	0
David Lang	DAL	27	23.2	0
Todd McNair	HOU	23	20.9	0
Irving Spikes	MIA	19	22.8	0
Ron Dickerson	KAN	21	22.5	0

DT/ST

RETURN SPECIALISTS

PLAYER	TEAM
Eric Metcalf	Atlanta Falcons
Mel Gray	Houston Oilers
Tyrone Hughes	New Orleans Saints
Brian Mitchell	Washington Redskins
Dave Meggett	New England Patriots
Darion Gordon	San Diego Chargers
Kevin Williams	Dallas Cowboys
Jack Jackson	Chicago Bears
Ronnie Humphreys	Indianapolis Colts
Joey Galloway	Seattle Seahawks
Rod Woodson	Pittsburgh Steelers
Tim Brown	LA Raiders
Glyn Milburn	Denver Broncos
Danan Hughes	Kansas City Chiefs
Dexter Carter	NY Jets
Napoleon Kaufman	LA Raiders
Raghib Ismail	LA Raiders
OJ McDuffie	Miami Dolpins
Andre Coleman	San Diego
Jeff Sydner	Cincinnati Bengals
Aaron Glen	NY Jets
Tamarick Vanover	Kansas City Chiefs
Clarence Verdin	Tampa Bay Buccaneers
Amp Lee	Minnesota Vikings
Herschel Walker	New York Giants
Robert Smith	Minnesota Vikings
Dwight Stone	Carolina Panthers
Ernest Givis	Jacksonville Jaguars
Jon Vaughn	Seattle Seahawks
Todd Kinchen	St. Louis Rams
Chuck Levy	Arizona Cardinals
Corey Sawyer	Cincinnati Bengals
Mike Miller	Cleveland Browns

DT/ST

215

PLAYER	TEAM
Kez McCorvey	Detroit Lions
Jeff Burris	Buffalo Bills
Sherman Williams	Dallas Cowboys

★11★

The Best of the New: The 1994 Rookie Freshman Class

QUICK REVIEW OF LAST SEASON'S ROOKIES

Last season was a comedown as far as rookies go. In fact only Marshall Faulk, William Floyd, Bam Morris and Erricht Rhett displayed fulltime potential as rookies. Which means that despite the talent and press clippings--rookies rarely make a huge dent their first year. Heath Shuler (QB/WAS) and Trent Dilfer (QB/TB) were thought to be the next Drew Bledsoe and Rick Mirer. Unfortunately both held out and both showed the rustiness and immaturity of great talented college QBs who get slapped silly on that first step onto the NFL hallowed fields. Last season rookie wide receivers Charles Johnson (PIT), Darnay Scott (CIN), Derrick Alexander (CLE), and Bert Emanuel (ATL) showed some brilliant flashes of what to expect in the future. This season all four should start and mature with their offenses. Thomas Lewis (NYG), Issac Bruce (STL), Bucky Brooks (BUF), Kevin Lee (NE), Lake Dawson (KC), Orlando Parker (NYJ) and Ryan Yarborough (NYJ) should also step up into starting roles for 1995. Remember, it takes receivers a little longer to pan out.

HOW ABOUT 1995's ROOKIES...ANY SPARK?

This season only two rookies jump at me with the ability to start right off and become top producers: Ki-Jana Carter and Rashaan Salaam. I really feel good about Carter because this Cincy club is taking on an exciting offensive look. Expect Carter to hit the line head on and show some breakaway ability that has been sorely missing in the Bengal Jungle. Rashaan may have to share the ball with Lewis Tillman and Raymont Harris, but if he shows up fit and ready to make the commitment to establish himself as a consistent runner...he will be a terrific offensive weapon for Chicago.

James Stewart (JAX) is a terrifically talented player who in college hooked up with Heath Shuler at Tennessee. Although a stud, how can you really feel that he can establish himself immediately in Jacksonville? Although the Jaguars' line has the enormous future All- Pro Tony Boselli and several decent linemen, it will be tough to gel and break loose Stewart.

Rookie receivers look to be in decent shape. Michael Westbrook (WAS) should land perhaps a starting job and become the next Michael Irvin, as Washington continues to become Dallas-East. Another super draft pick at receiver is the lightning quick Joey Galloway (SEA)--he will be a nice pick because Dennis Erickson's offense will utilize a speedster like Galloway!

Two tight ends that I have been writing about will also see starting time: Kyle Brady (NYJ) and Chris Fauria (SEA). Both are the new breed of tight end...they block...they catch...they run...they score. If you have noticed recently tight ends generally just block...and others just catch...and none can run (exception: Shannon Sharpe, Eric Green and Ben Coates). Watch Brady and Fauria as they will play pivotal roles.

As far as rookie QBs go, only one has a chance to start in 1995...Steve "Air" McNair. There is no guarantee, however, as of this writing Chris Chandler is listed ahead of McNair on the depth chart. I think sooner or later Houston will wake up to the fact that they are a rebuilding team and they may give McNair an early shot. As much as I like the Collins boys (Kerry and Todd) neither should make much of a dent unless injuries knock out the starters. Both will have highly successful NFL careers. A real longshot at seeing playing time this season is Eric Zeier (CLE). But if Vinny Testaverde gets hurt he could get the call. For the record I would like to state that this is a terrific QB and I don't care if he is only 6' tall. This kid can play and the NFL shouldn't take itself so seriously when ranking by height. Look Gizmo, one or two inches are not going to make that much difference...measure the heart, desire and arm strength as well.

While I am discussing QBs the coolest one seems to be Stoney Case (great name..huh?) and he gets to play for Buddy Ryan. I am going to predict, right here and now, that Stoney will win over Buddy with his gritty tough style and could end up with the job sooner than anyone would expect. In closing my tip for drafting rookies is to expect little...but the gems will perform.

IMPACT ROOKIES

PLAYER	POS	TEAM
Ki-Jana Carter	RB	Cincinnati Bengals
Salaam Rashaad	RB	Chicago Bears
Kyle Brady	TE	New York Jets
Michael Westbrook	WR	Washington Redskins
Joey Galloway	WR	Seattle Seahawks
J.J. Stokes	WR	San Francisco 49ers
Napoleon Kaufman	RB	Los Angeles Raiders
Steve McNair	QB	Houston Oilers
Curtis Martin	RB	New England Patriots
Tyrone Wheatley	RB	New York Giants
Steve McLaughlin	K	St. Louis Rams
Mark Bruener	TE	Pittsburgh Steelers
Christian Fauria	TE	Seattle Seahawks
James Stewart	RB	Jacksonville Jaguars
Jack Jackson	RS	Chicago Bears
Tamarick Vanover	WR	Kansas City Chiefs
Chris Sanders	WR	Houston Oilers
Chris T. Jones	WR	Philadelphia Eagles
David Dunn	WR	Cincinnati Bengals

219

SEMI-IMPACT ROOKIES

PLAYER	POS	TEAM
Kerry Collins	QB	Carolina Panthers
Todd Collins	QB	Buffalo Bills
Ken Dilger	TE	Indianapolis Colts
Lovell Pinkney	TE	St. Louis Rams
Terrell Fletcher	RB	San Diego Chargers
Zack Crockett	RB	Indianapolis Colts
Pete Mitchell	TE	Miami Dolphins
Larry Jones	RB	Washington Redskins
Jimmy Oliver	WR	San Diego Chargers
Antonio Freeman	WR	Green Bay Packers
Joe Aska	RB	Los Angeles Raiders
William Henderson	RB	Green Bay Packers
Tony Cline	TE	Buffalo Bills
Kez McCorvey	WR	Detroit Lions
Mike Miller	WR	Cleveland Browns
James Stewart	RB	Minnesota Vikings
Michael Roan	TE	Houston Oilers
Eric Bjornson	WR	Dallas Cowboys
David Sloan	TE	Detroit Lions
Eric Zeier	QB	Cleveland Browns
Cory Schlesinger	RB	Detroit Lions
Ryan Christopherson	RB	Jacksonville Jaguars

★12★

Dick's Picks

It is funny how I receive notes, letters and thank you's when doing radio shows because of Dick's Picks. I originally started it as a cheat sheet for my draft. In the beginning (prior to doing these books), I would have friends ask me to jot down the top players so that they could draft past four rounds! Although the game has changed from when I first started playing...the premise is still the same--draft smart...draft to win!

THE CRITERIA FOR PLAYER RATING

1. Last several seasons' stats.
2. FFL track record. Does player have solid results or is he a one-year phenom?
3. Projected role: starter, scorer, performance rating (yardage, receptions, etc.).
4. Major force (primary position player) or secondary player.
5. Age, injuries
6. Player's NFL team. Is the team a force or farce?
7. Individual player's supporting cast (e.g., strong offensive line/good weapons).
8. Attitude (winner, solid citizen, work habits, egomaniac, sullen, or a loser).

9. Is he staying with the same team or is he a free agent?

10. Experience

Now all this may seem easy to the casual observer/reader but it actually is difficult. With so many leagues playing with different scoring rules, I attempt to incorporate all scoring methods. For example, if your league only wishes to use a scoring system and not performance scoring...no problem. The players that I list are weighted for both. One thing that I have recently noticed is that the NFL coaches and players realize that if a player can rush for 100 yards in a game, he certainly can score around the goal line. For example, the knock on both Barry Sanders and Thurman Thomas is that they do all the work trotting and rambling downfield...only to get replaced around the goal line and someone else scores the TD. With Derrick Moore getting traded to San Francisco, this should mean that perhaps Barry will lug the ball--he should!

FINAL QUESTIONS AND CONCERNS FOR 1995

1. Where will Derrick Moore fit into the San Francisco backfield equation? Will Moore's presence effect William Floyd's production? Will Derek Loville find a role replacing Dexter Carter or Ricky Watters?

2. Which ex-Cardinal wide receiver will regain prominence in Miami: Gary Clark or Randal Hill?

3. I have ranked Eric Green as the #1 tight end for 1995. Will he finally grow up and live up to his vast potential by actually *playing* a full season?

4. Will Mike Pritchard make it back from his kidney injury? Will he be able to take the pounding?

DICK'S
PICKS

5. Trent Dilfer is surrounded by perhaps one of the NFL's most potent and yet unknown offenses: WRs Alvin Harper, Lawrence

Dawsey, Courtney Hawkins, TE Jackie Harris, RB Errict Rhett. The real mystery here is whether Trent Dilfer can take control and become another Drew Bledsoe.

6. Brett Favre is a poorman's Steve Young, but can he hit the same strides as in 1994, without Sterling Sharpe? Without Sterling is Favre really a top-five quarterback?

7. Vinny Testaverde gets no respect. Can he shake the blunder years and lead his team of go-to guys: RBs Leroy Hoard, Lorenzo White, Tommy Vardell, WRs Andre Rison, Derrick Alexander and Michael Jackson?

8. With Vinny T. as one of 1995's draft steals, another guy with no respect and decent stats is Craig Erickson. Can he explode and be a sleeper with the following weapons: RB Marshall Faulk, WRs Willie Anderson, Floyd Turner, and Sean Dawkins?

9. With Barry Foster moving on to Carolina that should open things up for Bam Morris...but why the free agent signing of Erric Pegram? Who gets the totes and TDs?

10. Is it wrong to get excited thinking that Craig "Ironhead" Heyward will perhaps become one of the NFL/FFL's premiere running backs for 1995? After all, not counting Eric Metcalf, who will probaly run, catch, return, pass, kick, and pass out Gatorade on the sidelines for the Falcons, as of this writing Heyward is *the* lone back in that offense.

11. I ranked Terry Allen fairly high--how will he be used in Washington?

12. Without Terry in Minnesota...will it be Amp Lee or Robert Smith?

13. Am I liking Jeff Blake way too much are is his 1994 showing right on the money? Willd Scott Mitchell close out his bank account and start hooking up with Detroit receivers Herman Moore, Brett Perriman and Johnnie Morton?

Well, we're come to the end of the road, and if you don't have enough information already, I have one more list that will put you over the edge. I feel this is the strongest list put together thus far, and should help each of you draft a successful franchise. Of course, no one can predict injuries, trades or mid-season slumps that can throw any well-honed draft plan out the window, but I feel the final tip I can give you is try to go for proven winners that score, score, score. It's all about luck, and that's where we will leave it. So, my friend, good luck this season, and make sure you keep in touch with me to let me know your trials and tribulations in the wide, wacky, wonderful world of fantasy football.

TOP 150 SCORING AND PERFORMANCE PICKS

PLAYER	POS	TEAM
1. Steve Young	QB	San Francisco 49ers
2. Dan Marino	QB	Miami Dolphins
3. Emmitt Smith	RB	Dallas Cowboys
4. Drew Bledsoe	QB	New England Patriots
5. Brett Favre	QB	Green Bay Packers
6. Marshall Faulk	RB	Indianapolis Colts
7. Jeff George	QB	Atlanta Falcons
8. Jerry Rice	WR	San Francisco 49ers
9. Andre Rison	WR	Cleveland Browns
10. John Elway	QB	Denver Broncos

DICK'S PICKS

11.	Natrone Means	RB	San Diego Chargers
12.	Vinny Testaverde	QB	Cleveland Browns
13.	Chris Warren	RB	Seattle Seahawks
14.	Jeff Hostetler	QB	Los Angeles Raiders
15.	Tim Brown	WR	Los Angeles Raiders
16.	Barry Sanders	RB	Detroit Lions
17.	Randall Cunningham	QB	Philadelphia Eagles
18.	Carl Pickens	WR	Cincinnati Bengals
19.	Ki-Jana Carter	RB	Cincinnati Bengals
20.	Ricky Watters	RB	Philadelphia Eagles
21.	Herman Moore	WR	Detroit Lions
22.	Craig Erickson	QB	Indianapolis Colts
23.	Michael Irvin	WR	Dallas Cowboys
24.	Jerome Bettis	RB	St. Louis Rams
25.	Terance Mathis	WR	Atlanta Falcons
26.	William Floyd	RB	San Francisco 49ers
27.	Anthony Miller	WR	Denver Broncos
28.	Errict Rhett	RB	Tampa Bay Buccaneers
29.	Andre Reed	WR	Buffalo Bills
30.	Stan Humphries	QB	San Diego Chargers
31.	Bam Morris	RB	Pittsburgh Steelers
32.	Ironhead Heyward	RB	Atlanta Falcons
33.	Rick Mirer	QB	Seattle Seahawks
34.	Leroy Hoard	RB	Cleveland Browns
35.	Cris Carter	WR	Minnesota Vikings
36.	Alvin Harper	WR	Tampa Bay Buccaneers
37.	Rashaan Salaam	RB	Chicago Bears
38.	Robert Brooks	RB	Green Bay Packers
39.	Irving Fryar	WR	Miami Dolphins
40.	Gary Brown	RB	Houston Oilers
41.	Thurman Thomas	RB	Buffalo Bills
42.	Pete Stoyanovich	K	Miami Dolphins
43.	Jason Elam	K	Denver Broncos
44.	John Carney	K	San Diego Chargers
45.	Vincent Brisby	WR	New England Patriots
46.	Chris Boniol	K	Dallas Cowboys

DICK'S PICKS

47.	Henry Ellard	WR	Washington Redskins
48.	Brian Blades	WR	Seattle Seahawks
49.	Rodney Hampton	RB	New York Giants
50.	Mario Bates	RB	New Orleans Saints
51.	Rob Moore	WR	Arizona Cardinals
52.	Eric Green	TE	Miami Dolphins
53.	Ron Moore	RB	New York Jets
54.	Shannon Sharpe	TE	Denver Broncos
55.	Floyd Turner	WR	Indianapolis Colts
56.	Barry Foster	RB	Carolina Panthers
57.	Jeff Jaeger	K	Los Angeles Raiders
58.	Edgar Bennett	RB	Green Bay Packers
59.	Derrick Fenner	RB	Los Angeles Raiders
60.	Randal Hill	WR	Miami Dolphins
61.	Ben Coates	TE	New England Patriots
62.	Terry Allen	RB	Washington Redskins
63.	Terry Kirby	RB	Miami Dolphins
64.	Eric Metcalf	RB/WR	Atlanta Falcons
65.	David Meggett	RB	New England Patriots
66.	Fred Barnett	WR	Philadelphia Eagles
67.	Jeff Blake	QB	Cincinnati Bengals
68.	Leonard Russell	RB	Denver Broncos
69.	Garrison Hearst	RB	Arizona Cardinals
70.	J.J. Birden	WR	Atlanta Falcons
71.	Tony Martin	WR	San Diego Chargers
72.	Kevin Williams	WR	Dallas Cowboys
73.	Willie Davis	WR	Kansas City Chiefs
74.	Matt Stover	K	Cleveland Browns
75.	Fuad Reveiz	K	Minnesota Vikings
76.	Darnay Scott	WR	Cincinnati Bengals
77.	Courtney Hawkins	WR	Tampa Bay Buccaneers
78.	Michael Jackson	WR	Cleveland Browns
79.	Doug Pelfrey	K	Cincinnati Bengals
80.	Doug Brien	K	San Francisco 49ers
81.	Morten Anderson	K	New Orleans Saints
82.	Trent Dilfer	QB	Tampa Bay Buccaneers

DICK'S PICKS

226

83. Michael Haynes	WR	New Orleans Saints
84. Jake Reed	WR	Minnesota Vikings
85. Jim Everett	QB	New Orleans Saints
86. Gary Clark	WR	Miami Dolphins
87. Jim Kelly	QB	Buffalo Bills
88. Calvin Williams	WR	Philadelphia Eagles
89. Willie Anderson	WR	Indianapolis Colts
90. Keith Jackson	TE	Green Bay Packers
91. Michael Husted	K	Tampa Bay Buccaneers
92. Norm Johnson	K	Atlanta Falcons
93. Scott Mitchell	QB	Detroit Lions
94. Ernest Givins	WR	Jacksonville Jaguars
95. Quinn Early	WR	New Orleans Saints
96. Jason Hanson	K	Detroit Lions
97. Heath Shuler	QB	Washington Redskins
98. Brent Jones	TE	San Francisco 49ers
99. John Taylor	WR	San Francisco 49ers
100. Don Beebe	WR	Carolina Panthers
101. Glyn Milburn	RB	Denver Broncos
102. Herschel Walker	RB	New York Giants
103. Curtis Martin	RB	New England Patriots
104. Michael Westbrook	WR	Washington Redskins
105. Michael Timpson	WR	Chicago Bears
106. Harvey Williams	RB	Los Angeles Raiders
107. Chris Miller	QB	St. Louis Rams
108. Amp Lee	RB	Minnesota Vikings
109. Chris Jacke	K	Green Bay Packers
110. Raghib Ismail	WR	Los Angeles Raiders
111. Steve Christie	K	Buffalo Bills
112. Johnny Mitchell	TE	New York Jets
113. Charles Johnson	WR	Pittsburgh Steelers
114. Alexander Wright	WR	St. Louis Rams
115. J.J. Stokes	WR	San Francisco 49ers
116. Joey Galloway	WR	Seattle Seahawks
117. Mike Pritchard	WR	Denver Broncos
118. Mark Seay	WR	San Diego Chargers

DICK'S
PICKS

119. Derrick Alexander WR Cleveland Browns
120. Lawrence Dawsey WR Tampa Bay Buccaneers
121. Ken Davis RB Buffalo Bills
122. Reggie Brooks RB Washington Redskins
123. Greg Hill RB Kansas City Chiefs
124. Steve Bono QB Kansas City Chiefs
125. James Stewart RB Jacksonville Jaguars
126. Derrick Moore RB San Francisco 49ers
127. Bernie Parmalee RB Miami Dolphins
128. Mark Carrier WR Carolina Panthers
129. Frank Reich QB Carolina Panthers
130. Ricky Proehl WR Seattle Seahawks
131. Troy Drayton TE St. Louis Rams
132. Pete Metzelaars TE Carolina Panthers
133. Kevin Butler K Chicago Bears
134. Chip Lohmiller K Washington Redskins
135. Haywood Jeffires WR Free Agent
136. Webster Slaughter WR Houston Oilers
137. Brett Perriman WR Detroit Lions
138. Mike Sherrard WR New York Giants
139. Keith Byars RB Miami Dolphins
140. Johnny Johnson RB New York Jets
141. Napoleon Kaufman RB Los Angeles Raiders
142. John Kasay K Carolina Panthers
143. Neil O'Donnell QB Pittsburgh Steelers
144. Marcus Allen RB Kansas City Chiefs
145. Dave Brown QB New York Giants
146. Gary Anderson K Pittsburgh Steelers
147. Larry Centers RB Arizona Cardinals
148. Qadry Ismail WR Minnesota Vikings
149. Bert Emanuel WR Atlanta Falcons
150. Kevin Turner RB Philadelphia Eagles

DICK'S
PICKS

★13★

About the 1995 FFL Software

by Kathy Rowland and David C. Dewenter

1995 FFL Fantasy Football Software

Programmed and Developed by   David C. Yager
Michael B. Hughes
David C. Dewenter

Franchise Football League
PO Box 2698
Reston, Virginia 22091

Order Processing: 1-800-872-0335
Technical Support: 1-703-391-0395
(Monday-Friday 9 AM - 9 PM EST)

Using The Fantasy Football Software

Once you have recruited the people to create your league, the first thing you will want to do is to elect or designate a Commissioner from your pool of franchise owners. The Commissioner is responsible for conducting league business, arbitrating league disputes, recording all draft information, team line-ups and trades, and providing weekly scoring and standings reports to franchise owners. The Commissioner should have easy access to a computer during the season. Throughout this manual, **FFL** is used to refer to the **Fantasy Football** software.

To help your league get started, the FFL has provided your league with this simple, easy-to-use software that:

- organizes your league's NFL draft using current NFL rosters

- charts the weekly starting lineups for each franchise owner (up to 30 franchises)

- executes trades

- tracks released and injured reserve players

- tracks all essential statistics on NFL players each week

- automatically tabulates FFL scoring, based upon your league's system, to determine weekly winners and year-to-date leaders

- prints franchise owner mailing labels

- allows you to edit and track head-to-head schedules with playoffs

- automatically updates your league's NFL rosters with new players via the weekly scoring update services

- allows you to create unlimited number of play-types for your league to use, in addition to the over 50 categories already included through any of the stat services

- "reset season" option allows owners to test their scoring system before the season starts and save franchise information and rosters

The instructions for the computer operation are organized simply so that information will be easy to find. It is assumed that the user understands the concepts of Fantasy Football. This manual illustrates how to use the software to maintain the league information.

Computer Requirements

The 1995 version of the FFL program is very user friendly and easier to use than ever before. No matter what your level of computer experience, you should be able to read the instructions once and be ready to run the program. Once installed, you will have the commands listed at the bottom of the screen to help you. Online help is available anytime by pressing [F1]. However, only the League Commissioner should be concerned about the use of the computer.

Although it is not required, it would be helpful to have a basic knowledge and understanding of PC systems and DOS programs. In order to run the FFL Software, the following is the minimum configuration for your PC:

- 386SX/20Mhz or compatible computer (386DX Recommended)

- Monochrome Monitor and Graphics Card or better

- 3.5" 1.44 MB floppy disk drive

- Hard Disk Drive (10-20MB available for complete program and a season's statistics)

- Printer

- Mouse (optional)

- CONFIG.SYS file must have the following settings: **Files=50, Buffers=30.** The CONFIG.SYS file is located in your system's root directory. Consult your computer operating system manual for information on editing this file.

The Fantasy Football Software CANNOT be run with any menu system (Windows, DOS Shell, etc). Be sure to exit any of these programs before installing and running the programs.

Installation Instructions

Once you have acquired the appropriate PC system based on the minimum requirements, you are ready to install the program. These installation instructions assume your computer is running (booted) and you have a DOS prompt displayed (usually the letter of your hard drive). For purposes of explanation, we are assuming your hard drive is lettered "C". Commands you need to type are in **BOLD** and on a separate line.

IMPORTANT NOTE: The FFL 1995 program CANNOT be run with any menu system (i.e., Windows, DOS Shell, etc). Be sure to exit any of these programs before you install the programs. Failure to do so will cause the programs to function incorrectly and may cause corruption of your data. It is also assumed that the program is not being installed on a network. A network installation will cause memory conflicts and the program will not function correctly.

---

1. Place the FFL program Diskette #1 into your floppy drive.

2. Access your floppy drive.

> if your floppy drive is A: **A: [ENTER]**
> if your floppy drive is B: **B: [ENTER]**

Once you access your floppy drive, your prompt will change to the letter of your floppy drive.

3. Begin the installation program by typing:

> INSTALL **[ENTER]**

An installation window will be displayed. The program will prompt you for the directory in which to install the program. The system will default to the **C:\FFL95** directory. If that is the directory you wish to use, simply press **[ENTER]**. If you wish to install the program in a directory other than the default, simply type the directory name and press **[ENTER]**. If the directory does not exist on your system, the installation program will create it for you. When the program prompts you, place the FFL program Diskette #2 into the floppy drive and press **[ENTER]**. When the installation is complete, a message will display indicating a successful installation and prompt you to press any key to exit the installation program.

You can now load the program and begin using the software.

STARTING THE PROGRAM

To start the FFL program immediately after installation, type the following at the C:\FFL95 (or the directory where FFL is installed) prompt:

STARTFFL [ENTER]

If you are starting the software after booting your system, type:

C:[ENTER]
CD\FFL95 (or your league's FFL directory) [ENTER]
STARTFFL [ENTER]

The first time you run the FFL program, you will be prompted that the FFL is creating your roster. This is a one-time process and will only take a few minutes.

REMEMBER: You cannot run this program with any Menu system (Windows, DOS Shell) and it should not be installed on a network.

Before going any further, review the following list of Key Functions and Terminology. It will be easier for you if you are familiar with both of these before beginning.

FUNCTION KEYS

- [Arrow Keys]: Press the appropriate arrow key to move the highlight bar up and down or left and right.

- [ENTER]: Once you have placed the highlight bar on the desired option, press [ENTER] to execute the option.

- [END]: This will save what you have been entering. For example: if you are entering franchise information, pressing [END] will save the record.

- [DELETE]: This will erase information in a record. If you select to delete information, you will be prompted to confirm the deletion.

- [INSERT]: Pressing [INSERT] enables you to add new players or point assignments.

- [ESC]: Pressing [ESC] from most places in the software will take you back to the previous menu.

- [F1]: When the highlight bar is placed on a specific option, press [F1] to access the Help information on that option.

- [F8]: While accessing a data entry field, press [F8] to clear the entire field. You may remove individual characters by pressing [DEL], however, [F8] is faster if the entire field should be removed.

- [F9]: Enables you to sort a list for the module you are currently utilizing.

- [F10]: Enables you to search for a specific item based how the list is sorted. For example: if you have sorted your list of players by player position, pressing [F10] will prompt you which position you wish to search for. See [Quick Jump].

IMPORTANT NOTE: Other function keys are available in the different modules. See the section on the specific module to determine which function keys are available in that module, or hit [SHIFT F1] within a module to see all the function keys.

TERMINOLOGY

- **Menu Lettering**: You can type the highlighted letter corresponding to the option you wish to execute or you may use the arrow keys to highlight the option.

- **Mouse Functions**: Using the mouse will allow you to move through the options more quickly. The options will highlight as you move. However, this option may be disabled to make the program run more efficiently. See Page 248 for more details.

- **Quick Jump**: When searching for players by name, you can type the desired player's name to quickly display that player. When using **Quick Jump**, type the player's last name in all **CAPS**, followed by a comma, space and the player's first name. The first name should only have the first letter capitalized. For example: to **Quick Jump** to find Desmond Howard, type **HOWARD, Desmond**.

- **Select**: Anytime you see **Select**, you are being instructed to choose a menu selection, player or other option by moving the **Highlight Bar** using the **Arrow Keys**, typing the **Letter** preceding the option, or moving the **Mouse** until the desired option is highlighted. Press the [ENTER] key or the **Left Mouse Button** to execute the selection.

Using The Software

Once you have loaded the FFL software (see Installation Instructions), the following screen is displayed:

```
Mon Aug 28, 1995   Franchise Football League      1995 Season
                        LEAGUE NOT SET UP
Pre-Season              MAIN MENU OPTIONS              V8.20
```

```
A.  League Set Up Menu      F.  Update Weekly Stats
B.  Draft / Release Players G.  Reports
C.  Select Starting Players H.  Screen Reports
D.  Trade Players           I.  System Utilities
E.  Injured Reserve         X.  Exit Program
```

FFL Title Bar Layout

Mon Aug 28, 1995 - This is displaying the current system date.

Week 1 of 1: This displays the **Current Week** (the **first** number) you are working in and the **Latest Week** (the **second** number) you can access. The Latest Week is the next week you are able to update. Note: when you first install and access the programs, this will display "Pre-Season". Pre-Season indicates that your regular season has not begun. *Franchises will not be charged for transactions during Pre-Season.*

LEAGUE NOT SET UP - This will only be displayed prior to setting up your league name. Once set up, your **League Name** will be displayed.

V8.20 - This is the version number of the FFL program you are using. This number is important and should be referenced if you call for technical support on the program.

The following are the Main Menu options and a brief description their function. Note: Each Main Menu option may contain several options relevant to that topic.

[F2] - enables you to set the current week.

[F4] - will display the NFL Roster.

A. League Set Up Menu

From this module, you will set up your league. Included with the league set up is maintenance of the Franchises, Draft Order, Player Positions, Player Point Assignments, Divisions, Scheduling, etc. Each option is explained in detail.

B. Draft/Release Players

The Draft/Release Players module maintains all aspects of the draft. Drafted players are assigned to the appropriate franchise. This module also enables you to release a player from a franchise.

C. Select Starting Players

From this module, each franchise selects the players they wish to start for the week.

D. Trade Players

Just like the real NFL, the FFL allows you to make trades. This module allows you to track and maintain the trades made.

E. Injured Reserve

This module allows you to place a player on Injured Reserve.

F. Update Weekly Stats

This module is used to update your league's fantasy points every week.

G. Reports

This module allows you to print various reports that are useful during the entire Fantasy Football season.

H. Screen Reports

This module allows the Commissioner to look up information quickly on the screen.

I. System Utilities

Utility modules are used to help the FFL program function more efficiently.

X. Exit Program

Press [X] to exit the program and return to a DOS prompt.

A. LEAGUE SETUP

a. Enter League Name

Press [a] to enter the name of your league. A data entry field will be displayed. Enter the name of your league using from 1-25 letters. The League Name can be changed at any time during the season using this module. Once entered, press [ENTER] to return to the main League Setup menu.

b. Set Up Franchises

Press [b] to set up your franchises. You will have the choice of adding franchises, display/edit franchises, print franchises and print mailing labels. Choose A to enter new franchises. Enter the information in the fields as necessary:

Franchise Name

You may enter up to 30 franchise names that will be competing in your league this year. The franchise names can be up to 20 characters in length.

Division

If you are setting up divisions in your league, enter the division that this franchise should be assigned. If you are not setting up custom divisions, all franchises will *automatically* be placed in Division #1.

Drafting Allowance

If desired, a drafting allowance can be utilized to achieve a salary cap for the franchises. If you choose to use the drafting allowance feature, enter the total dollar amount the franchise is allocated for the draft. All players will have to have dollar amounts assigned to them (see Update Player information). During Draft Night, if a franchise attempts to draft a player that will put them over their drafting allowance, a warning message will be displayed notifying the Commissioner of the situation. You will still be allowed to complete the transaction if desired.

If you do not wish to use a drafting allowance, **DO NOT ENTER ANY INFORMATION IN THE DRAFTING ALLOWANCE FIELD.**

Draft Order

Enter the draft order for this franchise. If you leave the field blank, the system will place them in entry order.

Dues Paid

If this franchise has paid their dues, enter "Y" in this field. If they haven't paid their dues, enter "N" in this field.

237

Scoring Method

Enter the scoring method for this franchise. The following are the three possible settings and their meanings:

1. Drafted Player Performance

This is the most common scoring method and the system will default to this method if left blank. This method figures this franchise's score by the performance of the players this franchise has drafted. This method is the only scoring method that will allow the franchise into Draft / Release Players.

2. Average of Other Franchises

This method can be used if you need to set up an additional franchise for even schedule pairing. For example: if you have 9 franchises in your league, you could set up a "dummy" franchise so that you don't have to leave a franchise on a bye each week. By setting up the "dummy" to be scored based on the average of the other franchises, you don't have an occurrence of this franchise winning the season.

3. Fixed Points

This method simply assigns a fixed number of points for the franchise. If chosen, a field will be displayed in which to enter the franchise's fixed point assignment. As with the previous setting, this one only needs to be used if you need a "dummy" franchise for even pairing.

In most cases, you will set all your franchise's scoring method to #1. Scoring methods #2 and #3 only need to be used in special circumstances. ONLY FRANCHISES THAT HAVE METHOD #1 WILL BE ALLOWED INTO DRAFT / RELEASE PLAYERS. Any franchise with scoring methods of 2 or 3 will not be displayed in Draft / Release Players.

The name, address and phone number portion of the screen for the franchises is self-explanatory. Enter all the appropriate information. The module allows up to 4 owners for each franchise. Once you have entered the information for the franchise, press **[END]** to save the record and move to another blank record. Once all the franchises have been entered, press **[ESC]** to return to the previous menu.

c. Select Draft Order

This module enables you to set the method your league will use to enter your draft selections if you are drafting by round.

If you are entering the draft picks as the franchise owners make them, this will allow you to choose from two automatic drafting orders on Draft Night. Select the method you wish to use, then press [ENTER], and you will be returned to the **League Setup** menu. Examples are based on a 16-team league.

Normal Draft

This is a straight 1-16, 1-16, 1-16 drafting order. This means every franchise owner picks in the same order throughout the draft. The first franchise entered will pick first and the last franchise entered will pick last in every round of the draft.

Reverse Draft

This is a reverse of the normal method - 1-16, 16-1, 1-16, 16-1, etc. . Every other round, each franchise owner will pick in the reverse order. For example, in the first round the first franchise will draft first, the second franchise second, etc. In the next round, the sixteenth franchise will draft first, the fifteenth franchise will draft second, etc.

Reset Draft Order Each Round

This method allows you to reset your draft order before each round. The system will prompt you for the order before the next round begins.

Reset Current Drafting Order

This method allows you to set a custom draft order. Once entered, this order is saved as the default draft order.

*If your league uses some other form of determining the order from round to round you may also enter the owners' draft picks after completing the draft. You would enter them in the **Draft by Franchise** method in the **Draft /Release Players Module**.

*If you drop out of the draft in the middle of a round after customizing the order, you may need to complete that round using Draft by Franchise. These picks will not, however, appear on the Post Draft Report.

d. Set Up Divisions

This module allows you to set up your divisions, assign franchises to each division and print the division set up.

A. Set Up Divisions

From this module you will set up the divisions and assign names to each division. The system will display a screen listing each division by number. For each division you wish to use, type in a name. For example -- if you wish to have four divisions, assign names to Divisions 1 - 4. The FFL program will automatically assign Division #1. You can rename Division #1 to suit your league's needs. Once you assign a name to a division, you have set up that division in your league. Once your divisions have been set up, press [END] to save the information.

B. Assign Franchises to Divisions

Once you have set up the divisions, you need to assign franchises to the divisions. When this module is accessed, a screen will display listing the divisions that you have set up.

Place the highlight bar on the division you wish to assign first and press **[ENTER]**. A new screen will be displayed listing the available franchises on the left side and the franchises assigned to this division on the right. Place the highlight bar on the franchise name you wish to assign to this division and press **[ENTER]**. The franchise name will then move from the available window to the assigned window (left to right). Continue highlighting franchise names and pressing **[ENTER]** to assign them until you have assigned all the desired franchises to the specific division. When finished, press **[ESC]** to return to the previous menu. The list of divisions will be redisplayed. Select the next division to assign. Continue in this manner until all franchises have been assigned to the appropriate division.

If you choose not to assign franchises to divisions, all franchises will automatically be placed in Division #1.

C. Print Division Setup

Once the divisions have been set up and franchises assigned, this option allows you to print a report showing which franchises are assigned to each division.

e. Tie Breakers

This module enables you to specify how ties will be broken should they arise. There are two types of ties that may need to be broken: Franchise Standings and Head to Head competition.

A. Franchise Standings

The Franchise Standings module allows you to define how ties should be broken if they occur at the end of the season. This is used for the playoffs.

1. League Record
2. League Points
3. Division Record
4. Non-Division Record
5. Division Points
6. Head to Head Record
7. Head to Head Points

Place these items in the order you wish to use to break ties by entering the highest priority in the first slot. For example: If you want franchise standing ties to be broken first based on League Points, place #2 in the first slot of the screen. Continue in this manner until you have used all the selections.

B. Head to Head

Select [B] to define the Head to Head tie breakers. Head to Head tiebreakers occur when two franchises play each other during a week and tie. The following choices are displayed:

a. Allow Ties

Press [A] to allow ties to occur. For example: if Franchise A plays Franchise B and they both receive 34 points, select [A] to record a tie in the weekly reports.

b. Total Non-Starting Points

Press [B] to use the total non-starting points to be used for tie breakers. This option will compare Franchise A's Non-Starting Points to Franchise B's Non-Starting Points. Whichever franchise has the highest total of Non-Starting Points will receive a win for that week. NOTE: Both franchises will still receive 34 points.

c. Number of Scoring Plays

Select [C] to use the number of scoring plays for tie breakers. This option will compare the total number of scoring plays for both franchises. In this case, scoring plays are only considered play types 1-14. The franchise that has the highest number of scoring plays will receive a win for that week. NOTE: Both franchises will still receive 34 points.

d. Select Non-Starting Players

If you are using Total Non-Starting Points as a tie breaker, select [D] to select the Non-Starting Players to use for this purpose. If you select this option, each non-starting player will be compared individually in the order you have selected until the tie is broken. NOTE: Both franchises will still receive 34 points.

f. Scheduling

When you access the Scheduling module for the first time, the system looks at the number of franchises and the number of divisions. If there is a system defined schedule that matches your particular league set up, it is automatically assigned. For example: If you have a 12 franchise, 3 division league, the system will automatically assign a 12 team, 3 division schedule. If there is no system defined schedule that matches your league's setup, the system will display all the possible choices and ask you to select the schedule that is closest to your league's setup. Once the schedule has been determined, the following options are displayed:

A. Edit Current Schedule

This option will display the schedule for the week you select. If you wish to make changes to the schedule, you may do so through this option. Both regular season and playoff schedules can be modified on a week by week basis or for the entire season. First, select the week you wish to modify and press [ENTER] to display the schedule. Use the function keys at the bottom of the screen to make the desired schedule changes.

B. Print Current Schedule

This option allows you to print the current schedule. A standard print screen will be displayed.

C. Number of Weeks in a Season

This option allows you to customize the length of your season. The system defaults to 17 weeks in the entire season, including playoff weeks if your league uses playoffs. If you wish to shorten the number of weeks (maybe to 14), use this option to do so. NOTE: You cannot extend the season past 17 weeks, which is the length of the NFL season.

Note: Use the Franchise Schedule Reports and the Division Set Up Report in the Reports section to view the divisions and schedules.

---

g. Playoff Setup

This module allows you to customize the playoffs for your league.

A. Number of Franchises in Round One

Enter the number of franchises that will be participating in Round One of your playoffs. The system will automatically calculate the franchises in the subsequent weeks.

B. Playoff Starting Week

Enter the Starting Week for your playoffs.

C. Playoff Ending Week

Enter the Ending Week for your playoffs.

NOTE: When setting the Playoff Starting and Ending Weeks, make certain you are setting weeks that are consistent with the number of weeks in your season. For example: if you set your season to be 15 weeks, your playoffs should be along the lines of weeks 13 to 15.

h. Enter Player Positions

From this module, you define player positions, as well as how many players can be drafted and started per franchise. This is already set up to comply with the recommended totals as defined by the FFL (see below for recommended FFL setup).

Select **Enter Player Positions** from the **League Setup** menu and press **[ENTER]**.

Select either **Add a Position, Display/Edit Positions, Mass Delete Positions** or **Print Positions** from this menu. If you select **Add a Position**, you'll be given the next available slot to add a player position. You may create additional player positions such as **Assistant Coach** with a position code of **AC**. You may also set the total number of players to be drafted and started at each position, and whether the position is active.

To change information about an existing player position, select **Display/Edit Positions** and then select the position you wish to edit. You will prompted to enter the Position #, Position Code, Position Description, Draft Limit, Start Limit, Common Play Type (See **Enter Play Types**), and to define the position as active or inactive.

Position Number

Enter the new position number in this field for the position you are entering. Position numbers 1-15 are already utilized by the FFL program.

Position Code

Enter the two letter code for this position (i.e., AC for Assistant Head Coach). You may not duplicate a code that is already in use, such as QB.

Position Description

Enter the description for the position (i.e., Assistant Head Coach).

Draft Limit

Enter the total number of this position type each franchise may draft. For example: if you enter 4 in this field, each franchise will only be allowed to draft 4 of this specific position.

Start Limit

Enter the total number of this position type each franchise may start. For example: if you enter 4 in this field, each franchise will only be allowed to start 4 of this specific position.

Common Play Types

This defines the most common play type for this position. For example, a QB's Common Play Type is Pass/TD.

Active / Inactive

If a position type is active, the FFL program will import stats from the stat file for this position. If you choose to make a position type inactive, the FFL program will ignore all stats contained in the stat file for that position. For example, if your league drafts Defensive Teams, you may choose to make the LB, DL and DB positions inactive. This would speed up the update by not reading in stats for players your league does not use.

You can get a printout of these positions in the **Reports** section of the program or by selecting **Print Position Types** from the main **Position** menu. When you have finished with this section, use the **[ESC]** key to return to the **League Setup** menu.

FFL Recommended Players

Code	Position	#Draft	#Start	Active
QB	Quarterbacks	4	1	YES
RB	Running Backs	6	2	YES
WR	Wide Receivers	6	3	YES
TE	Tight Ends	2	1	YES
K	Kickers	2	1	YES
DT	Defensive/Special Teams	2	1	YES
LB	Linebackers			YES
DB	Defensive Backs			YES
DL	Defensive Linemen			YES
OL	Offensive Linemen			YES
P	Punter			YES
RS	Return Specialist			YES
ST	Special Teams Unit			YES
QT	Quarterback Team			YES
HC	Head Coach			YES
Total Draft Picks		*22*	*9*	

Mass Delete

This module allows you to delete all players at a position from the player database. For example, if your league does not want to use Linebackers, you could delete the Linebacker position. All the Linebackers in the player database would be deleted. If you select **Mass Delete Player Positions**, there are several important items to consider:

1. You CANNOT delete system defined positions. You can only delete positions that you have added.

2. The position MUST be marked as inactive in order to delete the players at that position.

3. The position is not actually deleted from the system. The players assigned to that position are deleted from the database.

i. Enter Play Types

In this section you will be able to create your own **Play Types** for your league to use to award points in addition to the standard FFL scoring system. Select **Set Up Play Types** from the **League Setup** menu and press **[ENTER]**.

You can either **Add Play Types, Display Play Types, or Print Play Types**. If you select **Add Play Types**, you will be given the next available slot to add a play type. The following screen will be displayed:

PLAY TYPE ENTRY

```
Play Type Number:
Play Type Description:
Type:
Active:
Decimal Places
```

Play Type Number

The system has play types 1 - 54 already assigned. You can begin assigning new play types with number 55. If you try to enter a new play type under an already assigned number, you will receive an error message indicating that the number is already assigned.

Play Type Description

Enter the specific description for the play type you are entering.

Type

Select the type of play you are entering based on the following. (Pressing **[F10]** will display these options.)

A. Scoring Play

This setting indicates that this play type is a scoring type play, meaning that points are awarded to the team based on the play. For example, a pass/TD is an example of a scoring play.

B. Statistic

This setting indicates that the play you have entered awards statistics, but no score is achieved by the play. Rushing Yardage is an example of a statistical play.

C. Both

This indicates that the play you have entered achieves both scoring points and statistics.

Active

Select whether this play type is active or inactive. If you are adding a new play, you would most likely have it as an active play type. NOTE: Inactive Play Types are not included in the stats.

Decimal Places

Enter the number of decimal places you want this play type to utilize on reports.

When you select **Display Play Types**, the standard **FFL Play Types** plus any additional play types you have added will be displayed. These are some of the more popular types of plays used today.

Even if you subscribe to any of the FFL Weekly Stats, you will need to manually enter plays for the play types that you created to be awarded points in the Update Weekly Scoring section each week.

You will be able to set up the point ranges for any play types you added in the **Player Point Assignment** section so that when these plays are entered into the update section, the points for that play will automatically be awarded.

You can get a printout of all play types in the **Reports** section of the program or by selecting **Print Play Types** from the main **Play Type** menu. When you are finished defining your new plays, press the **[ESC]** key to return to the **League Setup** menu.

j. Enter Point Assignments

This section allows you to add or modify point assignment ranges. Based on the **FFL Distance Scoring Ranges** and **FFL Performance Scoring Increments**, you can set up point ranges to account for any scoring system, and the specific number of times a player performs a task.

After selecting **Enter Point Assignments** from the **League Setup** menu, a screen is displayed that will allow you to enter both **FFL Distance Scoring Ranges** and **FFL Performance Scoring Increments**. **Ranges** are point assignments that your league wants to award for a play that falls within a specified range (i.e. *Touchdowns* or *Field Goals*). **Increments** are used if your league wants to award points for every time a play occurs (i.e. *Rushing Yardage, Interceptions,* or *Passing Completions*).

To modify an existing point assignment, move the highlight bar down using the **arrow** keys or the **[Page Down]** key until you see the play want. Press **[ENTER]** on that point assignment, and it will appear in the entry box on top. Move the highlight to the place you want to change and type in the value you desire. Press **[ENTER]** and then press **[END]** to save the change.

To add a new point assignment, press the **[Insert]** key to take you to the Point Assignment Entry box. Press **[ENTER]** to bring up the selections for the position or group for which you would like to have this play credited. Move the highlight bar to the position you desire and press **[ENTER]**. Then press **[ENTER]** again to bring up the list containing the play types. When you have highlighted the play type for which you wish to set up a point assignment, press **[ENTER]**.

For both Ranges and Increments, the following screen is displayed:

Position:	Start:	Points:
Play Type:	End:	Qnty:

Lower and upper ranges refer to yards a play may cover or the number of times a certain play may occur. For example,the following point range indicates that a *Quarterback* throwing a touchdown *pass* between *10* and *39* yards will get *9* points:

| Position: **QB** | Start: **10** | Points: 9 |
| Play Type: **Pass / TD** | End: **39** | |

Notice we did not enter a Quantity for this assignment. This is a range assignment and therefore no Quantity is required.

To enter a point assignment **increment**, player point assignments may be created for performance related stats, such as rushing yardage, passing yardage, receiving yardage, sacks, interceptions, fumbles, or any other category your league might think of to award/penalize points for.

| Position: | Start: | Points: |
| Play Type | End: | Qnty: |

For example, if you wanted to reward a *Running Back* for *rushing* at least *100* yards in a game *10* points, then you would want to set up a point assignment like this:

| Position: **RB** | Start: **100** | Points: **10** |
| Play Type: **Rushing Yards Gained** End: **100** | | Qnty: **1** |

Then, lets reward the same ***Running Back*** another *1* point for every additional *10* yards he *rushes* in that game.

| Position: **RB** | Start: **101** | Points: **1** |
| Play Type: **Rushing Yards Gained** End: **999** | | Qnty: **10** |

So if he rushes 98 yards in a game, he will get 0 points, but if he rushes 159, he will get 15 points. He gets 10 points for reaching 100 yards and another 5 points for the additional 59 yards rushed.

REMEMBER....For a range type plays, do NOT enter any information in the QNTY field. You only use the QNTY field to specify point assignments for every time that particular play occurs. The QNTY field will always increment the play and assign points based on the number in the QNTY field. If you enter information in the QNTY field on a range play, you will not get the point assignments you expect.

To delete any number of ranges, press the **[F5]** key to enter the mass delete module. You may now press **[F2]** to select individual lines you wish to delete, or you can press **[F5]** to delete the entire listing of Player Point Assignments and set up your own assignments. When you are ready to delete your selections, press **[F3]**. You can now press **[ESC]** to return to the main **Player Point Assignment** screen.

> **NOTE:** Deleted point assignments are unrecoverable and must be reentered manually. It is suggested that before making any changes to the point assignments, you should copy the "POINTS.*" files to a diskette for backup. To make this backup copy, insert a diskette in your drive, cd\FFL95 directory and type the following:

COPY POINTS.* A: [ENTER]

Set Number of Decimal Places

Use this option to set the number of decimal places that will be used on your reports.

Print Point Assignments

This option allows you to print a report of the Point Assignments. A standard print screen will be displayed allowing you to print to your printer or to the screen.

k. Roster Transaction Fees

This is an optional section which will allow you to set up and manage fees for any player transactions that your league owners make during the season. There is also a separate report in **Reports** to print this information.

A. Set Up Roster Transaction Fees

You can set up separate fees for each roster move a league owner makes throughout the season. The following screen is displayed:

```
TRANSACTION              AMOUNT
Draft...................0.00
Cut.....................0.00
Trade...................0.00
Place on I/R...........0.00
Take off I/R...........0.00
```

Enter the amount you wish to charge for each of the transactions. For example, your league may charge $1 for every player pickup or release and $2 for each trade. These can easily be tracked for you here. This information is included in the League Rules Report.

B. Delete Transactions

If during the season the Commissioner makes a mistake in a transaction and needs to delete the transaction so that the franchise's owner is not charged for it, this module is used. Here you can delete any transaction from any week during the season so that owners will be charged the correct amount for transactions at the end of the season. Note: this option does not reverse the transaction; it simply deletes the fee for the transaction.

C. Print Roster Transactions

This option will print all the Roster Transactions that have occurred for the franchises.

D. Print Roster Transaction Fees

This option prints a list of the Roster Transaction Fees.

l. Set Up Printer

The Set Up Printer option must be used before you can begin to print reports. Once accessed, a menu will be displayed. The first time, option A will say "Printer" indicating you need to select a printer. Press [F3]. A list of printers will be displayed. Select your printer and press [ENTER]. Once selected, you can press [F3] to test the selected printer. You will then be prompted to select your printer port. Highlight the port and press [ENTER]. Once you have entered this information, the system will default to this printer. NOTE: most parallel printers default to LPT1. Most serial printers default to either COM1 or COM2.

You will also need to select the number of lines per page you wish to print. Press [F4]. Enter the number of lines you wish printer per page.

> **Important Note:** You must set your lines per page before you begin printing ANY reports, including reports printed to the screen. Failure to set the number of lines will cause you to get one line per page on all reports.

m. Miscellaneous Setup

This module enables you to determine your monitor type, as well as set the program to run with a mouse. Use Option A to determine if the program will run with a mouse. You will be prompted to select **YES** or **NO** for mouse operation. Option B allows you to specify your monitor type:

A. Monitor Automatically set by FFL

If you select option A, the FFL program will determine the best monitor type for your system and set the program accordingly.

B. Monochrome Monitor

If you are utilizing a monochrome monitor, select option B.

C. Color Monitor

If you are using a color monitor, select option C.

249

B. Draft/Release Players

Draft Players

The **Draft Players** option is used on your league's draft night. Tonight's the night you and your fellow franchise owners begin to put together your dream teams for the season. Distributing copies of the **1995 NFL Roster** to your fellow franchise owners can make conducting the draft much easier.

The **NFL Roster** can be printed from the **Reports** section in the Main Menu or by pressing the **[F4]** key under **League Setup**. Franchise owners may draft NFL players who are not on this list. Although the **Draft Players** section allows for the addition of players not listed, the weekly stat files will automatically update and add new players to the player database. If your league is not entering the draft picks directly into the computer during the draft, the **Draft Night Player List** is a helpful report for the Commissioner to use. This report prints out the same **NFL Roster** list, but with space available to record the franchise that drafts the player. This makes it much easier for the Commissioner to enter the draft picks later.

From the **Main Menu**, select **Draft/Release Players** and you will then be asked to Select Draft Method:

Method 1 - Draft by Round:

This should be used by leagues that have access to a computer during Draft Night. This method tracks draft selection order by round and allows one pick per franchise for each round, similar to an actual NFL draft. It rotates from franchise to franchise based on the draft order you selected during the **League Setup** portion of the **Main Menu**. For an explanation of the draft order, see pages 237-238.

Set up the computer in a central location so that each franchise owner has access to it during the draft. The Commissioner may want to operate the program or assist other owners. The left window will display those players available to draft. The right window will display the name of the franchise and its selected players. The current round and pick will be displayed above the two windows.

When the first franchise drafting picks the player it wants to draft, the Commissioner or franchise owner should scroll through the list of players, using the **arrow** keys or the **[F10]** key, to locate player's name with the highlight bar and press **[ENTER]**. This moves the player off the **Available NFL Players** window (left) and places him in the franchise window (right) and onto that franchise's team. At this point you may either press **[F1]** to record the pick and move on to the next selection, or **[F2]** to reverse the pick allowing you to select another player.

*If you drop out of the draft in the middle of a round after customizing the order, you may need to complete that round using Draft by Franchise. These picks will not, however, appear on the Post Draft Report.

If the wrong player is drafted, press [ESC] to get to the options menu: **Draft by Round** or **Draft by Franchise**. Select **Draft by Franchise**; when the box of franchises appears, select the franchise that drafted the wrong player. Using the **right arrow** key, move the highlight bar over to the franchise window and onto the wrong player selected, press [ENTER] and the player will be moved back to the **Available NFL Players** list. Now use the **left arrow** key to move the highlight bar back to the **Available NFL Players** list, select the player the franchise wants, and press [ENTER] again to move the player onto that franchise. After that, press [ESC] twice to go back to the options menu and re-select **Draft by Round**. You will return to the current round and current pick.

It is important that when you take one player off a franchise, you put one back on that franchise. Otherwise the round-pick sequence will be incorrect and will be re-set to round 1, pick 1, however, you will not lose any of the previous picks.

Following a draft by round, the Commissioner may choose to print the Post Draft Report. This report displays a round by round listing of the players drafted to each franchise.

Method 2 - Draft by Franchise:

This should be used by leagues that do not have access to a computer during the draft or wish to enter their draft picks following Draft Night. It allows the Commissioner to input all drafted players for each franchise at the same time, rather than one pick per franchise. This method can be used by **all leagues** to make adjustments, such as adding players, correcting errors, drafting players released by other franchises, or for leagues that have a supplemental draft. After Week 1, the program defaults to Draft by Franchise and Draft by Round is no longer available.

After you select **Draft by Franchise**, a window will appear listing the franchises. Select a franchise by using the **arrow** keys to move the highlight bar and press [ENTER]. Now, two windows will appear. The left **Available NFL Players** window contains a list of the available 1995 NFL Players. The right window displays the franchise name that is drafting. Have each franchise's list of drafted players handy.

Scroll through the list of players in the left window to locate the player, place the highlight bar on the name and press [ENTER]. This moves the player off the **Available NFL Players** list and into the franchise window. The highlight bar will automatically move back to the **Available NFL Players** window. Simply select the next player to be drafted and press [ENTER]. When all the players for that franchise have been drafted, press [ESC]. Repeat this procedure for the next franchise to draft.

To **remove** a player from a franchise, use the right **arrow** key to move the highlight bar to the franchise window. Place the bar on that player, press [ENTER], and the player's name will reappear in the **Available NFL Players** window.

At any time during the draft, the Commissioner can take a break by simply pressing the [ESC] key twice to return to the **Main Menu**. The FFL program records all draft choices, and the Commissioner can continue the draft at any time.

Both Method 1 and Method 2 Users:

After the draft has been completed, it's a good idea to print **Franchise Rosters** and **Starting Lineup Worksheets**. Return to the **Main Menu** and select **Reports**. Make sure your printer is **ON**. Select **Print Franchise Rosters** from the **Player Information** menu. Then select **Starting Lineup Worksheets** from the **Weekly Reports** menu and distribute to each franchise owner to track weekly starting lineups.

Important Keys to Make Your Draft Easier:

There are a number of special features that can be used during the draft to aid the Commissioner/franchise owner in picking players for their teams.

- Searching for a player's name can be done by simply typing (in **CAPS**) the player's last name. As you type each letter you will see the list of players scroll closer to the player you are looking for. If you make a mistake in typing, just press any of the arrow keys to reset the search mode. You can start typing the name again. This can be used in any window that contains player information sorted by **Player's Name**.

- Arrow Keys Up & Down: Moves the highlight bar vertically to scroll through the list of available and drafted players in both windows.

- Arrow Keys Right and Left: Moves the highlight bar from the **Available NFL Players** window to the **Franchise** window and back.

- [SHIFT] + [F1]: Lists all available options.

- [F1]: Help window available throughout FFL program.

- [F3]: Displays Player Performance Summary.

- [F4]: Lists all NFL players who have been drafted to that point. To access this option, press **[F4]**. A window will appear on the screen. To return to player windows, press **[ESC]**.

- [F6:] Displays the Roster Summary.

- [F7]: With a specific player highlighted, this will add the player at a different position.

- [F8]: Allows you to enable and disable the warning messages. The warning messages simply notify you when you have exceeded your league's salary or drafting limits for players.

- [F9]: Changes the order in which players are displayed, both in the **Available NFL Players** window and the **Franchise** window. Players can be displayed alphabetically, by position, or by NFL team. Players are initially displayed in alphabetical order. A window will appear on the screen. Select the desired display order, then press **[ENTER]**. Players are immediately listed in selected order. To return to player window, press **[ESC]**.

- [F10]: Quickly locates specific player by name, position, or team. If players are displayed alphabetically, the **[F10]** key will quickly locate a specific player by typing in his last name in **CAPS**. If the players are displayed by position, the **[F10]** key will quickly locate a specific group of player positions. If players are displayed by NFL team, the **[F10]** key will quickly locate a specific NFL team. A list of players, positions, or teams will appear. Select the appropriate option, press **[ENTER]**. To return to player window, press **[ESC]**.

> **Note: All entries must be typed exactly as they appear. Last names in UPPER case and first names in upper and lower case (i.e. SANDERS, Barry).**

- To Edit a Player: The **[F5]** key allows you to edit a player in either the **Available NFL Players** window or the **Franchise** window. Using the **arrow** keys, scroll through the list until you find the player you want to edit, then press **[F5]**. Now using the **arrow** keys, move the highlight bar to where you want to edit. When you are done, press **[END]** to save the change or **[ESC]** to cancel the change.

Note: You will notice that there are three name fields for the players, Last, First and Full Name. The Full Name field is for reports only. The system utilizes the Last and First Name fields.

- To Delete a Player from the NFL Roster: Place the highlight bar on the player to be deleted and press **[DEL]**. One last window will appear asking for confirmation before deleting the player.

- To Insert a New Player's Name: The FFL provides a comprehensive up-to-date **1995 NFL Roster**; additionally, if you subscribe to any of the stat update services the program will update and add new players throughout the season when you import each weekly stat file.

If a franchise wants to draft a player whose name does not appear in the **Available NFL Players** (left) window, select this option by pressing **[Insert]**, while in the left-hand side window, to enter a new player's information. A window will appear allowing the Commissioner/franchise owner to type in the player's last name and first name, and to select the player's position, NFL team name and price. (If you decide not to add this player to the list after the window has appeared on the screen, simply press **[ESC]**.) Press **[END]** to record new player's information.

For those leagues that want to split players into multiple positions, it can be accomplished quickly. For example, if an RB or WR also returns punts (such as David Meggett), he can be set up as a Return Specialist (RS) so that more than one franchise may draft him. One franchise may draft the player at his original position and receive all stats and scores awarded to him at that position, while another franchise may draft the player at his new position and receive all his RS stats and scores. Under the **Draft / Release Players** module, simply highlight the player you wish to split into a different position, and press **[F7]**. You will be presented with a list of available positions. Highlight the position at which you wish to insert the new player. The new player should then appear at his new position in the **Available Players** window.

Note: Do not use the **[INS]** key to add these players if they already exist in the database. For example, if you wish to add David Meggett as an RS as well as an RB, you must use the **[F7]** key instead of the **[INS]** key.

This may also be done for those leagues that want separate Defensive Teams (DT) stats and scores from Special Teams (ST) data. Highlight a DT, and press [F7]. Select ST and the new Special Team Unit will appear. Remember to use RS for players and ST for teams so that the correct stats will be awarded.

This feature works only for splitting DB, WR and RB into RS, and DT stats into DT and ST stats. While the program will allow you to split any position into any other position, stats will not be split for those new positions.

When you exit Draft Night, you will be asked if you are ready to start the regular season. If you select "Yes", the program will move to Week 1 of 1 and all future roster transactions will be counted and charged to the franchises.

Release Players

If a player seems no longer useful to a franchise and the owner wishes to draft or pick another available player, you must first release or take the unwanted player off the franchise. Select **Draft/Release Players** from the **Main Menu**. Select the franchise with the highlight bar and press **[ENTER]**. Two windows will appear; on the left is the franchise roster and on the right is the Released Players list. Select the player to be released by moving the highlight bar with the **arrow** keys and press **[ENTER]**. The player will automatically be moved onto the Released Players list and off the franchise roster. To put a player back on a franchise's roster, or if an error was made, simply re-draft the player to the appropriate franchise. *Note:* Players become eligible to be drafted again by other franchises after being released.

C. Select Starting Players

Immediately after your draft, you must select the starting players prior to the first week's NFL games. Thereafter, the starting lineups are automatically carried over to the next week after you run the **Update Weekly Scoring**. Once you have processed the scoring plays, a window will appear asking to "**Reset Current Week?**" If you are confident that you are finished with this week's updating, you should select **Yes**. The FFL program will automatically set up the next week's starting lineups based on the present week's lineups. You will still be able to make changes to the starting lineups in the **Select Starting Players** section.

Every week, the Commissioner records each franchise's starting lineup using the FFL program.

Choose **Select Starting Players** from the **Main Menu**. A window will appear listing the names of each franchise in the league. Use the highlight bar to select the desired franchise and press [**ENTER**]. Now, two windows will appear.

The left window displays the franchise's **Non-Starting Players**. The right window displays the franchise's **Starting Players**. To move the highlight bar from window to window, use the right and left **arrow** keys.

To select a starting player, place the highlight bar on the desired player in the left window and press [**ENTER**]. This automatically moves the player's name from the left **Non-Starters** window and places it in the right **Starters** window. Select each starting player using the same process until there are the appropriate number of starting players on each franchise. When complete, press [**ESC**] to select the next franchise.

To bench or delete a player from the starting lineup of a franchise, place the highlight bar on the desired player in the right window and press [**ENTER**]. The player's name automatically moves from the right window of **Starting Players** to the left window of **Non-Starting Players**.

To see a list of other options within this module, press [**SHIFT + F1**].

When the starting lineups for each franchise in the league have been recorded, press [**ESC**] twice to end and return to the **Main Menu**.

D. Trade Players

The Commissioner records all trades using the FFL program. Select **Trade Players** from the **Main Menu**. After the window appears, use the highlight bar to select the first franchise involved in the trade, and press **[ENTER]**. Now a second window will appear. Again using the highlight bar, select the second franchise involved in the trade and press **[ENTER]**.

Two windows will appear on the screen. The left window displays the roster of all players on the first franchise and the right window displays the roster of the second franchise. To make a trade, select the player to be traded from the first franchise by placing the highlight bar on his name, and press **[ENTER]**. The player's name will automatically move from the left window to the right window.

Trade players from the second franchise to the first franchise using the same procedure. If you are making a 2-for-1 or 3-for-2 trade, use the right and left **arrow** keys to change windows and select players.

To reverse a trade, follow the same steps as above, using the highlight bar and **[ENTER]** key. If you make a mistake, simply go to the other franchise and highlight the player placed there in error. Press **[ENTER]** to move the player back to the original team, then re-select the correct player. No harm is done if a trade is reversed in the same week, and when a player has not scored in that or successive weeks. Press **[ESC]** twice to end the trading and return to the **Main Menu**.

Note: If you have roster transaction fees set up for trades, the fee will be assessed against the franchises that are involved in the trade.

E. Injured Reserve

If, during the season, NFL players become injured, they can be placed on **Injured Reserve** by their NFL teams. This means they are not available to play, and are not available for other teams to pick up. If a player is unable to play in the NFL, an FFL franchise owner may place the player on Injured Reserve in order to hold on to him, but only if the NFL team does that as well. The FFL recommends that the Commissioner limit owners to four such transactions during the season to prevent stockpiling of talent.

Select **Injured Reserve** from the **Main Menu**. Select the franchise with the highlight bar and press **[ENTER]**. Two windows will appear; on the left is the franchise roster and on the right is the **Injured Reserve**. Select the player to be placed on the **Injured Reserve** and press **[ENTER]**. The player will automatically move onto the **Injured Reserve**. To put a player back on a team's roster or if an error was made, use the right **arrow** key to access the right window, place the highlight bar on the player's name, and press **[ENTER]**. To exit, press **[ESC]** twice to return to **Main Menu**.

While on IR, a player's salary counts against a franchise's salary cap.

To print a list of any players on Injured Reserve, print the **Injured Reserve** report from the **Player Information** reports section.

F. Update Weekly Stats

This option is used to update your league's fantasy points every week. If you are using any of the update services (i.e. **PRODIGY, CompuServe, The Microsoft Network, Fantasy Sports BBS**), be sure you have downloaded the weekly file (i.e. **FFLSTAT.1** before you enter this section on the **Main Menu**. These instructions are explained in the **Subscribing To Weekly Scoring Updates** section of this manual.

COMMISSIONERS USING AN UPDATE SERVICE

The following options will be displayed if you are using an update service.

Note: if you did not add any players to your database under Draft / Release Players, the menu option A will not appear; option B will appear as option A, option C as B, etc.

A. Match User Created Players

If the program detects the stat file for the week you have selected, it will import the stat file and assign points to the plays for the week based on your league's point assignments. If you manually inserted a player into the database under Draft / Release Players, this section will appear. Selecting item A presents you with a list of all the players you manually added to the database. The following steps will allow you to match the player you created to the player found in the download file.

At this time, you can manually update these plays with the correct player name by highlighting the player's name and pressing **[ENTER]**. You may now press **[F10]** to bring up the current master roster of players. The program will attempt to match the closest name, but you may need to scroll up and down to be sure. If you cannot find the correct match, this player might be a new player to be added to your league. In almost all cases these players will be new players. If you do find the player's correct name, first highlight him and press **[ENTER]** then **[END]** to save him in the play file. His name should now disappear from the list of unmatched names. Once you have finished matching the players, press **[ESC]** to return to the previous menu. Any unmatched players may be added under Section C.

B. Add / Edit Player Stats

This section allows you to edit players' stats or insert stats for any players not listed in the download file. Upon selecting this option, you will be presented with a Enter / Edit Player Stats screen.

This screen displays all players that have stats for the week. To edit a player's stats, you have two options. If you select **[F2]** you can view the player's scoring plays (such as touchdowns, field goals, etc) for the week.

```
          ENTER SCORING PLAYS FOR WEEK 1
Plyr:    AIKMAN, Troy            QB      Dallas
Fran:    6                       Points:  0
```

```
        SCORING TYPE            QTY           POINTS
   1    Pass / TD               45             12
   2    Rush / TD               12.0           18
   3    2 Point Pass             1              2
```

To edit a scoring play type, move the highlight bar to the appropriate play type. Press [F10] to edit the play type itself, or move the highlight bar to the quantity or points field to modify those values. If you change the value in the quantity field, the points will change based on your point assignments. Once you have finished modifying any scoring plays, press [ESC] to return to the previous screen.

If you select [F3] you can view the player's statistical plays (such as rushing yards gained, interceptions, etc) for the week.

```
          ENTER PLAYER STATS FOR WEEK 1
Plyr:    AIKMAN, Troy            QB        Dallas
Fran:    6                       Stat Points: 4
```

```
     STAT CATEGORY            QTY           POINTS
     Rushing Attempts          1              0
     Rushing Yards Gained      1              2
     Rushing Average          4.5             0
     Rushing Touchdowns        1              1
     Yards From Scrimmage     235             0
     Passing Attempts          21             0
     Passing Completions       31             0
     Passing Completion %     67.7            0
     Passing Yards Gained     234             0
     Passing Average          11.1            0
```

To edit a statistical play type, move the highlight bar to the appropriate play type. If you change the value in the quantity field, the points will change based on your point assignments. Once you have finished modifying any statistical plays, press [ESC] to return to the previous screen.

C. Update Roster

Select option [C] to automatically add new players to the roster. This will take any players from section A that were not matched up and add them to your player database.

D. Update this Week's Stats

Select **[D]** to post the weekly stat records to the program's data files. Your players and franchise's weekly stats are now recorded and the information can be viewed through the Reports section. Once the update process has completed, you will be prompted to reset the week and pass your league's lineups forward. If you feel you made a roster lineup or point assignment error choose **NO**, otherwise choose **YES** and the program will set up your league's next week lineups. You may still go back make changes but you may need to manually move your lineups forward. If you need to manually move your lineups, there is a special option under System Utilities (See Page 269). If you make only a starting roster change, then you won't need to run the update process again.

E. Recalculate Points

Press **[E]** to recalculate your points. This function zeros out points assessed to the stats in a week and forces the program to recalculate the points. Generally, you will only need to do this if, for any reason, you had to modify your player point assignments after running an update.

F. Reload Stat File

Press **[F]** to reload the stat file from a disk drive or other subdirectory should the need arise.

G. Purge This Week's Stats

This option should not need to be used often. The stats are automatically purged when you run the update program. However, if you ever need to manually purge the stats, this option can be used.

COMMISSIONERS UPDATING MANUALLY

The following options will be displayed if you are NOT using an update service and are entering your stats manually.

A. Add / Edit Player Stats

This section allows you to add and edit player stats. Upon selecting this option, you will be presented with an Enter / Edit Player Stats screen.

The Enter / Edit Player Stats screen allows you to enter all players that have stats for the week. To add and edit a player's stats, you have two options. If you select [F2] you can add the player's scoring plays (such as touchdowns, field goals, etc) for the week.

```
        ENTER SCORING PLAYS FOR WEEK 1
Plyr:   AIKMAN, Troy            QB      Dallas
Fran:   6                              Points:  0
```

	SCORING TYPE	QTY	POINTS
1	Pass / TD	45	12
2	Rush / TD	12.0	18
3	2 Point Pass	1	2

To add a scoring play type, move the highlight bar to the appropriate play type. Press [F10] to edit the play type itself, or move the highlight bar to the quantity or points field to modify those values. If you change the value in the quantity field, the points will change based on your point assignments. Once you have finished adding any scoring plays, press [ESC] to return to the previous screen.

If you select [F3] you can add the player's statistical plays (such as rushing yards gained, interceptions, etc) for the week.

```
        ENTER PLAYER STATS FOR WEEK 1
Plyr:   AIKMAN, Troy            QB      Dallas
Fran:   6                              Stat Points:  4
```

STAT CATEGORY	QTY	POINTS
Rushing Attempts	1	0
Rushing Yards Gained	1	2
Rushing Average	4.5	0
Rushing Touchdowns	1	1
Yards From Scrimmage	235	0
Passing Attempts	21	0
Passing Completions	31	0
Passing Completion %	67.7	0
Passing Yards Gained	234	0
Passing Average	11.1	0

To add a statistical play type, move the highlight bar to the appropriate play type. If you change the value in the quantity field, the points will change based on your point assignments. Once you have finished adding any statistical plays, press [ESC] to return to the previous screen.

B. Update Roster

Select option [B] to automatically add new players to the roster. This will take any players from section A that were not matched up and add them to your player database.

C. Update this Week's Stats

Select [C] to post the weekly stat records to the program's data files. Your players and franchise's weekly stats are now recorded and the information can be viewed through the Reports section. Once the update process has completed, you will be prompted to reset the week and pass your league's lineups forward. If you feel you made a roster lineup or point assignment error choose **NO**, otherwise choose **YES** and the program will set up your league's next week lineups. You may still go back make changes but you may need to manually move your lineups forward. If you need to manually move your lineups, there is a special option under System Utilities (See Page 269). If you make only a starting roster change, then you won't need to run the update process again.

D. Recalculate Points

Press [D] to recalculate your points. This function zeros out points assessed to the stats in a week and forces the program to recalculate the points. Generally, you will only need to do this if you had to modify your player point assignments for any reason.

E. Reload Stat File

Press [E] to reload the stat file from a disk drive or other subdirectory should the need arise.

F. Purge This Week's Stats

This option should not need to be used often. The stats are automatically purged when you run the update program. However, if you ever need to manually purge the stats, this option can be used.

G. Reports

As has been mentioned several times throughout this manual, there are numerous reports within the FFL program that can be used to facilitate many tasks.

When you first access the **Reports** module, you will be prompted to select the output format for the report (print to a printer, to the screen or to a disk). Highlight the appropriate output. If you have not chosen your printer, option A will say "Printer" indicating you need to select a printer. Press **[F3]**. A list of printers will be displayed. Select your printer and press **[ENTER]**. Once selected, you can press **[F3]** to test the selected printer. You will then be prompted to select your printer port. Highlight the port and press **[ENTER]**. Once you have entered this information, the system will default to this printer. NOTE: most parallel printers default to LPT1. Most serial printers default to either COM1 or COM2.

You will also need to select the number of lines per page you wish to print. Press **[F4]**. Enter the number of lines you wish printed per page.

Important Note: You must set your lines per page before you begin printing ANY reports, including reports printed to the screen. Failure to set the number of lines will cause you to get one line per page on all reports.

---

a. Weekly Reports

A. User-Defined Weekly Reports

This prints out the reports you have selected under "Customize Weekly Reports".

B. Weekly Winning Report

Prints total starting and non-starting points for each franchise for that week and year-to-date. This can be printed with or without the newsletter.

C. Weekly League Summary Report

Will print league standings with current results and next weeks matchups. At the end of your league's regular season you will have the option to have the matchups reflect the playoffs. This also shows the 1995 NFL schedule, wins, losses, and ties, and the division and non-division records. This can be printed with or without the newsletter.

D. Weekly Winners Ranking

This report lists the overall points scored by each franchise. The information is listed by week and the teams are ranked from highest number of points in a week to lowest.

E. Player Scoring Report

Prints total starting and non-starting points for each player on each franchise for that week. The head to head matchups are placed together on the same page. You have the option of printed for all franchises or selecting specific franchises.

F. Scoring Plays Report

Prints all the scoring plays awarded to each player on a franchise, both starting and non-starting, for that week.

G. Starting Lineup Worksheets

Prints all players on a franchise, listed by franchise, and whether they were started the previous week. Additional space is provided for franchise owners to indicate whether they want the player to start this week. You have the option of printed for all franchises or selecting specific franchises.

H. Pre-Game Starting Players

Prints the upcoming week's games, with each head-to-head matchup on a separate page. Includes both starting and non-starting rosters with YTD points. At the end of your league's regular season you will have the option to have the matchups reflect the playoffs.

I. Starting Roster Report

Prints the starting roster results for the entire league.

J. Customize Weekly Reports

Here is where you can customize the **"User-Defined Weekly Reports"** discussed earlier. You can select all the reports your league wants to see on a weekly basis and be able to print them all by just selecting the **"User Defined Weekly Reports"** option.

b. League Setup Reports

A. Player Point Assignments

Prints the current scoring play ranges that the program uses for assigning point values to the play file in the **Update Weekly Scoring** section.

B. Player Positions

Prints both pre-defined and user-defined player positions.

C. Play Types

Prints both pre-defined and user-defined play types.

D. Division Setup

Print your league's divisional setup to hand out to league members before the season starts.

E. Mailing Labels

Print mailing labels for up to four owners per franchise. For dot-matrix printers use **Avery Labels #4145** and for laser printers use **Avery Labels #5161**.

Note: If you do not have franchise owners' names and addresses set up, the mailing labels will not print.

F. League Rules

This report prints miscellaneous league rule information such as tie breakers, head to head records, roster transaction fees, season length, division set up, draft order method, current draft order, etc.

. Player Information

A. NFL Roster

Prints the current database of NFL players available for drafting, listed by position or NFL team. This report is a very good handout for franchise owners on Draft Night.

B. Franchise Rosters

Prints each franchise's roster of players.

C. Draft Night Player List

Prints the same list of players as the NFL Roster Report, but also provides space for entering the franchise name that drafts that player. Very helpful report for Commissioners who are not entering the draft picks as they are made on Draft Night. This report now has the option to include player salaries if your league choose to implement a salary cap.

D. Weekly Player Scores Report

Prints a year-to-date scoring report for players with scoring listed by the week. You are given the option of printing for only non-drafted players, only drafted players, or for all players. By using the Non-Drafted Players option, this is very useful for franchise owners to locate a productive player not yet on a team.

E. Top 40 Point Leaders

Prints the top 40 players, by position, based on their year-to-date fantasy point scoring.

F. Released Players

Prints all players released by week.

G. Injured Reserve

Prints a history of all players placed on Injured Reserve.

H. Roster Transactions

Prints all player roster moves on a week-by-week basis. This includes moves such as trades, releases and newly drafted players.

I. Roster Transaction Fees

This report will print a franchise by franchise listing of all transaction fees charged throughout the season, if the fees were set up in the **League Set Up** section.

J. Post Draft Report

This new report can only be used by Commissioners using the **Draft by Round** option in **Draft / Release Players**. The **Post Draft Report** displays the round and pick for each franchise.

k. Player Salary Report

This report lists the information about the players' salaries (input by you). This report prints by franchise.

d. NFL & FFL Schedules

A. Schedules By Week

This will print your league's entire season schedule. It can print the entire 17-week schedule or just your league's regular season schedule based upon what is set up in the **Divisions/Schedules** section of **League Set Up**.

B. Schedules By Franchise

This will print what each franchise's regular season schedule is and what franchise they play from week to week. This can also can be set to reflect playoffs by showing you only your league's regular season.

C. Schedules With Playoff Report

This will appear to be the same report as Schedules By Week, but this report will also include your league's playoff format. Depending upon what week you generate this report, the program will attempt to match up what franchises it feels are in the playoffs based on the YTD records at the time the report is generated.

D. 1995 NFL Schedule

Print the entire 1995 NFL schedule or a single week. Single weeks are also printed in the **Weekly League Summary Report**.

e. Stat Reports

A. Drafted Stat Detail

Shows comprehensive NFL stats for all current players on each franchise. These are total year-to-date stats for each player regardless of which franchise(s) he has been assigned throughout the season. You have the option to print for all franchises or selected franchises.

B. Non-Drafted Stat Detail

Shows comprehensive NFL stats for all non-drafted players in your league. These are total year-to-date stats for each player whether he was ever on this franchise. You have the option to print for all franchises or selected franchises.

C. Franchise Stat History

Shows comprehensive NFL stats for all current and former players while they played for each specific franchise. You have the option to print for all franchises or selected franchises.

D. Top 40 Stat Leaders

Shows the top 40 players for each of the NFL stat categories included in the weekly stat update file or is manually entered. You have the option of printing all positions or selected positions.

E. Season Player Scoring Summary

Prints a spreadsheet-like report, similar to the one in the back of the FFL Journal, which displays all Distance scoring (NFL point scoring plays) information for each player with his YTD fantasy points. Can be sorted by player name, position or ranking. You have the option of printing for all franchises or selected franchises.

F. Box Score Report

This report prints a weekly box score report similar to those found in the sports section of your newspaper. Breaks down distance scoring plays based on time and quarter information from actual NFL games (if you get stats via update service). Also breaks down most other statistical info from players on either franchise for that week.

All Reports

Here you have quick access to all the reports the 1995 FFL program has to offer, without having to go through multiple menus. You can also use this option to flag multiple reports to print at one time.

Change Week

This allows you to print reports for a different week of the season. Once selected, you will be prompted to enter the week for which you want to print reports.

h. Printer Options

This option displays the same options displayed when you first accessed the **Reports** module. This allows you to change your printing output.

i. Enter Newsletter

This module enables you to create a custom newsletter to be sent to the franchises. Once accessed, a blank screen is displayed allowing you type the text of the newsletter. Each week, the newsletter you typed is saved into a system file, so that if you need to reprint a week's reports, you can easily reprint the newsletter if necessary.

H. Screen Reports

This is a very handy tool for the Commissioner to quickly look up information on a specific franchise's performance while he is on the phone with the franchise owner. When you select this option, you are prompted to select whether you want information on all players or only drafted players. If you select the **All Players** option, you are presented with a player roster. This roster may be sorted by either position or name using the [F9] key. To view a summary of the player stats, press [F3], which displays the same Player Performance Screen seen under Draft Night. The statistics shown on the Player Performance Screen are year-to-date. To view only a player's scoring plays, press [F2]. To view only a player's statistical plays, press [F4].

When you select the **Drafted Players** option, you a presented with a Franchise Summary Window, displaying each franchise with both their weekly and year to date points, and their overall and division record. Move the highlight bar to a specific franchise and press [ENTER]. You will then see a weekly summary of the franchise's starting and non-starting points. Pressing [ENTER] on a desired week displays the players on that given franchise in that week, and their starting or non-starting points. Pressing [ENTER] on the desired player displays the Player Performance Screen seen under Draft Night. The statistics shown on the Player Performance Screen are only for that week. To view a summary of the player stats, press [F3], which displays the same Player Performance Screen seen under Draft Night. To view only a player's scoring plays, press [F2]. To view only a player's statistical plays, press [F4].

I. System Utilities

A. File Indexing

From time to time during the season, it may become necessary to re-align the master files the program uses. This simply helps the program to run more smoothly if errors occur. Errors may be caused by the repeated adding, editing, or deleting of information in those files.

File Indexing does not reset the FFL program to the beginning of the season, but rather it re-aligns certain index markers that allows the program to work with that particular data file.

The files to be concerned about are:

- Point file - the file Player Point Assignments utilizes.
- Player file - NFL Player Rosters (Because this file will become quite large, you might not want to reindex each week, unless you have a lot of time on your hands. It is a good idea to do this after a week of heavy trades, releases, injuries, or other roster moves).
- Play file - the master file of Weekly Scoring Plays and Updated NFL Rosters.
- Franchise file - this file stores all the owner information of each franchise in your league.
- Division file - this file stores your league's divisional set up.
- Roster Transaction file - this file keeps track of your league's roster moves throughout the season.

B. Reset Season

This module allows you to test your league's scoring system before the season starts. You can run a few updates and get several weeks into your test season and then have the program reset itself back to the beginning without losing any team information or their rosters. This feature will, however, clear out all scoring plays and points from the master play file so that all franchises are back to zero points in pre-season. You can even reset the entire program without saving the franchise info, where the program will start over in pre-season with no franchise information or rosters.

In all cases, any play types, point assignments or other rules you have set up will be saved. Only the franchise info, roster, plays and current week status are changed.

C. Backup / Restore

This module allows you to backup your files, as well as restore from a backup should you ever have the need.

a. Create Backup File

Select option [a] to create a backup file. The system will prompt you to select the drive you wish to back up to. It is strongly recommended that you backup to a different drive from your hard disk drive. You are also encouraged to keep multiple backup sets. NOTE: The module will name the file the same name each time. Using different media (diskettes, tapes, etc), and dating them with allow you to have multiple sets in case you need to perform a restore.

b. Restore Backup

Select option [b] to restore information from a backup. Insert the appropriate media (if applicable) and press [b] to begin the restoration process. This will overwrite all current data files with the data files contained on the backup. For example, if your backup is from Week 2, and it is Week 7 of the season, after restoring, your data will be restored only to Week 2, and you will need to re-enter the information for Weeks 3 through 7.

D. Move Lineups Forward

In previous versions of the FFL program, the only way to move your lineups forward was through the **Update Weekly Stats** module. The **Move Lineups Forward** module allows you to move your lineups forward manually each week. This allows you to move your lineups forward without having to run the update process again. Generally, this should only be used if you answered "**NO**" to "**Re-Set Current Week**" at the end of your update, but do not need to re-run your update for any other reason.

Subscribing To Weekly Scoring Updates

A. FSPI Bulletin Board Service Update

Through the FSPI Service, your league can subscribe to receive the weekly scoring updates via download for use with the Franchise Football League's Fantasy Football game. All you need for this service is any standard communication software, such as Procomm Plus, which is available from any major software dealer, and a modem. In some cases you may be able to purchase both as part of a special offer bundle. **To subscribe,** just **call 1-800-872-0335** and we will set up your account. You can then download an entire season's worth of stats each Monday and Tuesday to update your league in just minutes.

How Does It Work?

Once you have installed your communication software, follow these steps on how to log onto the FSPI Public Bulletin Board Service, how to obtain further information about the FFL and how to subscribe to the Weekly Scoring Update service:

BBS Phone Lines:	1-703-860-0008
Hours of Operation:	3pm - 12pm EST (21 hours/day)
	(Subject to change without notice)
Settings:	N - Parity
	8- Data Pits
	1- Stop Bits
Baud Rates:	1200 - 14,400

After your communication software has called our **Fantasy Sports BBS**, you will see the welcome screen followed by prompts asking you to enter your **first name, last name** and **your password**. Your first time on you can create whatever password you wish. Write it down so that you don't forget it because you will need to enter it every time you sign on to the **Fantasy Sports BBS**.

From here all the your choices will appear on the screen for you to choose from. Depending on your security level (what services you have paid for) you have access to download the FFL Weekly Statistics about three hours after the final Sunday and Monday games.

The first stat file will be available on Sunday, September 3, 1995.

For new members just signing on to the bulletin board system, you can read all about **FSPI**, the upcoming **1996** version of the **FBL**, and future programs in **Fantasy Hockey** and **Fantasy Basketball**. You will be able to download full working demo versions of these programs as well as other sports related information. All users will be able to download modifications or changes made throughout the 1995 NFL season.

After you have downloaded the **FFLSTAT.1** file, which is the compressed Week #1 stat file, you will need to copy it from the directory of your communication software to the \FFL95 directory of our program.

For example, if you are using **Procomm Plus** software to download stats, you might type at the C:\FFL95 prompt:

Copy C:\pcplus\FFLSTAT.1 [ENTER]

In this case, the **PCPLUS** is the standard directory name for the Procomm Plus software.

Now start the FFL program and when you enter the **Update Weekly Stats** section, the program will look for and import these stats. If all goes well with the update, you can delete the **FFLSTAT.1** file to save space.

B. PRODIGY Service Update

Through the PRODIGY Service, your league can subscribe to receive the weekly scoring updates via download for use with the Franchise Football League's Fantasy Football game. All you need for this service is your PRODIGY Service Start-Up Kit, which is available from any Sears location or any major software dealer, and a modem. In some cases you may be able to purchase both as part of a special offer bundle.

How Does It Work?

Once you have installed your PRODIGY Service software and logged on to the service, follow these steps to obtain further information about the FFL and how to subscribe to the Weekly Scoring Update service:

When the **PRODIGY Service HIGHLIGHTS** screen appears, type:

J [ENTER]

and then when the box appears, type:

FFL [ENTER]

Answer the questions under the ordering section. You will need a major credit card (VISA, Mastercard) to charge your enrollment fee covering the entire season of weekly downloads. You can also arrange to pay by check, but you will need to contact a Prodigy Custom Services Representative for more information. Each week of the NFL season, scoring updates and NFL game results will be available via PRODIGY Service download around three hours after the last Sunday and Monday's game (subject to statistics availability).

The first download will be available Sunday September 3, 1995.

Once the season has started, each week's stat file will be labeled and kept on-line all season long for you to download. Once you have selected the week you wish to download, the system will prompt you with the default FFL directory and that week's file name, so yo can change either the directory name or the disk drive (C: is the default drive setting) yc wish the file to be copied to.

For example, in week 4 of the season you may be asked if this is the path you wish to us when copying the stat file to your computer:

\FFL95\FFLSTAT.4

which would copy the week 4 scoring file to the FFL95 directory on your C: drive.

Once you have exited PRODIGY Service and are now at your **C:\FFL95** prompt sta your FFL program and **SET CURRENT WEEK** to Week 4 (in this case), and th program will look for and read the **"FFLSTAT.4"** stat file containing the scoring pla for that week. Now, you are ready to update your league's stats.

For more information on the PRODIGY service, you may call: 1-800-PRODIGY.

C. Microsoft Network

When the Microsoft Network Service main screen (MSN Central) appears, type:

[ALT] E G O **[ENTER]**

and then when the box appears, type:

FFL **[ENTER]**

Answer the questions under the ordering section. You will need a major credit card (VIS. Mastercard) to charge your enrollment fee covering the entire season of weekly dow loads. You can also arrange to pay by check, but you will need to contact a Microsc Network Customer Service Representative for more information. Each week of the NI season, scoring updates and NFL game results will be available via Microsoft Netwo download around three hours after the last Sunday and Monday's game (subject statistics availability).

The first download will be available Sunday September 3, 1995.

Once the season has started, each week's stat file will be labeled and kept on-line all seas long for you to download. Once you have selected the week you wish to download, tl system will prompt you with the default FFL directory and that week's file name, so y can change either the directory name or the disk drive (C: is the default drive setting) y wish the file to be copied to.

For example, in week 4 of the season you may be asked if this is the path you wish to u when copying the stat file to your computer:

\FFL95\FFLSTAT.4

which would copy the week 4 scoring file to the FFL95 directory on your C: drive.

Once you have exited Microsoft Network and are now at your **C:\FFL95** prompt start your FFL program and **SET CURRENT WEEK** to Week 4 (in this case), and the program will look for and read the **"FFLSTAT.4"** stat file containing the scoring plays for that week. Now, you are ready to update your league's stats.

D. CompuServe

When the CompuServe main screen appears, type:

[CTRL]-G **[ENTER]**

and then when the box appears, type:

SIFFL **[ENTER]**

answer the questions under the ordering section. You will need a major credit card (VISA, Mastercard) to charge your enrollment fee covering the entire season of weekly downloads. You can also arrange to pay by check, but you will need to contact a CompuServe Customer Service Representative for more information. Each week of the NFL season, scoring updates and NFL game results will be available via CompuServe download around three hours after the last Sunday and Monday's game (subject to statistics availability).

The first download will be available Sunday September 3, 1995.

Once the season has started, each week's stat file will be labeled and kept on-line all season long for you to download. Once you have selected the week you wish to download, the system will prompt you with the default CompuServe download directory (C:\CSERVE\DOWNLOAD) and that week's file name, so you can change either the directory name or the disk drive (C: is the default drive setting) you wish the file to be copied to.

For example, in week 4 of the season you may be asked if this is the path you wish to use when copying the stat file to your computer:

\CSERVE\DOWNLOAD\FFLSTAT.4

You will need to change the path in the download file dialog box to C:\FFL95, which will copy the week 4 scoring file to the FFL95 directory on your C: drive.

Once you have exited CompuServe and are now at your **C:\FFL95** prompt start your FFL program and **SET CURRENT WEEK** to Week 4 (in this case), and the program will look for and read the **"FFLSTAT.4"** stat file containing the scoring plays for that week. Now, you are ready to update your league's stats.

E. Facsimile Update Service

This method will provide you with the weekly FFL scoring plays and selected perform ance statistics. These plays and statistics will be sent via fax 4-5 hours following the Monday Night Football game so you will have them waiting for you first thing Tuesday morning. This will save you a lot of time not having to fumble through the Monday and Tuesday sports pages for the box scores. You will be able to easily enter all the week's scoring plays into the **Scoring Plays Entry Screen** (see **Update Weekly Scoring**) right from this fax.

F. Next/Second Day Diskette Update Service

Through this method, you will receive the weekly scoring updates on diskette on the **Wednesday** (for **Next Day** Service) or **Thursday** (for **Second Day** Service) following that Monday night's game.

Frequently Asked Questions

• **Can I run more than one league using this software?** Yes, all you will need to do is to install the software in a separate directory for each league you want to run. For example, the first league will be in C:\FFL95 and the second might be in C:\FFL952, etc.

• **Will this software run on a Macintosh computer?** Only if it set up to run DOS programs with a program such as SoftPC. However, we do not offer technical support for those who choose to run this program on a Macintosh.

• **Can I run this program from Windows?** No! This program is not meant to be run from *any* menu system. If you try to run it from Windows it will crash and you may lose important data that is unrecoverable, forcing you to start the entire season over.

• **Can I customize which reports my league wants to see each week?** Yes, from the Weekly Reports menu in Fantasy you can select all the reports you want to see every week to print at the same time.

• **How can I backup all my league's data each week?** From within the program, simply choose **System Utilities** from the main menu, then choose **Backup / Restore**.

Software Troubleshooting

> **Please read the following section on software troubleshooting. Although we do not anticipate any errors occurring in your FFL program, any problems you may experience probably will be minor and easily correctable.**

Here are the most commonly asked questions and their solutions:

- My program won't start or run properly when I start it from Windows or a menu? Th FFL program is not meant to be run from any menu system. If you try to run it fror Windows it will crash and you may lose important data that is unrecoverable, forcin you to start the entire season over. It also is not designed to run on a network.

- What do I do if I get error codes across the top of the screen in certain places of th program? First, re-index the Play file and/or Player file, then try the task again. Als make sure you are not running the FFL program from a menu program such as DOS Shell or Windows. (*Consult your menu software manual* on how to exit the menu the DOS prompt.) Also check your CONFIG.SYS file, located in the main roc directory on your computer's hard drive, to make sure these settings appear:

    Files=50

    Buffers=30

If you need to make changes to this file, *consult your computer's operating system manua* on how to make these modifications. You can also use a Boot-Diskette to bypass thes menus without making major changes to your software.

- How do I set up a Boot-Disk for my computer? First place a blank diskette in the *A* drive of your system and type from the DOS prompt of C:\

    Format a:/s **[ENTER]**

The computer will format the diskette and copy the file necessary to enable your compute to start up from the diskette, instead of the hard disk drive. Press **[ENTER]** when you ar asked to label the diskette, and type **N** for no when asked if you would like to form another. Now, again type from the DOS prompt of C:\

    Copy Con A:\Config.sys **[ENTER]**

You will then see a blank line after you press **[ENTER]**, so now type:

    Files=50 **[ENTER]**

Buffers=30 **[ENTER]**

^Z **[ENTER]**
(hold **[CTRL]** key and **Z** down at the same time.)

You should now see the message of "1 File(s) copied" and then the C:\ prompt again. Now leave the diskette in the disk drive and hold the **[CTRL][ALT]** and **[DEL]** keys down at the same time to re-boot your computer. You should see the computer access the A:\ drive with the diskette in it, then the DOS prompt of A:\ appear on the screen when it is done. Now type:

C:\ **[ENTER]** (or the drive in which the FFL game is located)

CD\FFL95 **[ENTER]**

Now try the FFL program again.

• I get "out of memory" errors while running the FFL program! Make sure you are not running any memory resident programs at the same time as the FFL program, such as menus, or other TSR (terminate-stay-resident) programs. You should be able to bypass this error if you use the boot-disk discussed earlier. If you are using DOS 5.0 or higher consult your DOS manual on how to load your operating system and other device drivers into upper memory.

• None of the reports will print out! Make sure all power and cable connections between the printer and the computer are tightly plugged in. Turn the printer off then back on, and make sure you see the "Ready" or "On-line" light activate on the front of your printer showing that it is ready. Now, try to print again.

• When I print reports I either get just the heading and nothing else, double-spaced information, or garbage? You need to make sure that your printer is able to and set up for Epson emulation. Please consult your printer's Owners Manual on how to check this.

• How can I conserve space from each week after I have finished updating that weeks scores? After you have updated successfully for a given week and are satisfied with the results you can copy that weeks FFLSTAT.# file to a floppy disk for backup and delete it from your hard drive. This can save as much as 70K of space per week.

Also, you can reduce more space each week by deleting all the .PRN and .RPT files that re created when you generate/view any reports.

This can be done by typing at the C:\FFL95 prompt:

Erase *.prn **[ENTER]**

Erase *.rpt **[ENTER]**

Information Hotlines

The **FFL Technical Support Lines** are open from **9am - 9pm (EST) Monday throug** **Friday**. If you need support with the latest version of the program, be sure you have fir looked through the previous section on **Software Troubleshooting** to see if there is solution listed for your situation. If you can still not resolve your situation, give us a cal

You **must** have these few items of information so we may help you correct any problen

- Brand name or model of the computer you are using (Compaq, IBM, NEC, Tand etc.).

- The processor and speed of your computer (486SX, 16mhz, etc.).

- Amount of RAM your computer has (640K, 2MB, etc.).

- Operating system version number (DOS 5.0, DOS 3.3, etc.).

- Type of disk drive you are using (3.5" High Density 1.44 or Double-Sided Double Density 720K).

- Make and model of printer (HP LaserJet IIP, NEC P5200 dot matrix, etc.).

- What steps you were performing right before the error occurred.

- The contents of your CONFIG.SYS file.

Fantasy Football
Technical Support Line:
1-703-391-0395
Monday-Friday (9 am - 9 pm EST)

Technical Support Bulletin Board: Leave a message for the System Operator (SysOp) c the FSPI Bulletin Board. Be sure to include any and all important information so we ca respond to your problem promptly. You may also leave us e-mail on the Prodigy Servic Write to us by typing

[JUMP]:sports bb and selecting **Football-Fantasy**
or directly to our **Technical Support** ID# **GDXS68F**.

Write to: Franchise Football League
                 Technical Support Department
                 P.O. Box 2698
                 Reston, VA 22091

FFL Order Processing Department
1-800-872-0335

Write to: Fantasy Sports Properties, Inc.
                Order Processing Department
                P.O. Box 2698
                Reston, VA 22091

```
+------------------------------------------------------------+
|                                                            |
|                    Fantasy Football                        |
|                Technical Support Line:                     |
|                    1-703-391-0395                          |
|            Monday-Friday (9 am - 9 pm EST)                  |
|                                                            |
+------------------------------------------------------------+
```

APPENDIX A
1995 NFL SCHEDULE

Week 1
Cincinnati Bengals at Indianapolis Colts
Cleveland Browns at New England Patriots
Houston Oilers at Jacksonville Jaguars
Carolina Panthers at Atlanta Falcons
San Francisco 49ers at New Orleans Saints
Tampa Bay Buccaneers at Philadelphia Eagles
St.Louis Rams at Green Bay Packers
Detroit Lions at Pittsburgh Steelers
New York Jets at Miami Dolphins
San Diego Chargers at Los Angeles Raiders
Kansas City Chiefs at Seattle Seahawks
Arizona Cardinals at Washington Redskins
Minnesota Vikings at Chicago Bears
Buffalo Bills at Denver Broncos, SUN
Dallas Cowboys at New York Giants, MON

Week 2
Miami Dolphins at New England Patriots
Los Angeles Raiders at Washington Redskins
Pittsburgh Steelers at Houston Oilers
New Orleans Saints at St.Louis Rams
Detroit Lions at Minnesota Vikings
Carolina Panthers at Buffalo Bills
New York Giants at Kansas City Chiefs
Tampa Bay Buccaneers at Cleveland Browns
Denver Broncos at Dallas Cowboys
Indianapolis Colts at New York Jets
Seattle Seahawks at San Diego Chargers
Jacksonville Jaguars at Cincinnati Bengals
Atlanta Falcons at San Francisco 49ers
Philadelphia Eagles at Arizona Cardinals, SUN
Green Bay Packers at Chicago Bears, MON

Week 3
San Diego Chargers at Philadelphia Eagles
Indianapolis Colts at Buffalo Bills
Los Angeles Raiders at Kansas City Chiefs
Cleveland Browns at Houston Oilers
St.Louis Rams at Carolina Panthers
Atlanta Falcons at New Orleans Saints
Arizona Cardinals at Detroit Lions
New York Giants at Green Bay Packers

New England Patriots at San Francisco 49ers
Cincinnati Bengals at Seattle Seahawks
Jacksonville Jaguars at New York Jets
Washington Redskins at Denver Broncos
Chicago Bears at Tampa Bay Buccaneers
Dallas Cowboys at Minnesota Vikings, SUN
Pittsburgh Steelers at Miami Dolphins, MON

Week 4
Chicago Bears at St.Louis Rams
New Orleans Saints at New York Giants
Washington Redskins at Tampa Bay Buccan
Minnesota Vikings at Pittsburgh Steelers
New York Jets at Atlanta Falcons
Denver Broncos at San Diego Chargers
Houston Oilers at Cincinnati Bengals
Kansas City Chiefs at Cleveland Browns
Arizona Cardinals at Dallas Cowboys
Philadelphia Eagles at Los Angeles Raiders
Green Bay Packers at Jacksonville Jaguars,
San Francisco 49ers at Detroit Lions, MON
Byes: Buffalo Bills, Carolina Panthers, Indi
Colts, Miami Dolphins, New England Patri
Seattle Seahawks

Week 5
New England Patriots at Atlanta Falcons
Miami Dolphins at Cincinnati Bengals
Tampa Bay Buccaneers at Carolina Panther
Philadelphia Eagles at New Orleans Saints
Dallas Cowboys at Washington Redskins
St.Louis Rams at Indianapolis Colts
Kansas City Chiefs at Arizona Cardinals
Jacksonville Jaguars at Houston Oilers
Denver Broncos at Seattle Seahawks
San Diego Chargers at Pittsburgh Steelers
New York Giants at San Francisco 49ers
Los Angeles Raiders at New York Jets, SUN
Buffalo Bills at Cleveland Browns, MON
Byes: Chicago Bears, Detroit Lions, Green
Packers, Minnesota Vikings

eek 6
ncinnati Bengals at Tampa Bay Buccaneers
:w York Jets at Buffalo Bills
ttsburgh Steelers at Jacksonville Jaguars
·een Bay Packers at Dallas Cowboys
ashington Redskins at Philadelphia Eagles
irolina Panthers at Chicago Bears
)uston Oilers at Minnesota Vikings
:veland Browns at Detroit Lions
dianapolis Colts at Miami Dolphins
attle Seahawks at Los Angeles Raiders
izona Cardinals at New York Giants
nver Broncos at New England Patriots, SUN
n Diego Chargers at Kansas City Chiefs, MON
es: Atlanta Falcons, New Orleans Saints
Louis Rams, San Francisco 49ers

:ek 7
anta Falcons at St.Louis Rams, THUR
ittle Seahawks at Buffalo Bills
w England Patriots at Kansas City Chiefs
ladelphia Eagles at New York Giants
troit Lions at Green Bay Packers
nnesota Vikings at Tampa Bay Buccaneers
i Francisco 49ers at Indianapolis Colts
cago Bears at Jacksonville Jaguars
imi Dolphins at New Orleans Saints
w York Jets at Carolina Panthers
shington Redskins at Arizona Cardinals
las Cowboys at San Diego Chargers
 Angeles Raiders at Denver Broncos, MON

ek 8
cinnati Bengals at Pittsburgh Steelers, THUR
iston Oilers at Chicago Bears
mi Dolphins at New York Jets
sonville Jaguars at Cleveland Browns
v Orleans Saints at Carolina Panthers
toit Lions at Washington Redskins
nnesota Vikings at Green Bay Packers
inta Falcons at Tampa Bay Buccaneers
sas City Chiefs at Denver Broncos
anapolis Colts at Los Angeles Raiders
 Diego Chargers at Seattle Seahawks
 Francisco 49ers at St.Louis Rams
falo Bills at New England Patriots, MON

Byes: Arizona Cardinals, Dallas Cowboys, New York
Giants, Philadelphia Eagles

Week 9
Jacksonville Jaguars at Pittsburgh Steelers
New York Jets at Indianapolis Colts
Cleveland Browns at Cincinnati Bengals
Dallas Cowboys at Atlanta Falcons
St.Louis Rams at Philadelphia Eagles
Green Bay Packers at Detroit Lions
Carolina Panthers at New England Patriots
Buffalo Bills at Miami Dolphins
Seattle Seahawks at Arizona Cardinals
New Orleans Saints at San Francisco 49ers
Tampa Bay Buccaneers at Houston Oilers
New York Giants at Washington Redskins, SUN
Chicago Bears at Minnesota Vikings, MON
Byes: Denver Broncos, Kansas City Chiefs,
Los Angeles Raiders, San Diego Chargers

Week 10
Buffalo Bills at Indianapolis Colts
New England Patriots at New York Jets
Houston Oilers at Cleveland Browns
Detroit Lions at Atlanta Falcons
St.Louis Rams at New Orleans Saints
Green Bay Packers at Minnesota Vikings
Washington Redskins at Kansas City Chiefs
Pittsburgh Steelers at Chicago Bears
Los Angeles Raiders at Cincinnati Bengals
Carolina Panthers at San Francisco 49ers
Arizona Cardinals at Denver Broncos
New York Giants at Seattle Seahawks
Miami Dolphins at San Diego Chargers, SUN
Philadelphia Eagles at Dallas Cowboys, MON
Byes: Jacksonville Jaguars, Tampa Bay Buccaneers

Week 11
Indianapolis Colts at New Orleans Saints
Los Angeles Raiders at New York Giants
Atlanta Falcons at Buffalo Bills
New England Patriots at Miami Dolphins
Cincinnati Bengals at Houston Oilers
Seattle Seahawks at Jacksonville Jaguars
Carolina Panthers at St.Louis Rams
Tampa Bay Buccaneers at Detroit Lions

Chicago Bears at Green Bay Packers
Kansas City Chiefs at San Diego Chargers
San Francisco 49ers at Dallas Cowboys
Minnesota Vikings at Arizona Cardinals
Denver Broncos at Philadelphia Eagles, SUN
Cleveland Browns at Pittsburgh Steelers, MON
Byes: New York Jets, Washington Redskins

Week 12
Seattle Seahawks at Washington Redskins
Jacksonville Jaguars at Tampa Bay Buccaneers
Indianapolis Colts at New England Patriots
Pittsburgh Steelers at Cincinnati Bengals
St.Louis Rams at Atlanta Falcons
Arizona Cardinals at Carolina Panthers
New York Giants at Philadelphia Eagles
Detroit Lions at Chicago Bears
Green Bay Packers at Cleveland Browns
San Diego Chargers at Denver Broncos
Buffalo Bills at New York Jets
Dallas Cowboys at Los Angeles Raiders
New Orleans Saints at Minnesota Vikings
Houston Oilers at Kansas City Chiefs, SUN
San Francisco 49ers at Miami Dolphins, MON

Week 13
Minnesota Vikings at Detroit Lions, THUR
Kansas City Chiefs at Dallas Cowboys, THUR
Miami Dolphins at Indianapolis Colts
New England Patriots at Buffalo Bills
Cincinnati Bengals at Jacksonville Jaguars
Chicago Bears at New York Giants
Philadelphia Eagles at Washington Redskins
Tampa Bay Buccaneers at Green Bay Packers
Denver Broncos at Houston Oilers
New York Jets at Seattle Seahawks
Pittsburgh Steelers at Cleveland Browns
St.Louis Rams at San Francisco 49ers
Atlanta Falcons at Arizona Cardinals
Carolina Panthers at New Orleans Saints, SUN
Los Angeles Raiders at San Diego Chargers, MON

Week 14
New York Giants at Arizona Cardinals, THUR
Indianapolis Colts at Carolina Panthers
Cincinnati Bengals at Green Bay Packers

Houston Oilers at Pittsburgh Steelers
Atlanta Falcons at Miami Dolphins
New Orleans Saints at New England Patriots
St.Louis Rams at New York Jets
Tampa Bay Buccaneers at Minnesota Vikings
Jacksonville Jaguars at Denver Broncos
Kansas City Chiefs at Los Angeles Raiders
Cleveland Browns at San Diego Chargers
Washington Redskins at Dallas Cowboys
Philadelphia Eagles at Seattle Seahawks
Buffalo Bills at San Francisco 49ers, SUN
Chicago Bears at Detroit Lions, MON

Week 15
Cleveland Browns at Minnesota Vikings, SAT
Arizona Cardinals at San Diego Chargers, SAT
Buffalo Bills at St.Louis Rams
New York Jets at New England Patriots
Indianapolis Colts at Jacksonville Jaguars
New Orleans Saints at Atlanta Falcons
San Francisco 49ers at Carolina Panthers
Dallas Cowboys at Philadelphia Eagles
Chicago Bears at Cincinnati Bengals
Detroit Lions at Houston Oilers
Seattle Seahawks at Denver Broncos
Pittsburgh Steelers at Los Angeles Raiders
Washington Redskins at New York Giants
Green Bay Packers at Tampa Bay Buccaneers,
Kansas City Chiefs at Miami Dolphins, MON

Week 16
New England Patriots at Pittsburgh Steelers, SA
Green Bay Packers at New Orleans Saints, SAT
Jacksonville Jaguars at Detroit Lions
Miami Dolphins at Buffalo Bills
Cincinnati Bengals at Cleveland Browns
New York Jets at Houston Oilers
Atlanta Falcons at Carolina Panthers
Arizona Cardinals at Philadelphia Eagles
Tampa Bay Buccaneers at Chicago Bears
Washington Redskins at St.Louis Rams
Denver Broncos at Kansas City Chiefs
San Diego Chargers at Indianapolis Colts
New York Giants at Dallas Cowboys
Los Angeles Raiders at Seattle Seahawks, SUN
Minnesota Vikings at San Francisco 49ers, MO

Week 17

San Diego Chargers at New York Giants, SAT
Detroit Lions at Tampa Bay Buccaneers, SAT
New England Patriots at Indianapolis Colts, SAT
Pittsburgh Steelers at Green Bay Packers
Houston Oilers at Buffalo Bills
Seattle Seahawks at Kansas City Chiefs
Cleveland Browns at Jacksonville Jaguars
San Francisco 49ers at Atlanta Falcons
Philadelphia Eagles at Chicago Bears
New Orleans Saints at New York Jets
Minnesota Vikings at Cincinnati Bengals
Carolina Panthers at Washington Redskins
Denver Broncos at Los Angeles Raiders
Miami Dolphins at St.Louis Rams, SUN
Dallas Cowboys at Arizona Cardinals, MON

FRANCHISE FOOTBALL LEAGUE'S - 1994 FINAL FANTASY RANKINGS

#	Player	Pos	Team	Total Fantasy Points	Basic - Distance Pts.	Perform. Scoring Pts.	Passing '1-9	Passing '10-39	Passing '40+	Rushing '1-9	Rushing '10-39	Rushing '40+	Receiving '1-9	Receiving '10-39	Receiving '40+	FG '10-39	FG '40-49	FG '50+	PATs	Def.-ST TDs	Total TDs
1	YOUNG, Steve	QB	San Francisco	427	358	69	20	10	5	7											42
2	MARINO, Dan	QB	Miami	348	267	81	11	15	4	1											31
3	FAVRE, Brett	QB	Green Bay	346	299	47	11	21	1	1	1										35
4	BLEDSOE, Drew	QB	New England	272	189	83	13	11	1												25
5	SANDERS, Barry	RB	Detroit	236	72	164				2	4	1	1								8
6	MOON, Warren	QB	Minnesota	232	159	73	7	7	4												18
7	SMITH, Emmitt	RB	Dallas	231	141	90				20	1		1								22
8	EVERETT, Jim	QB	New Orleans	223	187	36	7	13	2												22
9	ELWAY, John	QB	Denver	219	202	17	3	10	3	3	1										20
10	GEORGE, Jeff	QB	Atlanta	216	191	25	10	9	4												23
11	RICE, Jerry	WR	San Francisco	211	140	71					2		7	4	2						15
12	KELLY, Jim	QB	Buffalo	201	204	-3	6	14	2		1										23
13	SHARPE, Sterling	WR	Green Bay	197	138	59							8	10							18
14	WARREN, Chris	RB	Seattle	195	101	94				4	5		1	1							11
15	WATTERS, Ricky	RB	San Francisco	192	123	69				5	1	1	2	2							11
16	CUNNINGHAM, Randall	QB	Philadelphia	189	186	3	4	8	4	2	1										19
17	HOSTETLER, Jeff	QB	LA Raiders	174	198	-24	6	10	4	2											22
18	FAULK, Marshall	RB	Indianapolis	166	102	64				8	2	1			1						12
19	MONTANA, Joe	QB	Kansas City	161	128	33	8	6	2												16
20	SAN DIEGO	DT	San Diego	160	84	76														7	7
21	CARNEY, John	K	San Diego	159	159											27	5	2	33		
22	ERICKSON, Craig	QB	Tampa Bay	159	166	-7	3	8	5	1											17
23	REVEIZ, Fuad	K	Minnesota	155	155											25	8	1	30		
24	MATHIS, Terance	WR	Atlanta	152	88	64							7	2	2						11
25	PICKENS, Carl	WR	Cincinnati	151	87	64							6	3	2						11
26	FRYAR, Irving	WR	Miami	150	70	80							2	2	3						7
27	HUMPHRIES, Stan	QB	San Diego	150	152	-2	7	4	6												17
28	TESTAVERDE, Vinny	QB	Cleveland	149	165	-16	4	9	3	2											18
29	SAN FRANCISCO	DT	San Francisco	145	72	73														6	6
30	BLAKE, Jeff	QB	Cincinnati	144	139	5	5	5	4	1											15
31	MINNESOTA	DT	Minnesota	144	75	69														7	7
32	HOARD, Leroy	RB	Cleveland	142	105	37				4	1		1	2	1						9
33	ESIASON, Boomer	QB	NY Jets	141	139	2	7	9	1												17
34	MEANS, Natrone	RB	San Diego	141	81	60				9	3										12
35	BENNETT, Edgar	RB	Green Bay	140	93	47				4	1		2	2							9
36	ELAM, Jason	K	Denver	140	140											22	7	1	29		
37	PELFREY, Doug	K	Cincinnati	140	140											17	9	2	24		
38	INDIANAPOLIS	DT	Indianapolis	138	78	60														7	7
39	ANDERSEN, Morten	K	New Orleans	134	134											19	9	2	32		
40	CHRISTIE, Steve	K	Buffalo	134	134											17	5	2	38		

FRANCHISE FOOTBALL LEAGUE'S - 1994 FINAL FANTASY RANKINGS

#	Player	Pos	Team	Total Fantasy Points	Basic - Distance Pts.	Perform. Scoring Pts.	Passing '1-9	Passing '10-39	Passing '40+	Rushing '1-9	Rushing '10-39	Rushing '40+	Receiving '1-9	Receiving '10-39	Receiving '40+	Field Goals '10-39	Field Goals '40-49	Field Goals '50+	PATs	Def.-ST ST TDs	Total TDs
41	DALLAS	DT		134	57	77														5	5
42	REED, Andre	WR	Buffalo	134	72	62							1	6							8
43	DETROIT	DT		132	82	50														7	7
44	WASHINGTON	DT		131	79	52														7	7
45	ELLARD, Henry	WR	Washington	130	57	73							2	1	3						6
46	STOYANOVICH, Pete	K	Miami	130	130											15	8	1	35		
47	THOMAS, Thurman	RB	Buffalo	128	75	53				4	3		2								9
48	BROWN, Tim	WR	LA Raiders	127	81	46							2	5	2						9
49	JAEGER, Jeff	K	LA Raiders	127	127											12	8		31		
50	BONIOL, Chris	K	Dallas	126	126											16	6		48		
51	STOVER, Matt	K	Cleveland	126	126											18	8		32		
52	ANDERSON, Gary a	K	Pittsburgh	125	125											16	7	1	32		
53	BAHR, Matt	K	New England	125	125											23	4		36		
54	CARTER, Cris	WR	Minnesota	124	61	63							4	1	2						7
55	CLEVELAND	DT		124	54	70														5	5
56	MOORE, Herman	WR	Detroit	124	84	40							6	4	1						11
57	NEW ORLEANS	DT		124	57	67														5	5
58	IRVIN, Michael	WR	Dallas	123	54	69							1	4	1						6
59	BYARS, Keith	RB	Miami	122	90	32				2			2	3							7
60	COATES, Ben	TE	New England	114	54	60							4	2	1						7
61	KRIEG, Dave	QB	Detroit	114	112	2	7	6	1												14
62	PHILADELPHIA	DT		114	37	77														3	3
63	BRIEN, Doug	K	San Francisco	113	113											11	4		60		
64	AIKMAN, Troy	QB	Dallas	112	120	-8	4	8	1	1											14
65	BUTLER, Kevin	K	Chicago	111	111											14	5		24		
66	ELLIOTT, Lin	K	Kansas City	111	111											22	3		30		
67	HARPER, Alvin	WR	Dallas	111	78	33								6	2						8
68	LA RAIDERS	DT		111	48	63														5	5
69	JOHNSON, Norm	K	Atlanta	110	110											16	4	1	32		
70	RISON, Andre	WR	Atlanta	110	68	42							3	4	1						8
71	BIASUCCI, Dean	K	Indianapolis	109	109											9	5	2	37		
72	JACKE, Chris	K	Green Bay	109	109											16	2	1	41		
73	KANSAS CITY	DT		109	32	77						1									
74	PITTSBURGH	DT		109	24	85															
75	MILLER, Chris	QB	LA Rams	108	135	-27	5	9	2	4											16
76	WALKER, Herschel	RB	Philadelphia	108	84	24								2							8
77	LOHMILLER, Chip	K	Washington	107	107											14	5	1	30		
78	MARTIN, Tony	WR	San Diego	107	66	41							2	2	1					2	7
79	METCALF, Eric	RB	Cleveland	107	99	8							2	2						3	7
80	MILLER, Anthony	WR	Denver	107	50	57								4	1					2	5

#	Player	Pos	Team	Total Fantasy Points	Basic-Distance Pts	Perform. Scoring Pts	Passing '1-9	Passing '10-39	Passing '40+	Rushing '1-9	Rushing '10-39	Rushing '40+	Receiving '1-9	Receiving '10-39	Receiving '40+	FG '10-39	FG '40-49	FG '50+	PATs	Def.-ST TDs	Total TDs
81	HUSTED, Michael	K	Tampa Bay	104	104											18	4	1	20		
82	KASAY, John	K	Seattle	104	104											13	6	1	25		
83	HANSON, Jason	K	Detroit	103	103											13	5		39		
84	CENTERS, Larry	RB	Arizona	102	63	39				4	1		1	1							7
85	BARNETT, Fred	WR	Philadelphia	101	57	44								1	4						5
86	GREEN BAY	DT		101	33	68														3	3
87	MURRAY, Eddie	K	Philadelphia	100	100											19	2		33		
88	NY JETS	DT		100	33	67														3	3
89	SEATTLE	DT		99	37	62														3	3
90	LOWERY, Nick	K	NY Jets	98	98											14	6		26		
91	ALLEN, Terry	RB	Minnesota	97	56	41				6	2										8
92	NEW ENGLAND	DT		97	18	79														2	2
93	DAVIS, Greg	K	Arizona	96	96											13	6	1	17		
94	ODONNELL, Neil	QB	Pittsburgh	96	123	-27	4	7	2	1											14
95	ATLANTA	DT		95	30	65														3	3
96	LA RAMS	DT		95	49	46														4	4
97	PARMALEE, Bernie	RB	Miami	95	59	36				4	1	1	1								7
98	RHETT, Errict	RB	Tampa Bay	94	44	50				7											7
99	THOMPSON, Leroy	RB	New England	91	78	13				2			4	1							7
100	NY GIANTS	DT		90	32	58														2	2
101	SCOTT, Darnay	WR	Cincinnati	89	54	35								2	3						5
102	FRIESZ, John	QB	Washington	88	86	2	4	4	2												10
103	WILLIAMS, Harvey	RB	LA Raiders	88	68	20				4			2	1							7
104	ARIZONA	DT		87	16	71														1	1
105	DEL GRECO, Al	K	Houston	87	87											8	7	1	18		
106	HAMPTON, Rodney	RB	NY Giants	87	41	46				5	1										6
107	RUSSELL, Leonard	RB	Denver	87	63	24				6	3										9
108	SHULER, Heath	QB	Washington	86	98	-12	3	2	5												10
109	ZENDEJAS, Tony	K	LA Rams	84	84											17	1		28		
110	WILSON, Charles	WR	Tampa Bay	83	66	17								2	4						6
111	HOUSTON	DT		82	25	57														2	2
112	BETTIS, Jerome	RB	LA Rams	81	34	47				3			1								4
113	MOORE, Rob	WR	NY Jets	81	55	26							2	3	1						6
114	MILBURN, Glyn	RB	Denver	80	57	23					1		1	2	3						6
115	ANDERSON, Willie	WR	LA Rams	79	54	25							1	2	1						4
116	MEGGETT, David	RB	NY Giants	79	69	10				3	1			2							6
117	GRAHAM, Jeff	WR	Chicago	78	50	28							1	2	1						7
118	KRAMER, Erik	QB	Chicago	78	76	2	2	4	2												8
119	FOSTER, Barry	RB	Pittsburgh	74	36	38				3	2										5
120	SHERRARD, Mike	WR	NY Giants	74	54	20							2	2	2						6

FRANCHISE FOOTBALL LEAGUE'S - 1994 FINAL FANTASY RANKINGS

	Player	Pos	Team	Total Fantasy Points	Basic-Distance Pts	Perform. Scoring Pts	Passing '1-9	Passing '10-39	Passing '40+	Rushing '1-9	Rushing '10-39	Rushing '40+	Receiving '1-9	Receiving '10-39	Receiving '40+	FG '10-39	FG '40-49	FG '50+	PATs	Def.-ST TDs	Total TDs
121	HOWARD, Desmond	WR	Washington	73	50	23								4	1						5
122	MIAMI	DT	Minnesota	73	12	61														1	1
123	REED, Jake	WR	Minnesota	73	36	37								4							4
124	MORRIS, Byron	RB	Pittsburgh	72	45	27				6	1										7
125	BROOKS, Robert	WR	Green Bay	70	60	10								4						2	6
126	JONES, Brent	TE	San Francisco	70	71	-1							5	3	1						9
127	DAVIS, Willie	WR	Kansas City	69	50	19							1	2	2						5
128	CHANDLER, Chris	QB	LA Rams	68	78	-10	1	4	2	1											8
129	JACKSON, Keith	TE	Miami	68	59	9							2	5							7
130	MAJKOWSKI, Don	QB	Indianapolis	68	87	-19	1	5		3											9
131	ISMAIL, Qadry	WR	Minnesota	67	48	19							1	2	2						5
132	ALLEN, Marcus	RB	Kansas City	66	47	19				6	1										7
133	TILLMAN, Lewis	RB	Chicago	66	45	21				6	1										7
134	CINCINNATI	DT		65	16	49														1	1
135	JEFFIRES, Haywood	WR	Houston	64	54	10							2	4							6
136	SMALL, Torrance	WR	New Orleans	64	44	20							2	2	1						5
137	WALSH, Steve	QB	Chicago	64	87	-23	5	5		1											11
138	BROWN, Dave	QB	NY Giants	63	120	-57	6	4	2	2											14
139	CHICAGO	DT		63	12	51														1	1
140	JOHNSON, Johnny	RB	NY Jets	63	42	21				3			2								5
141	BUFFALO	DT		62	10	52														1	1
142	HARMON, Ronnie	RB	San Diego	62	35	27					1			1							2
143	INGRAM, Mark	WR	Miami	62	51	11							2	3	1						6
144	MITCHELL, Scott	QB	Detroit	61	87	-26	5	5		1											11
145	ALEXANDER, Derrick	WR	Cleveland	60	20	40							1		1						2
146	BONO, Steve	QB	Kansas City	60	41	19		3	1												4
147	BRISBY, Vincent	WR	New England	60	39	21							2	3							5
148	BIRDEN, J.J.	WR	Kansas City	58	35	23							1	3							4
149	HARBAUGH, Jim	QB	Indianapolis	57	75	-18	3	5	1												9
150	MITCHELL, Brian	RB	Washington	57	50	7							1							2	3
151	TIMPSON, Michael	WR	New England	57	24	33							1	2							3
152	TREADWELL, David	K	NY Giants	57	57	-1										10	1		22		
153	CARRIER, Mark	WR	Cleveland	56	57	-1							2	3	1						6
154	SEAY, Mark	WR	San Diego	56	45	11							4	1	1						6
155	BATES, Mario	RB	New Orleans	55	42	13				4	2										6
156	CONWAY, Curtis	WR	Chicago	54	41	13		1						1	1						3
157	HAYNES, Michael	WR	New Orleans	54	45	9							1	3	1						5
158	WHITE, Lorenzo	RB	Houston	54	33	21				2	1		1								4
159	WILLIAMS, John L.	RB	Pittsburgh	54	36	18				1			1	1							3
160	TAMPA BAY	DT		53	12	41														1	1

FRANCHISE FOOTBALL LEAGUE'S - 1994 FINAL FANTASY RANKINGS

#	Player	Pos	Team	Total Fantasy Points	Basic-Distance Pts.	Perform. Scoring Pts.	Pass 1-9	Pass 10-39	Pass 40+	Rush 1-9	Rush 10-39	Rush 40+	Rec 1-9	Rec 10-39	Rec 40+	FG 10-39	FG 40-49	FG 50+	PATs	Def.-ST TDs	Total TDs
161	EMANUEL, Bert	WR	Atlanta	52	39	13								3	1						4
162	BUTTS, Marion	RB	New England	51	51					7	1										8
163	DAWKINS, Sean	WR	Indianapolis	51	42	9							1	4							5
164	MOORE, Ron	RB	Arizona	51	41	10				3	1		1								5
165	TOMCZAK, Mike	QB	Pittsburgh	51	41	10		3													4
166	TURNER, Kevin	RB	New England	51	36	15				1			1	1							3
167	HUGHES, Tyrone	DB	New Orleans	50	48	2														4	4
168	DALUISO, Brad	K	NY Giants	49	49											8	2	1	5		
169	DENVER	DT	Denver	49	49																
170	HEYWARD, Craig	RB	Atlanta	49	54	-5				7			1								8
171	MORGAN, Anthony	WR	Green Bay	49	39	10								3	1						4
172	PERRIMAN, Brett	WR	Detroit	48	37	11							1	3							4
173	SHARPE, Shannon	TE	Denver	48	37	11							2	1	1						4
174	WILLIAMS, Calvin	WR	Philadelphia	48	24	24							1	2							3
175	BEEBE, Don	WR	Buffalo	45	36	9							1	2	1						4
176	DRAYTON, Troy	TE	LA Rams	45	45								3	3							6
177	ERVINS, Ricky	RB	Washington	45	36	9				3				1							4
178	JOHNSON, Charles	WR	Pittsburgh	45	30	15							2	1							3
179	KINCHEN, Todd	WR	LA Rams	45	48	-3						1	1	2							4
180	MIRER, Rick	QB	Seattle	45	83	-38	7	3	1												11
181	BROWN, Derek	RB	New Orleans	44	36	8				3				1							4
182	TURNER, Floyd	WR	Indianapolis	44	45	-1							3	3							6
183	COBB, Reggie	RB	Green Bay	43	39	4				2	1			1							4
184	GARNER, Charlie	RB	Philadelphia	42	21	21				2	1										3
185	METZELAARS, Pete	TE	Buffalo	42	42								1	4							5
186	MITCHELL, Johnny	TE	NY Jets	42	30	12							2	2							4
187	SANDERS, Deion	DB	Atlanta	42	36	6														3	3
188	TAYLOR, John	WR	San Francisco	42	33	9							4	1							5
189	THIGPEN, Yancey	WR	Pittsburgh	42	42								2	2							4
190	VAUGHN, Jon	RB	Seattle	41	44	-3				1			1		2						4
191	BLADES, Brian	WR	Seattle	40	26	14							4								4
192	BUCHANAN, Ray	DB	Indianapolis	40	30	10														3	3
193	EARLY, Quinn	WR	New Orleans	40	30	10							2	2							4
194	FLOYD, William	RB	San Francisco	39	39					5	1										6
195	ISMAIL, Raghib	WR	LA Raiders	39	39								2	3							5
196	JOHNSTON, Daryl	RB	Dallas	39	36	3				2			2								4
197	JOSEPH, James	RB	Philadelphia	39	39						1		2								3
198	PROEHL, Ricky	WR	Arizona	39	39								3	1							3
199	MCDANIEL, Terry	DB	LA Raiders	37	30	7								1	1					3	5
200	MONK, Art	WR	NY Jets	37	27	10								3							3

FRANCHISE FOOTBALL LEAGUE'S - 1994 FINAL FANTASY RANKINGS

#	Player	Pos	Team	Total Fantasy Points	Basic-Distance Pts.	Perform. Scoring Pts.	Passing '1-9	Passing '10-39	Passing '40+	Rushing '1-9	Rushing '10-39	Rushing '40+	Receiving '1-9	Receiving '10-39	Receiving '40+	Field Goals '10-39	Field Goals '40-49	Field Goals '50+	PATs	Def.-ST TDs	Total TDs
201	PARKER, Anthony	DB	Minnesota	37	33	4	2													3	3
202	RICHARDSON, Bucky	QB	Houston	37	67	-30		3	1	1											7
203	ANDERS, Kimble	RB	Kansas City	36	24	12				2			1								3
204	BROWN, Gary	RB	Houston	36	42	-6				4											5
205	HAWKINS, Courtney	WR	Tampa Bay	36	36	12							3	1							5
206	LEE, Amp	RB	Minnesota	36	24	12							2	2							2
207	SLAUGHTER, Webster	WR	Houston	36	15	21							1	1							2
208	WASHINGTON, Dewayne	DB	Minnesota	36	33	3														3	3
209	GREEN, Robert	RB	Chicago	35	30	5							1	1							2
210	WALL, Wesley	TE	New Orleans	35	35								1	3							4
211	GRAY, Mel	WR	Detroit	34	36	-2														3	3
212	JEFFERSON, Shawn	WR	San Diego	33	33		3							1							3
213	TOLLIVER, Billy Joe	QB	Houston	33	73	-40		3		2					2						8
214	FENNER, Derrick	RB	Cincinnati	32	24	8				1				1							2
215	HARRIS, Jackie	TE	Tampa Bay	32	32								2	2	1						3
216	McDUFFIE, O.J.	WR	Miami	32	24	8							1	2							3
217	PRITCHARD, Mike	WR	Denver	32	12	20									1						1
218	CLARK, Gary	WR	Arizona	31	9	22								1							1
219	MONTGOMERY, Tyrone	RB	LA Raiders	31	24	7									1						1
220	PEETE, Rodney	QB	Dallas	31	36	-5		2	1												4
221	POTTS, Roosevelt	RB	Indianapolis	31	24	7				1					1						2
222	LEWIS, Mo	LB	NY Jets	30	21	9														2	2
223	PIERCE, Aaron	TE	NY Giants	30	30	5							2	2							4
224	ANDERSON, Richie	RB	NY Jets	29	24	23							2	1							2
225	BAILEY, Johnny	RB	LA Rams	29	6	8				1											1
226	GARRETT, Jason	QB	Dallas	29	21	-1		1	1												2
227	HESTER, Jessie	WR	LA Rams	29	30	4								2	1						3
228	GORDON, Darrien	DB	San Diego	28	24	-2														2	2
229	GREEN, Eric	TE	Pittsburgh	28	30	14							2	2							4
230	KIRBY, Terry	RB	Miami	28	14	4				2											2
231	RICHARD, Stanley	DB	San Diego	28	24															2	3
232	BRUCE, Isaac	WR	LA Rams	27	27	6								3							3
233	COLLINS, Andre	LB	Washington	27	21	9														2	2
234	DAWSON, Lake	WR	Kansas City	27	18	-10								2							2
235	FREROTTE, Gus	QB	Washington	26	36	-1	3	2													5
236	GEDNEY, Chris	TE	Chicago	26	27	2								3							3
237	McDONALD, Tim	DB	San Francisco	26	24															2	2
238	SCHROEDER, Jay	QB	Cincinnati	26	36	-10		2	1												4
239	WOODSON, Rod	DB	Pittsburgh	25	18	7														2	2
240	BAVARO, Mark	TE	Philadelphia	24	24								1	2							3

#	Player	Pos	Team	Total Fantasy Points	Basic - Distance Pts	Perform. Scoring Pts.	Passing '1-9	Passing '10-39	Passing '40+	Rushing '1-9	Rushing '10-39	Rushing '40+	Receiving '1-9	Receiving '10-39	Receiving '40+	FG '10-39	FG '40-49	FG '50+	PATs	Def.-ST TDs	Total TDs
241	BAXTER, Brad	RB	NY Jets	24	24					4											4
242	CRITTENDEN, Ray	WR	New England	24	24								1	2							3
243	CROSS, Howard	TE	NY Giants	24	24								4								4
244	HEARST, Garrison	RB	Arizona	24	24			1		1											2
245	JENKINS, James	TE	Washington	24	24								4								4
246	MATTHEWS, Aubrey	WR	Detroit	24	24								1	2							3
247	MOORE, Derrick	RB	Detroit	24	24					4											4
248	SMITH, Irv	TE	New Orleans	24	24								1	2							3
249	SMITH, Steve	RB	Seattle	24	24					2			1								3
250	WRIGHT, Alexander	WR	LA Raiders	24	24										2						2
251	COLEMAN, Andre	WR	San Diego	23	24	-1														2	2
252	GARDNER, Carwell	RB	Buffalo	23	24	-1				4											4
253	GIVINS, Ernest	WR	Houston	23	24	-1									1					1	2
254	VARDELL, Tommy	RB	Cleveland	23	18	5								1							1
255	WILLIAMS, Kevin	WR	Dallas	23	24	-1														2	2
256	WINANS, Tydus	WR	Washington	23	23									1	1						2
257	BENNETT, Tony	LB	Indianapolis	22	12	10														1	1
258	GREEN, Harold	RB	Cincinnati	22	18	4				1			1								2
259	RYPIEN, Mark	QB	Cleveland	22	29	-7	3	1													4
260	TILLMAN, Cedric	WR	Denver	22	6	16							1								1
261	TURNER, Eric	DB	Cleveland	22	12	10		1													1
262	BRISTER, Bubby	QB	Philadelphia	21	15	6	1	1		1											3
263	CARTER, Anthony	WR	Detroit	21	21								2	1							3
264	HORTON, Ethan	TE	Washington	21	21								2	1							3
265	JENNINGS, Keith	TE	Chicago	21	21								2	1							3
266	MORTON, Johnnie	WR	Detroit	21	18	3							1							1	2
267	REYNOLDS, Ricky	DB	New England	21	21															2	2
268	SMITH, Chuck	DL	Atlanta	21	9	12														1	1
269	CALLOWAY, Chris	WR	NY Giants	20	21	-1								1	1						2
270	COLEMAN, Pat	WR	Houston	20	9	11								1							1
271	DAWSEY, Lawrence	WR	Tampa Bay	20	9	11								1							1
272	GRAHAM, Kent	QB	NY Giants	20	24	-4	2														2
273	HEBRON, Vaughn	RB	Philadelphia	20	15	5					1										1
274	PAUP, Bryce	LB	Green Bay	20	9	11														1	1
275	WALKER, Derrick	TE	San Diego	20	21	-1								1	1						2
276	CRAVER, Aaron	RB	Miami	19	2	17															
277	GILBERT, Gale	QB	San Diego	18	24	-6	1	2													3
278	HASTINGS, Andre	WR	Pittsburgh	18	18									2							2
279	JACKSON, Greg	DB	Philadelphia	18	12	6														1	1
280	LOGAN, Marc	RB	San Francisco	18	18					1			1								2

FRANCHISE FOOTBALL LEAGUE'S - 1994 FINAL FANTASY RANKINGS

#	Player	Pos	Team	Total Fantasy Points	Basic- Distance Pts	Perform. Scoring Pts	Pass '1-9	Pass '10-39	Pass '40+	Rush '1-9	Rush '10-39	Rush '40+	Rec '1-9	Rec '10-39	Rec '40+	FG '10-39	FG '40-49	FG '50+	PATs	Def.-ST TDs	Total TDs
281	MARTIN, Kelvin	WR	Seattle	18	9	9															1
282	MCDOWELL, Anthony	RB	Tampa Bay	18	18									1							1
283	SINGLETON, Nate	WR	San Francisco	18	18								1		1						2
284	TOLBERT, Tony	DL	Dallas	18	12	6														1	1
285	TURNER, Nate	RB	Buffalo	18	18									1							1
286	CLARK, Derrick	RB	Denver	17	18	-1				3											3
287	TURNER, Marcus	DB	NY Jets	17	12	5														1	1
288	VINCENT, Troy	DB	Miami	17	12	5														1	1
289	WEST, Ed	TE	Green Bay	17	17								1	1							2
290	WOODSON, Darren	DB	Dallas	17	12	5														1	1
291	BEUERLEIN, Steve	QB	Arizona	16	42	-26	5			1											6
292	COLLINS, Mark	DB	Kansas City	16	12	4														1	1
293	HARRIS, Raymont	RB	Chicago	16	6	10				1											1
294	WALKER, Darnell	DB	Atlanta	16	12	4														1	1
295	BAYLESS, Martin	DB	Washington	15	12	3					1										2
296	DAVIS, Kenneth	RB	Buffalo	15	15					1			1								2
297	EVANS, Jerry	TE	Denver	15	15								1	1							2
298	GLOVER, Andrew	TE	LA Raiders	15	15								1	1							2
299	JACKSON, Michael	WR	Cleveland	15	15								1	1							2
300	KLINGLER, David	QB	Cincinnati	15	48	-33	3	2	1												6
301	NOVACEK, Jay	TE	Dallas	15	15								1	1							2
302	PUPUNU, Alfred	TE	San Diego	15	15								1	1							2
303	SMITH, Anthony	DL	LA Raiders	15	9	6														1	1
304	SMITH, Darrin	LB	Dallas	15	9	6														1	1
305	WOODEN, Terry	LB	Seattle	15	12	3														1	1
306	BENNETT, Donnell	RB	Kansas City	14	15	-1				1				1							2
307	BROOKS, Bill	WR	Buffalo	14	15	-1							1	1							2
308	JOHNSON, Mike	LB	Detroit	14	12	2														1	1
309	MCCANTS, Keith	LB	Tampa Bay	14	12	2														1	1
310	SAWYER, Corey	DB	Cincinnati	14	12	2														1	1
311	STRONG, Mack	RB	Seattle	14	15	-1				1	1										2
312	VANHORSE, Sean	DB	San Diego	14	12	2														1	1
313	ZORDICH, Mike	DB	Arizona	14	9	5														1	1
314	BROUSSARD, Steve	RB	Cincinnati	13	17	-4				1	1										2
315	CORYATT, Quentin	LB	Indianapolis	13	12	1														1	1
316	DISHMAN, Cris	DB	Houston	13	9	4														1	1
317	GREENE, Kevin	LB	Pittsburgh	13		13														1	1
318	HALEY, Charles	DL	Dallas	13		13														1	1
319	HARRIS, James	LB	Minnesota	13	9	4														1	1
320	LYGHT, Todd	DB	LA Rams	13	12	1														1	1

FRANCHISE FOOTBALL LEAGUE'S - 1994 FINAL FANTASY RANKINGS

#	Player	Pos	Team	Total Fantasy Points	Basic - Distance Pts	Perform. Scoring Pts	Passing '1-9	Passing '10-39	Passing '40+	Rushing '1-9	Rushing '10-39	Rushing '40+	Receiving '1-9	Receiving '10-39	Receiving '40+	FG '10-39	FG '40-49	FG '50+	PATs	Def.- ST TDs	Total TDs
321	RANDLE, John	DL	Minnesota	13		13															
322	SMITH, Neil	DL	Kansas City	13		13															
323	WILLIAMS, Alfred	DL	Cincinnati	13		9															
324	BAILEY, Robert	DB	LA Rams	12	4															1	1
325	BALDWIN, Randy	RB	Cleveland	12	12															1	1
326	BYNER, Earnest	RB	Cleveland	12	12					2											2
327	CARTER, Dexter	RB	San Francisco	12	12								2								2
328	CASH, Keith	TE	Kansas City	12	12															1	2
329	CLAY, Willie	DB	Detroit	12	9	3															1
330	COTHRAN, Jeff	RB	Cincinnati	12	12								1							1	1
331	GRAHAM, Scottie	RB	Minnesota	12	12					2											2
332	GREEN, Darrell	DB	Washington	12	9	3														1	1
333	GRIFFITH, Howard	RB	LA Rams	12	12								1							1	1
334	HARVEY, Ken	LB	Washington	12		12	1														1
335	JOHNSON, Lee	K	Cincinnati	12	12																
336	JOHNSON, Tracy	RB	Seattle	12	12					2											2
337	MCAFEE, Fred	RB	Arizona	12	12					2											2
338	MCCAFFREY, Ed	WR	San Francisco	12	12								2								2
339	ONEAL, Leslie	LB	San Diego	12		12															
340	SMITH, Cedric	RB	Washington	12	12								1								1
341	THOMAS, Blair	RB	New England	12	12					2											2
342	TRUITT, Olanda	WR	Minnesota	12	12										1						1
343	TUPA, Tom	QB	Cleveland	12	12																
344	TURNER, Vernon	WR	Tampa Bay	12	12															1	1
345	WASHINGTON, Lionel	DB	LA Raiders	12	9	3														1	1
346	WATTERS, Orlando	DB	Seattle	12	9	3														1	1
347	WRIGHT, Toby	DB	LA Rams	12	12															1	1
348	BREWER, Dewell	RB	Indianapolis	11	12	-1															
349	CONNOR, Darion	LB	Atlanta	11		11															
350	JOHNSON, Maurice	TE	Philadelphia	11	12	-1							2								2
351	LATHON, Lamar	LB	Houston	11	4	7															
352	LLOYD, Greg	LB	Pittsburgh	11		11															
353	MUSTER, Brad	RB	New Orleans	11	6	5				1											1
354	NEWMAN, Anthony	DB	LA Rams	11	9	2														1	1
355	RIVERS, Reggie	RB	Denver	11	12	-1				2											
356	SPIKES, Irving	RB	Miami	11	12	-1				2											2
357	SWANN, Eric	DL	Arizona	11	4	7															2
358	WILLIAMS, James	LB	New Orleans	11	9	2															
359	CROSS, Jeff	DL	Miami	10		10														1	1
360	FULLER, William	DL	Philadelphia	10		10															

FRANCHISE FOOTBALL LEAGUE'S - 1994 FINAL FANTASY RANKINGS

#	Player	Pos	Team	Total Fantasy Points	Basic-Distance Pts.	Perform. Scoring Pts.	Passing '1-9	Passing '10-39	Passing '40+	Rushing '1-9	Rushing '10-39	Rushing '40+	Receiving '1-9	Receiving '10-39	Receiving '40+	Field Goals '10-39	Field Goals '40-49	Field Goals '50+	PATs	Def.-ST TDs	Total TDs
361	HARMON, Andy	DL	Philadelphia	10		10															
362	HEBERT, Bobby	QB	Atlanta	10	19	-9	1	1													2
363	HUMPHREY, Ronald	RB	Indianapolis	10	12	-2														1	1
364	MARTIN, Wayne	DL	New Orleans	10		10															
365	MIMS, Chris	DL	San Diego	10		10															
366	PETERSON, Todd	K	Arizona	10	10											2			4		
367	THOMAS, Derrick	LB	Kansas City	10		10															
368	BAILEY, Victor	WR	Philadelphia	9	9									1							1
369	BROWN, Chad	LB	Pittsburgh	9		9															
370	BRUNELL, Mark	QB	Green Bay	9	12	-3				1											1
371	CAMPBELL, Jeff	WR	Denver	9	9									1							1
372	COOK, Marv	TE	Chicago	9	9									1							1
373	COOPER, Adrian	TE	Seattle	9	9									1							1
374	COPELAND, Russell	WR	Buffalo	9	9									1							1
375	GELBAUGH, Stan	QB	Seattle	9	9			1													1
376	GREEN, Paul	WR	Seattle	9	9									1							1
377	HURST, Maurice	DB	New England	9		9															
378	JACK, Eric	DB	Atlanta	9	9															1	1
379	JACKSON, Mark	WR	NY Giants	9	9									1							1
380	JONES, Sean	DL	Green Bay	9		9															
381	MARTIN, Eric	WR	Detroit	9	9									1							1
382	MCGEE, Tim	WR	Cincinnati	9	9									1							1
383	MCGLOCKTON, Chester	DL	LA Raiders	9		9															
384	MCKNIGHT, James	WR	Seattle	9	9									1							1
385	MCMURTRY, Greg	WR	Chicago	9	9									1							1
386	MILLEN, Hugh	QB	Denver	9	14	-5	2														2
387	MORRISON, Darryl	DB	Washington	9	9															1	1
388	ROSS, Jermaine	WR	LA Rams	9	9									1							1
389	RUSSELL, Derek	WR	Denver	9	9									1							1
390	SANDERS, Ricky	WR	Atlanta	9	9									1							1
391	SMITH, Bruce	DL	Buffalo	9		9															
392	SMITH, Robert	RB	Minnesota	9	9						1										1
393	SPIELMAN, Chris	LB	Detroit	9		9															
394	WHITE, Reggie	DL	Green Bay	9		9														1	1
395	WILLIAMS, Aeneas	DB	Arizona	9		9															
396	YARBOROUGH, Ryan	WR	NY Jets	9	9									1							1
397	BATES, Michael	WR	Seattle	8	12	-4									1						1
398	BROOKS, Reggie	RB	Washington	8	12	-4				2											2
399	BURNETT, Rob	DL	Cleveland	8		8															2
400	CASH, Kerry	TE	Indianapolis	8	9	-1									1						1

	Player	Pos	Team	Total Fantasy Points	Basic - Distance Pts.	Perform. Scoring Pts.	Passing '1-9	Passing '10-39	Passing '40+	Rushing '1-9	Rushing '10-39	Rushing '40+	Receiving '1-9	Receiving '10-39	Receiving '40+	FG '10-39	FG '40-49	FG '50+	PATs	Def.-ST TDs	Total TDs
401	DOLEMAN, Chris	DL	Atlanta	8		8															
402	EVANS, Vince	QB	LA Raiders	8	18	-10	1		1												2
403	FLETCHER, Simon	LB	Denver	8		8															
404	HASTY, James	DB	NY Jets	8		8															
405	JOHNSON, Leshon	RB	Green Bay	8		8															
406	JOYNER, Seth	LB	Arizona	8		8															
407	KINCHEN, Brian	TE	Cleveland	8	9	-1								1							1
408	MILLS, Ernie	WR	Pittsburgh	8	9	-1								1							1
409	SLADE, Chris	LB	New England	8		8															
410	SPELLMAN, Alonzo	DL	Chicago	8		8															
411	STUBBLEFIELD, Dana	DL	San Francisco	8		8															
412	ARMSTRONG, Trace	DL	Chicago	7		7															
413	GEATHERS, Jumpy	DL	Atlanta	7		7															
414	HANKS, Merton	DB	San Francisco	7		7															
415	HENNINGS, Chad	DL	Dallas	7		7															
416	JEFFCOAT, Jim	DL	Dallas	7		7															
417	MCNAIR, Todd	RB	Kansas City	7		7															
418	MICKELL, Darren	DL	Kansas City	7		7															
419	PERRY, Darren	DB	Pittsburgh	7		7															
420	SEALS, Ray	DL	Pittsburgh	7		7															
421	THOMAS, William	LB	Philadelphia	7		7															
422	WILLIAMS, Gerald	DL	Pittsburgh	7	6	1							1							1	1
423	ARMSTRONG, Tyji	TE	Tampa Bay	6	6								1								1
424	BANKSTON, Michael	DL	Arizona	6		6															
425	BATY, Greg	TE	Miami	6	6								1								1
426	BAXTER, Fred	TE	NY Jets	6	6								1								1
427	BERNSTINE, Rod	RB	Denver	6		6															
428	CARTER, Pat	TE	Houston	6	6								1								1
429	DAVIDSON, Kenny	DL	Pittsburgh	6		6															
430	DRONETT, Shane	DL	Denver	6		6															
431	GREENE, Tracy	TE	Kansas City	6	6								1								1
432	HAMILTON, Keith	DL	NY Giants	6		6															
433	HARTLEY, Frank	TE	Cleveland	6	6								1								1
434	HAYES, Jon	TE	Pittsburgh	6	6								1								1
435	HILL, Travis	LB	Cleveland	6		6															
436	HOWARD, Erik	DL	NY Giants	6		6														1	1
437	JUNKIN, Trey	TE	Seattle	6	6								1								1
438	LEE, Shawn	DL	San Diego	6		6															
439	LEWIS, Nate	WR	Chicago	6	6								1								1
440	LODISH, Mike	DL	Buffalo	6		6														1	1

FRANCHISE FOOTBALL LEAGUE'S - 1994 FINAL FANTASY RANKINGS

#	Player	Pos	Team	Total Fantasy Points	Basic-Distance Pts.	Perform. Scoring Pts.	Pass '1-9	Pass '10-39	Pass '40+	Rush '1-9	Rush '10-39	Rush '40+	Rec '1-9	Rec '10-39	Rec '40+	FG '10-39	FG '40-49	FG '50+	PATs	Def.-ST TDs	Total TDs
441	MCCALLUM, Napoleon	RB	LA Raiders	6	6					1											1
442	MCCOY, Tony	DL	Indianapolis	6		6															
443	MCGEE, Tony	TE	Cincinnati	6	6								1								1
444	MILLER, Scott	WR	Miami	6	6								1								1
445	REEVES, Bryan	WR	Arizona	6	6								1								1
446	REEVES, Walter	TE	Cleveland	6	6								1								1
447	SEAU, Junior	LB	San Diego	6		6															
448	SIMMONS, Clyde	DL	Arizona	6		6															
449	THOMAS, Henry	DL	Minnesota	6		6															
450	WADDLE, Tom	WR	Chicago	6	6								1								1
451	WALKER, Adam	RB	San Francisco	6	6					1											1
452	WETNIGHT, Ryan	TE	Chicago	6	6								1								1
453	WYCHECK, Frank	TE	Washington	6	6								1								1
454	YOUNG, Bryant	DL	San Francisco	6		6															
455	YOUNG, Duane	TE	San Diego	6	6								1								1
456	YOUNG, Robert	DL	LA Rams	6		6															
457	BENNETT, Cornelius	LB	Buffalo	5		5															
458	BUCKLEY, Terrell	DB	Green Bay	5		5															
459	CHILDRESS, Ray	DL	Houston	5		5															
460	CLARK, Vinnie	DB	Atlanta	5		5															
461	COLEMAN, Lincoln	RB	Dallas	5	6	-1				1											1
462	COLEMAN, Marco	LB	Miami	5		5															
463	DEL RIO, Jack	LB	Minnesota	5		5															
464	FRANCIS, James	LB	Cincinnati	5		5															
465	GLENN, Vencie	DB	Minnesota	5		5															
466	GRIFFIN, Don	DB	Cleveland	5		5															
467	GROSSMAN, Burt	DL	Philadelphia	5		5															
468	HANSEN, Phil	DL	Buffalo	5		5															
469	HARRISON, Nolan	DL	LA Raiders	5		5															
470	HILL, Greg	RB	Kansas City	5	6	-1				1											1
471	JOHNSON, D.j.	DB	Atlanta	5		5															
472	JONES, Jimmy	LB	LA Rams	5		5															
473	KENNEDY, Cortez	DL	Seattle	5		5															
474	KIRKLAND, Levon	LB	Pittsburgh	5		5															
475	KOSAR, Bernie	QB	Miami	5	6	-1	1														
476	LEWIS, Darryll	DB	Houston	5		5															
477	NEAL, Lorenzo	RB	New Orleans	5	6	-1				1											1
478	PEGRAM, Erric	RB	Atlanta	5	6	-1				1											1
479	PRITCHETT, Kelvin	DL	Detroit	5		5															
480	SABB, Dwayne	LB	New England	5		5															

FRANCHISE FOOTBALL LEAGUE'S - 1994 FINAL FANTASY RANKINGS

	Player	Pos	Team	Total Fantasy Points	Basic - Distance Pts.	Perform. Scoring Pts.	Passing '1-9	'10-39	'40+	Rushing '1-9	'10-39	'40+	Receiving '1-9	'10-39	'40+	Field Goals '10-39	'40-49	'50+	PATs	Def.-ST TDs	Total TDs
481	SPENCER, Jimmy	DB	New Orleans	5		5															
482	THOMAS, Broderick	LB	Detroit	5		5															
483	TURNBULL, Renaldo	LB	New Orleans	5		5															1
484	WARE, Derek	TE	Arizona	5	6	-1							1								
485	WASHINGTON, James	DB	Dallas	5		5															
486	WILKINSON, Dan	DL	Cincinnati	5		5															
487	WOOLFORD, Donnell	DB	Chicago	5		5															
488	WORLEY, Tim	RB	Chicago	5	6	-1				1											1
489	ADAMS, Sam	DL	Seattle	4		4															
490	ARMSTEAD, Jessie	LB	NY Giants	4		4															
491	ATKINS, Gene	DB	Miami	4		4															
492	BARKER, Roy	DL	Minnesota	4		4															
493	BROWN, Larry	DB	Dallas	4		4															
494	BROWN, Vincent	LB	New England	4		4															
495	BUTLER, Leroy	DB	Green Bay	4		4															
496	COX, Bryan	LB	Miami	4		4															
497	CULPEPPER, Brad	DL	Minnesota	4		4															
498	DARBY, Matt	DB	Buffalo	4		4															
499	FONTENOT, Albert	DL	Chicago	4		4															
500	HALL, Rhett	DL	Tampa Bay	4		4															
501	HOAGE, Terry	DB	Arizona	4		4															
502	JACKSON, Ricky	LB	San Francisco	4		4															
503	JONES, Aaron	DL	New England	4		4															
504	LAGEMAN, Jeff	DL	NY Jets	4		4															
505	LETT, Leon	DL	Dallas	4		4															
506	MASSEY, Robert	DB	Detroit	4		4															
507	MCGINEST, Willie	LB	New England	4		4															
508	OLIVER, Louis	DB	Miami	4		4															
509	PLEASANT, Anthony	DL	Cleveland	4		4															
510	ROBINSON, Eugene	DB	Seattle	4		4															
511	ROMANOWSKI, Bill	LB	Philadelphia	4		4															
512	ROSS, Kevin	DB	Atlanta	4		4															
513	SINCLAIR, Michael	DL	Seattle	4		4															
514	SIRAGUSA, Tony	DL	Indianapolis	4		4															
515	SPITULSKI, Bob	LB	Seattle	4		4															
516	STRAHAN, Michael	DL	NY Giants	4		4															
517	SWILLING, Pat	LB	Detroit	4		4															
518	TOVAR, Steve	LB	Cincinnati	4		4															
519	WARREN, Frank	DL	New Orleans	4		4															
520	WASHINGTON, Marvin	DL	NY Jets	4		4															

FRANCHISE FOOTBALL LEAGUE'S - 1994 FINAL FANTASY RANKINGS

	Player	Pos	Team	Total Fantasy Points	Basic - Distance Pts.	Perform. Scoring Pts.	Passing '1-9	'10-39	'40+	Rushing '1-9	'10-39	'40+	Receiving '1-9	'10-39	'40+	Field Goals '10-39	'40-49	'50+	PATs	Def.-ST TDs	Total TDs
521	WILLIAMS, James	DB	Denver	4		4															
522	WOODS, Tony	DL	Washington	4		4															
523	ZORICH, Chris	DL	Chicago	4		4															
524	ALLEN, Eric	DB	Philadelphia	3		3															
525	BALL, Jerry	DL	LA Raiders	3		3															
526	BARNETT, Harlan	DB	New England	3		3															
527	BOOTY, John	DB	NY Giants	3		3															
528	BOWENS, Tim	DL	Miami	3		3															
529	BROWN, Dennis	DL	San Francisco	3		3															
530	BROWN, Gilbert	DL	Green Bay	3		3															
531	BROWN, J.b.	DB	Miami	3		3															
532	CARRINGTON, Darren	DB	San Diego	3		3															
533	CARTER, Tom	DB	Washington	3		3															
534	DOTSON, Santana	DL	Tampa Bay	3		3															
535	DOUGLASS, Maurice	DB	Chicago	3		3															
536	FREDRICKSON, Rob	LB	LA Raiders	3		3															
537	GILBERT, Sean	DL	LA Rams	3		3															
538	GOAD, Tim	DL	New England	3		3															
539	HARPER, Dwayne	DB	San Diego	3		3															
540	HENLEY, Darryl	DB	LA Rams	3		3															
541	HOUSTON, Bobby	LB	NY Jets	3		3															
542	HUNTER, Patrick	DB	Seattle	3		3															
543	JONES, Henry	DB	Buffalo	3		3															
544	JONES, James	DL	Cleveland	3		3															
545	JONES, Mike	DL	New England	3		3															
546	KELLY, Joe	LB	NY Jets	3		3															
547	MARYLAND, Russell	DL	Dallas	3		3															
548	MILLER, Jamir	LB	Arizona	3		3															
549	MINCY, Charles	DB	Kansas City	3		3															
550	MONTGOMERY, Glenn	DL	Houston	3		3															
551	NICKERSON, Hardy	LB	Tampa Bay	3		3															
552	PHIFER, Roman	LB	LA Rams	3		3															
553	POPE, Marquiz	DB	LA Rams	3		3															
554	PORCHER, Robert	DL	Detroit	3		3															
555	REICH, Frank	QB	Buffalo	3	9	-6		1													
556	ROBERTSON, Marcus	DB	Houston	3		3															
557	SPARKS, Phillippi	DB	NY Giants	3		3															
558	STAMS, Frank	LB	Cleveland	3		3															
559	STEWART, Michael	DB	Miami	3		3															
560	TATE, David	DB	NY Giants	3		3															1

FRANCHISE FOOTBALL LEAGUE'S - 1994 FINAL FANTASY RANKINGS

	Player	Pos	Team	Total Fantasy Points	Basic - Distance Pts.	Perform. Scoring Pts.	Passing '1-9	'10-39	'40+	Rushing '1-9	'10-39	'40+	Receiving '1-9	'10-39	'40+	Field Goals '10-39	'40-49	'50+	PATs	Def.-ST TDs	Total TDs
561	TEAGUE, George	DB	Green Bay	3		3															
562	TRUDEAU, Jack	QB	NY Jets	3	9	-6		1													1
563	VEASEY, Craig	DL	Miami	3		3															
564	WASHINGTON, Mickey	DB	Buffalo	3		3															
565	WASHINGTON, Ted	DL	Denver	3		3															
566	WHEELER, Mark	DL	Tampa Bay	3		3															
567	WILLIAMS, Darryl	DB	Cincinnati	3		3															
568	ALBERTS, Trev	LB	Indianapolis	2		2															
569	ALEXANDER, Elijah	LB	Denver	2		2															
570	AMBROSE, Ashley	DB	Indianapolis	2		2															
571	ANDERSON, Eddie	DB	LA Raiders	2		2															
572	BARNETT, Tony	DL	New England	2		2															
573	BARROW, Michael	LB	Houston	2		2															
574	BEAVERS, Aubrey	LB	Miami	2		2															
575	BIEKERT, Greg	LB	LA Raiders	2		2															
576	BISHOP, Blaine	DB	Houston	2		2															
577	BLADES, Bennie	DB	Detroit	2		2															
578	BRAXTON, Tyrone	DB	Miami	2		2															
579	BRIM, Mike	DB	Cincinnati	2		2															
580	BROOKS, Michael	LB	NY Giants	2		2															
581	BROWN, Reggie	WR	Houston	2	2																
582	BUCK, Vince	DB	New Orleans	2		2															
583	BUCKNER, Brenston	DL	Pittsburgh	2		2															
584	CAMPBELL, Jesse	DB	NY Giants	2		2															
585	CARRIER, Mark a	DB	Chicago	2		2															
586	CARTER, Dale	DB	Kansas City	2		2															
587	CASE, Scott	DB	Atlanta	2		2															
588	COPELAND, Horace	WR	Tampa Bay	2	2																
589	CROCKETT, Ray	DB	Denver	2		2															
590	CURRY, Eric	DL	Tampa Bay	2		2															
591	DANIEL, Eugene	DB	Indianapolis	2		2															
592	DENT, Richard	DL	San Francisco	2		2															
593	EDWARDS, Antonio	DL	Seattle	2		2															
594	FLORES, Mike	DL	Philadelphia	2		2															
595	FOOTMAN, Dan	DL	Cleveland	2		2															
596	GAYLE, Shaun	DB	Chicago	2		2															
597	GILDON, Jason	LB	Pittsburgh	2		2															
598	GRAY, Carlton	DB	Seattle	2		2															
599	GRBAC, Elvis	QB	San Francisco	2	12	-10	2														2
600	GUYTON, Myron	DB	New England	2		2															

FRANCHISE FOOTBALL LEAGUE'S - 1994 FINAL FANTASY RANKINGS

	Player	Pos	Team	Total Fantasy Points	Basic - Distance Pts.	Perform. Scoring Pts.	Passing '1-9	'10-39	'40+	Rushing '1-9	'10-39	'40+	Receiving '1-9	'10-39	'40+	Field Goals '10-39	'40-49	'50+	PATs	Def.- ST TDs	Total TDs
601	HALL, Dana	DB	San Francisco	2		2															
602	HARPER, Roger	DB	Atlanta	2		2															
603	HARRIS, Tim	LB	San Francisco	2		2															
604	HASSELBACH, Harald	DL	Denver	2		2															
605	HILLIARD, Randy	DB	Denver	2		2															
606	JACOBS, Tim	DB	Cleveland	2		2															
607	JOHNSON, Pepper	LB	Cleveland	2		2															
608	JONES, Rondell	DB	Denver	2		2															
609	KELLY, Todd	DL	San Francisco	2		2															
610	LAKE, Carnell	DB	Pittsburgh	2		2															
611	LANGHAM, Antonio	DB	Cleveland	2		2															
612	LEE, Carl	DB	Minnesota	2		2															
613	LYLE, Keith	DB	LA Rams	2		2															
614	LYNCH, Lorenzo	DB	Arizona	2		2															
615	MARION, Brock	DB	Dallas	2		2															
616	MARSHALL, Leonard	DL	Washington	2		2															
617	MAYHEW, Martin	DB	Tampa Bay	2		2															
618	MCDANIEL, Ed	LB	Minnesota	2		2															
619	MCDONALD, Devon	LB	Indianapolis	2		2															
620	MCGILL, Lenny	DB	Green Bay	2		2															
621	MCMICHAEL, Steve	DL	Green Bay	2		2															
622	MCMILLIAN, Mark	DB	Philadelphia	2		2															
623	MILLER, Corey	LB	NY Giants	2		2															
624	MILLS, Sam	LB	New Orleans	2		2															
625	MOSS, Winston	LB	LA Raiders	2		2															
626	NASH, Joe	DL	Seattle	2		2															
627	OWENS, Dan	DL	Detroit	2		2															
628	PARRELLA, John	DL	San Diego	2		2															
629	PATTON, Marvcus	LB	Buffalo	2		2															
630	PERRY, Michael dean	DL	Cleveland	2		2															
631	PHILLIPS, Joe	DL	Kansas City	2		2															
632	PORTER, Rufus	LB	Seattle	2		2															
633	ROBINSON, Gerald	DL	LA Rams	2		2															
634	RUCKER, Keith	DL	Arizona	2		2															
635	SCROGGINS, Tracy	DL	Detroit	2		2															
636	SINGLETON, Chris	LB	Miami	2		2															
637	SMITH, Al	LB	Houston	2		2															
638	SMITH, Kevin	DB	Dallas	2		2															
639	SMITH, Rod	DB	New England	2		2															
640	STEED, Joel	DL	Pittsburgh	2		2															

FRANCHISE FOOTBALL LEAGUE'S - 1994 FINAL FANTASY RANKINGS

	Player	Pos	Team	Total Fantasy Points	Basic-Distance Pts	Perform.-Scoring Pts.	Passing '1-9	'10-39	'40+	Rushing '1-9	'10-39	'40+	Receiving '1-9	'10-39	'40+	Field Goals '10-39	'40-49	'50+	PATs	Def.-ST TDs	Total TDs
641	STEPHENS, Rod	LB	Seattle	2		2															
642	STONE, Dwight	WR	Pittsburgh	2	2																
643	TOWNSEND, Greg	DL	Philadelphia	2		2															
644	TUBBS, Winfred	LB	New Orleans	2		2															
645	WALLACE, Aaron	LB	LA Raiders	2		2															
646	WASHINGTON, Brian	DB	NY Jets	2		2															
647	WHITE, Alberto	DL	LA Raiders	2		2															
648	WHITE, William	DB	Kansas City	2		2															
649	WILLIAMS, Brent	DL	Seattle	2		2															
650	WILLIAMS, Jarvis	DB	NY Giants	2		2															
651	WILLIS, James	LB	Green Bay	2		2															
652	WILSON, Bobby	DL	Washington	2		2															
653	WILSON, Karl	DL	San Francisco	2		2															
654	WILSON, Troy	DL	San Francisco	2		2															
655	AHANOTU, Chidi	DL	Tampa Bay	1		1															
656	ARCHAMBEAU, Lester	DL	Atlanta	1		1															
657	ATWATER, Steve	DB	Denver	1		1															
658	BANKS, Carl	LB	Cleveland	1		1															
659	BARNETT, Oliver	DL	Buffalo	1		1															
660	BATES, Bill	DB	Dallas	1		1															
661	BEAMON, Willie	DB	NY Giants	1		1															
662	BELSER, Jason	DB	Indianapolis	1		1															
663	BLACKMON, Robert	DB	Seattle	1		1															
664	BOOTH, Isaac	DB	Cleveland	1		1															
665	BOYD, Malik	DB	Minnesota	1		1															
666	BRADFORD, Ronnie	DB	Denver	1		1															
667	BUSSEY, Barney	DB	Tampa Bay	1		1															
668	CALDWELL, Mike	LB	Cleveland	1		1															
669	CARTER, Marty	DB	Tampa Bay	1		1															
670	CASILLAS, Tony	DL	Dallas	1		1															
671	COLON, Harry	DB	Detroit	1		1															
672	CONLAN, Shane	LB	LA Rams	1		1															
673	COOK, Toi	DB	San Francisco	1		1															
674	COPELAND, John	DL	Cincinnati	1		1															
675	COVINGTON, Tony	DB	Tampa Bay	1		1															
676	DAVEY, Don	DL	Green Bay	1		1															
677	DAVIS, Eric	DB	San Francisco	1		1															
678	DILLARD, Stacey	DL	NY Giants	1		1															
679	DIMRY, Charles	DB	Tampa Bay	1		1															
680	DIXON, Gerald	LB	Cleveland	1		1															

	Player	Pos	Team	Total Fantasy Points	Basic - Distance Pts.	Perform. Scoring Pts.	Passing			Rushing			Receiving			Field Goals			PATs	Def.- ST TDs	Total TDs
							'1-9	'10-39	'40+	'1-9	'10-39	'40+	'1-9	'10-39	'40+	'10-39	'40-49	'50+			
681	DRAKEFORD, Tyrone	DB	San Francisco	1		1															
682	EDWARDS, Dixon	LB	Dallas	1		1															
683	EMTMAN, Steve	DL	Indianapolis	1		1															
684	EPPS, Tory	DL	Chicago	1		1															
685	EVANS, Byron	LB	Philadelphia	1		1															
686	EVANS, Doug	DB	Green Bay	1		1															
687	EVERETT, Thomas	DB	Tampa Bay	1		1															
688	FARR, Dmarco	DL	LA Rams	1		1															
689	FIGURES, Deon	DB	Pittsburgh	1		1															
690	FOX, Mike	DL	NY Giants	1		1															
691	FRANK, Donald	DB	San Diego	1		1															
692	FRASE, Paul	DL	NY Jets	1		1															
693	GANT, Kenneth	DB	Dallas	1		1															
694	GOLDBERG, Bill	DL	Atlanta	1		1															
695	GOUVEIA, Kurt	LB	Washington	1		1															
696	GRANT, Alan	DB	Cincinnati	1		1															
697	GREEN, Victor	DB	NY Jets	1		1															
698	GRIGGS, David	LB	San Diego	1		1															
699	GROW, Monty	DB	Kansas City	1		1															
700	HAGER, Britt	LB	Philadelphia	1		1															
701	HARRIS, Robert	DL	Minnesota	1		1															
702	HAYWORTH, Tracy	LB	Detroit	1		1															
703	HENRY, Kevin	DL	Pittsburgh	1		1															
704	HERROD, Jeff	LB	Indianapolis	1		1															
705	HILL, Eric	LB	Arizona	1		1															
706	HOLLIER, Dwight	LB	Miami	1		1															
707	HOLLINQUEST, Lamont	LB	Washington	1		1															
708	HUMPHRIES, Leonard	DB	Indianapolis	1		1															
709	JACKSON, Steve	DB	Houston	1		1															
710	JAMISON, George	LB	Kansas City	1		1															
711	JENKINS, Carlos	LB	Minnesota	1		1															
712	JETER, Tommy	DL	Philadelphia	1		1															
713	JOHNSON, Bill	DL	Cleveland	1		1															
714	JOHNSON, Joe a	DL	New Orleans	1		1															
715	JOHNSON, Keshon	DB	Chicago	1		1															
716	JOHNSON, Raylee	DL	San Diego	1		1															
717	JOHNSON, Tim	DL	Washington	1		1															
718	JONES, Gary	DB	Pittsburgh	1		1															
719	JONES, Roger	DB	FREE AGENT	1	2	1															
720	JORDAN, Andrew	TE	Minnesota	1		-1															

FRANCHISE FOOTBALL LEAGUE'S - 1994 FINAL FANTASY RANKINGS

	Player	Pos	Team	Total Fantasy Points	Basic - Distance Pts.	Perform. Scoring Pts.	Passing '1-9	'10-39	'40+	Rushing '1-9	'10-39	'40+	Receiving '1-9	'10-39	'40+	Field Goals '10-39	'40-49	'50+	PATs	Def.-ST TDs	Total TDs
721	KOONCE, George	LB	Green Bay	1		1															
722	KRUMRIE, Tim	DL	Cincinnati	1		1															
723	LEGETTE, Tyrone	DB	New Orleans	1		1															
724	LEWIS, Albert	DB	LA Raiders	1		1															
725	LINCOLN, Jeremy	DB	Chicago	1		1															
726	LOTT, Ronnie	DB	NY Jets	1		1															
727	LUMPKIN, Sean	DB	New Orleans	1		1															
728	MACK, Milton	DB	Tampa Bay	1		1															
729	MADDOX, Mark	LB	Buffalo	1		1															
730	MALONE, Darrell	DB	Miami	1		1															
731	MANN, Charles	DL	San Francisco	1		1															
732	MARSHALL, Wilber	LB	Arizona	1		1															
733	MATTHEWS, Clay	LB	Atlanta	1		1															
734	MCCRARY, Michael	DL	Seattle	1		1															
735	MCDANIELS, Pallom	DL	Kansas City	1		1															
736	MCDONALD, Ricardo	LB	Cincinnati	1		1															
737	MCGRIGGS, Lamar	DB	Minnesota	1		1															
738	MCGRUDER, Michael	DB	Tampa Bay	1		1															
739	MCNEIL, Ryan	DB	Detroit	1		1															
740	MECKLENBURG, Karl	LB	Denver	1		1															
741	MOORE, Stevon	DB	Cleveland	1		1															
742	NOGA, Al	DL	FREE AGENT	1		1															
743	NORTON, Ken	LB	San Francisco	1		1															
744	NOTTAGE, Dexter	DL	Washington	1		1															
745	NUNN, Freddie Joe	LB	Arizona	1		1															
746	OLIVER, Muhammad	DB	Miami	1		1															
747	OTTIS, Brad	DL	LA Rams	1		1															
748	PALMER, Sterling	DL	Washington	1		1															
749	PHILLIPS, Anthony	DB	Atlanta	1		1															
750	PITTS, Mike	DL	New England	1		1															
751	PLUMMER, Gary	LB	San Francisco	1		1															
752	RANDOLPH, Thomas	DB	NY Giants	1		1															
753	RAY, Terry	DB	New England	1		1															
754	RAYMOND, Corey	DB	NY Giants	1		1															
755	ROBINSON, Jeff	DL	Denver	1		1															
756	ROBINSON, Rafael	DB	Seattle	1		1															
757	SHEPPARD, Ashley	LB	Minnesota	1		1															
758	SMITH, Ben	DB	Denver	1		1															
759	SMITH, Dennis	DB	Denver	1		1															
760	SMITH, Frankie	DB	Miami	1		1															

FRANCHISE FOOTBALL LEAGUE'S - 1994 FINAL FANTASY RANKINGS

	Player	Pos	Team	Total Fantasy Points	Basic - Distance Pts.	Perform. Scoring Pts.	Passing '1-9	'10-39	'40+	Rushing '1-9	'10-39	'40+	Receiving '1-9	'10-39	'40+	Field Goals '10-39	'40-49	'50+	PATs	Def.-ST TDs	Total TDs
761	SMITH, Otis	DB	Philadelphia	1		1															
762	SMITH, Thomas	DB	Buffalo	1		1															
763	SMITH, Vinson	LB	Chicago	1		1															
764	STARGELL, Tony	DB	Tampa Bay	1		1															
765	STOKES, Fred	DL	LA Rams	1		1															
766	STOWE, Tyronne	LB	Washington	1		1															
767	STRICKLAND, Fred	LB	Green Bay	1		1															
768	TAYLOR, Jay	DB	Kansas City	1		1															
769	TAYLOR, Terry	DB	FREE AGENT	1		1															
770	THOMAS, Mark	DL	San Francisco	1		1															
771	THOMPSON, Bennie	DB	Kansas City	1		1															
772	TRAPP, James	DB	LA Raiders	1		1															
773	TUGGLE, Jesse	LB	Atlanta	1		1															
774	WATTS, Damon	DB	Indianapolis	1		1															
775	WHIGHAM, Larry	DB	Seattle	1		1															
776	WIDMER, Corey	LB	NY Giants	1		1															
777	WILKINS, Gabe	DL	Green Bay	1		1															
778	WILLIAMS, Dan	DL	Denver	1		1															
779	WILSON, Bernard	DL	Tampa Bay	1		1															
780	WOODALL, Lee	LB	San Francisco	1		1															
781	WRIGHT, Jeff	DL	Buffalo	1		1															
782	YOUNG, Lonnie	DB	NY Jets	1		1